United Nations Economic Commission for Europe
Population Activities Unit

Socio-Economic Status and Living Arrangements of Older Persons in Finland

Jarl Lindgren
Anneli Miettinen
Mauri Nieminen

UNITED NATIONS
New York and Geneva, 1999

The Population Research Institute of Väestöliito

Explanatory Notes

The designations employed and the presentation of the material in this publication do not imply the expression of any opinion whatsoever on the part of the Secretariat of the United Nations concerning the legal status of any country, territory, city or area, or of its authorities, or concerning the delimitation of its frontiers or boundaries.

The views expressed herein are those of the individual authors and do not necessarily reflect the views of the United Nations nor the institutions with which the authors are affiliated.

The following symbols have been used throughout this paper:

A dash (-) indicates nil or negligible.
Two dots (..) indicate not available or not pertinent.

UNITED NATIONS PUBLICATION
Sales No. E.99.II.E.19
ISBN 92-1-116721-3 ISSN 1014-4994

PREFACE

Population ageing is now widely recognized as one of the most salient long-term developments in the countries of Europe and North America. It has profound economic and social implications, and poses unique public policy challenges. Although differences in demographic history and in current social, economic, and political realities create different priorities across countries and subregions, there is a common understanding of the need to address these issues through a coherent system of policy measures based on sound research on its social and economic consequences. The increasing importance of population ageing is reflected in the attention paid to its opportunities and challenges by various international and national forums. In recognition of that, the United Nations has designated 1999 as the International Year of Older Persons. It has also developed several instruments on ageing, including the International Plan of Action on Ageing, the United Nations Principles for Older Persons and the United Nations Targets on Ageing for the Year 2001.

The United Nations Economic Commission for Europe (UN/ECE), with the financial support of the United Nations Population Fund (UNFPA) and the United States National Institute on Aging (NIA), has long been active in addressing issues related to population ageing. Its work in the field is guided, among other things, by the understanding that older persons are a heterogeneous and rapidly changing group and that they make social and economic contributions, which makes population ageing not only a challenge, but also an opportunity for social and economic development. Recognizing the urgent need for better information and data collection as well as research on which to base well-informed and effective policy-making, UN/ECE has been coordinating various data-collection and research activities in the field of population ageing.

Most of the UN/ECE work in the field is performed as part of a programme carried out by its Population Activities Unit (PAU). One of the two main objectives of the programme was to assemble a set of cross-nationally comparable micro-data samples based on the 1990-round of population and housing censuses in countries of Europe and North America. The samples are designed so as to allow research on a wide range of issues related to ageing (most of them include oversampling with age), as well as on other social phenomena. A common set of nomenclatures and classifications, derived from a study of census data comparability in Europe and North America, was adopted as standards for recoding. Fifteen countries have so far contributed datasets as part of this programme. The second main objective of the PAU programme is to use the assembled data collection and study the social and economic conditions of older persons. Two types of studies will be produced within the programme's research component: country studies, like the present one, that focus on the process of population ageing and the status of older persons in individual participating countries; and regional comparative studies that focus on specific issues related to the status of older persons from a cross-country comparative perspective. The aim of both types of studies is to enhance national capacities to formulate and evaluate programmes and policies targeted towards older people, through increased knowledge of the determinants of the social and economic status of older persons, and through better understanding of the existing range of policy instruments in this field.

The list of persons and institutions that have contributed to the success of the PAU programme on population ageing is a long one. The work would not have been possible without the financial assistance of UNFPA and NIA, nor without the active cooperation and support of the national statistical offices and other institutions in the participating countries. The programme also benefited greatly from the guidance and counsel provided by the members of its Advisory Board (Ms. J. Gierveld, Mr. A. Klinger, Mr. G. C. Myers, Mr. S. Preston and Mr. R. Suzman).

This report is one of the outcomes of these activities. It is the second in a series of country studies to be published. We take this opportunity to also thank the authors of this monograph, Mr. Jarl Lindgren, Ms. Anneli Miettinen and Mr. Mauri Nieminen, for their efforts and patience whilst working on it. Thanks are also due to Mr. John Steinhard and Mr. Mark Bloch, who performed the editing and facilitated the publication of the monograph.

Miroslav Macura
Chief, Population Activities Unit
Economic Analysis Division
United Nations Economic
   Commission for Europe

Ismo Söderling
Director, The Population
Research Institute
The Family Federation of Finland

CONTENTS

Chapter Six

Some Concluding Remarks

List of Tables in Appendix One

The first figure and table numbers given in brackets refer to their location in this research paper. Subsequent PAU table numbers in brackets refer to the standard Population Activities Unit tables on which they are based.

List of Tables in Appendix Two

Introduction

The tendency for populations to age seems to be an unavoidable and irreversible demographic trend. It is already a reality in the highly industrialized nations of Europe and North America and is gradually spreading to the developing world. Given the widely held belief that society should strive to avoid the untimely death of its citizens, it is to be expected that average lifespans will increase, with more and more people living to an advanced age. A significant factor underlying the trend is the simultaneous decline in fertility.

The trend is of a historically unprecedented magnitude, and is projected to bring in its wake completely new problems demanding solutions in the near future.

In this context Finland's situation is arguably unique in Europe. Although one of the last countries to experience the demographic shifts typical of industrialization, it seems to be one of the first to face full-scale ageing of the population. Within ten to twenty years the large age groups born after the Second World War will reach the age of retirement. The proportion of senior citizens will almost double. The growing cost of old-age pensions is often perceived as a thorny problem, despite the confidence of many economists who take a sanguine view of sustained long-term economic growth. Concern over future funding has moreover been sharpened by current moves to cut social security costs.

Several Finnish studies have been carried out in order to shed light on especially economic effects of population ageing. Many of them were compiled prior to the Finnish recession, in the early 1990s, when population ageing was first recognized as a serious problem. People had been retiring earlier and a labour shortage was imminently expected. Then the ensuing recession caused the predicted labour shortage to be overtaken by massive unemployment, so interest in the problems of ageing waned.

In recent years some research into the living conditions of senior citizens and population ageing has been published, usually focusing on a specific topic. For more general and versatile information on elderly persons we can avail ourselves of the population censuses, formerly undertaken every ten years, more recently every five. Since 1990 population censuses are based on data from registers.

Among the publications published during the 1980s and 1990s it is worth mentioning research into future social expenditure (e.g. Ministry of Social Affairs and Health, 1987; Palm, 1988; Parkkinen and Järviö, 1988; Parkkinen, 1986 and 1995) and reports on living conditions, financial circumstances and old-age policy (e.g. Puhakka, 1988; Ministry of Social Affairs and Health, 1988 and 1994; Committee Report, 1996:1; Väestöliitto, 1997). There are also reports which form part of an international research project on the demographic and socio-economic effects of ageing (Lindgren, 1990 and 1992) including monographs discussing issues around ageing (e.g. EVA, 1989; Väestöliitto, 1990 and 1998).

This report will furnish useful information on several aspects of living conditions and provision for aged persons. However, as it is mainly intended for the purposes of international comparison, its findings are usually presented as percentages.

Besides a short overview of the demographic and economic background, the research project has provided information on the living arrangements and economic circumstances of those aged 50 and over. Living arrangements are examined in private households in terms of household size, generations and kin present. In addition, the extent of institutionalization is studied. The economic situation is analysed in terms of economic activity and income sources. Size of dwelling, household amenities and disability status are dealt with. The items are analysed by gender, marital status, age and number of generations present in the household.

Besides the data collated by the Population Activities Unit, some additional sources of information have been used. However, it has not generally been possible to provide data over time, as comparable data from previous years are seldom available.

Finally, the report includes a technical annex with information on the reliability of data and methodology. The standard tabulations are available at the end of the report as an appendix to the tables.

This study was supported by a grant from the Alli Paasikivi Foundation.

Chapter One

Social, Economic and Demographic Background

1.1 Demographic trends

As elsewhere in Europe, the population of Finland increased rather rapidly from the beginning of the nineteenth century. In 1850 there were 1.6 million inhabitants in Finland. Fifty years later the population had risen by one million, and by 1920 it had almost doubled to reach 3.1 million. This population growth was a consequence of the demographic transition, a decrease in mortality and a more or less unaltered fertility. Not until the beginning of the first decade of the twentieth century did total fertility begin to tail off.

The total fertility rate by periods of five years was almost equally high from 1856 to 1910 or 4.8-4.7. In 1906-1910 the total fertility rate was still 4.6. The expectation of life at birth of women grew during the same period from 44 to 50 years. Among men the increase was somewhat less (Koskinen and Martelin, 1994). The natural increase, the excess of births over deaths, which was only 9 per thousand in 1851-1865 stabilized to 13-14 per thousand during the following decades (Strömmer, 1969).

The Second World War pushed demographic change in an entirely new direction. After the war, social development was characterized by far-reaching structural change, in many respects more rapid than that seen in other European countries. The proportion of the economically active population in agriculture declined from 46 per cent in 1950 to 8 per cent in 1995. Internal migration was intense: in 1950 32 per cent of the population lived in urban municipalities, by 1995 this proportion was 65 per cent. At the same time the population employed in service industries increased from 26 to 64 per cent. The fertility decline which had started already in the 1910s was interrupted by a baby boom at the end of the 1940s and the early 1950s. The total fertility rate culminated in 1947 when it was 3.7. After the baby boom, fertility continued to decline.

Later in the 1970s fertility ceased to decline, stabilizing below the replacement level, i.e. the total fertility rate (children per woman) was below 1.9. Since the middle of the 1980s the annual total fertility rate per woman has been 1.7-1.8. At the beginning of the 1970s mortality stabilized at a relatively low level and population growth had markedly slowed down.

Despite low fertility there has been an annual excess of births over deaths which is almost solely a result of the declining death rate. Since the end of the 1950s when the excess of births over deaths was 10 per thousand, it has continuously dropped, to three per thousand in the early 1990s (fig. 1.1). In 1995 the population of Finland was 5.1 million.

FIGURE 1.1

Population development in Finland in 1900-1996

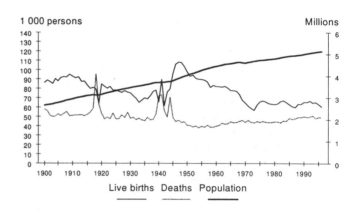

Source: Väestöliitto, 1998

The population age distribution has radically changed during the last 50 years. In 1950 the age distribution still resembled a pyramid (fig. 1.2) with a broad base provided by the large cohort of babies born in the late 1940s. Over the subsequent decades, as a consequence of declining fertility, the youngest age groups have become significantly smaller and more uniform. Now the middle aged form the largest age groups. In 1950 children aged 0-14 accounted for 30 per cent of the population, falling to 19 per cent by 1995. Simultaneously, the working aged population has grown from 63 per cent to 67 per cent. The proportion of persons aged 65 or more has doubled, from 7 to 14 per cent. Even more remarkable has been the growth of the older population. Fifty years ago persons aged 80 or more amounted to 0.8 per cent of the total population. In 1995 their proportion had quadrupled to 3.2 per cent, of which men constituted only 36 per cent.

FIGURE 1.2

Age distribution in 1950 and 1996

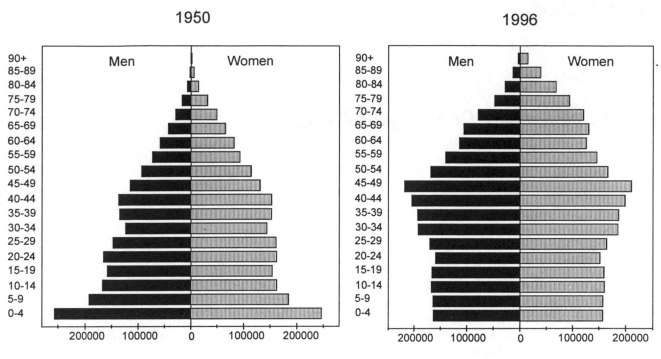

Source: Väestöliitto, 1998

Declining mortality, firstly characteristic only of children but now becoming typical of older age groups, has gradually affected the sex ratio. At the beginning of the century female preponderance was already evident among those in their thirties. As more male children than female children are born and mortality is decreasing there are now more men than women in the cohorts up to the age of fifty. On the contrary, the male-female ratio among the older age groups, those 80 or over, has changed significantly in the opposite direction, from six men per ten women at the beginning of the century to four per ten.

The mean expectation of life at birth has increased rather rapidly. In 1995 the life expectancy at birth was 72.8 for men and 80.2 for women (fig. 1.3). The reasons behind the high male death rate are largely a matter for conjecture. Among explanations cited are accidents among young men, cardiovascular mortality and violent deaths among middle-aged men caused by heavy drinking, an increasing incidence of lung cancer caused by smoking, unresolved social conflicts and homelessness (Ministry of Social Affairs and Health, 1988). During the last decade the excess male mortality has declined somewhat. The reason is a decrease in the typical causes of death among males such as cardiovascular diseases and lung cancer. This is mainly a consequence of changed living conditions and dietary habits among men. Even the tendency to equality between sexes has contributed to the decline of the longevity difference when habits typical of men have been adopted by women. Hence e.g. smoking and drinking have been more and more common among women, tending to increase female mortality (Koskinen and Martelin, 1994).

FIGURE 1.3

Expectation of life at birth in 1901-1995

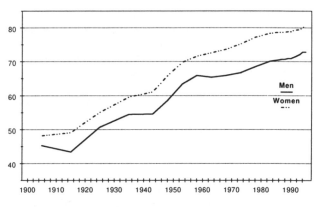

Source: Väestöliitto, 1998

The life expectancy of aged persons remained largely unchanged during the early part of the century. In the early 1940s the mean expectation of life at age 65 was 10.5 for men and 12.9 for women, figures which had changed little since the turn of the century. During subsequent decades longevity at the older ages increased rapidly, especially for women. By the beginning of the 1960s the expectation of life at age 65 had risen to 11.5 for men and 13.8 for women (Kolari, 1980). In 1995 the expectation of life at 65 was 14.5 for men and 18.6 for women (fig.1.4). Proportionally, the increase of life expectancy has been still greater among the oldest persons. Since the beginning of this century, life expectancy at age 80 has increased from 4.4 to 6.4 years among men and from 4.9 to 7.9 among women.

FIGURE 1.4

Expectation of life at age 65 in 1901-1995

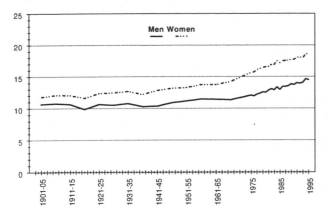

Source: Väestöliitto, 1998.

According to the latest population projection (Statistics Finland, 1997) the total population will increase until 2013 and after that slowly decrease. At the end of the projection period, in 2030, the age distribution is fairly uniform, meaning that the age pyramid has become more rectangular (fig. 1.5). As in all EU countries the projections show a growing number and proportion of senior citizens. In Finland the growth in proportion of senior citizens, especially the very old, is projected to be more rapid than the EU average (fig. 1.6).

In 2010-2020 the large age groups born at the end of the 1940s will reach the age of retirement. A great increase in the number of senior citizens will take place and their proportion in the population will grow gradually. In 2030 the proportion of the population aged 65 or over is calculated to be 25 per cent, or nearly twice that at the turn of the millennium. The mean expectation of life is projected to grow until 2010, reaching 76.1 for men and 82.4 for women.

The number of older persons, those aged 80 and over, will more than double, to 7.3 per cent of the population. The number of older men will grow significantly more than that of women. In 2030 there will be six men for every ten women among those over 80, compared to a ratio of four to ten in 1995. As a consequence of the faster growth of male longevity, the proportion of widows will decrease in all age groups and the proportion of widowers increase especially in the older age groups (Lindgren, 1990).

Even the pattern of marriage has changed significantly during recent decades. The changes are mostly noticeable in the younger age groups. The proportion of married people has decreased somewhat, mostly because consensual unions have become more common. The trend towards consensual union has not yet affected the proportion of those married among senior citizens but evidently will in the future. As a consequence of the difference in longevity between men and women, married men are much more common than married women, and this increases with age (table 1.1). Among seniors, the proportion of people never married has remained roughly constant over the last several decades: only a very slight decline may be observed. The pattern of widowhood has remained more or less stable over the decades, the percentage increasing rapidly with age, especially among women. The divorce rate rose rapidly in the early 1970s but has since levelled off. Among aged persons the rate is low, with somewhat more divorced women than men (Lindgren, 1990).

1.2 Economic and social development

On the whole, during recent years economic development in Finland has been satisfactory. The economic dependency ratio (the ratio of economically inactive to economically active persons) was sustainable until the beginning of the 1990s, thanks to a fairly young population age structure, a high employment ratio and favour-

TABLE 1.1

Distribution of persons aged 50 or more by marital status, in 1990 (*percentage*)

Men	Never married	Married	Widowed	Divorced or separated
50-54	12.9	72.8	1.4	12.9
55-59	12.1	74.6	2.4	10.9
60-64	11.7	75.1	4.1	9.0
65-69	9.5	76.2	7.3	7.0
70-74	7.2	75.1	12.4	5.4
75-79	6.7	68.4	20.5	4.4
80-84	6.9	57.8	32.1	3.2
85+	7.2	39.2	50.9	2.7
Total	**10.6**	**72.7**	**7.9**	**8.9**

Women	Never married	Married	Widowed	Divorced or separated
50-54	9.5	69.5	6.7	14.2
55-59	9.8	65.7	12.1	12.4
60.64	10.4	59.2	20.3	10.1
65-69	11.2	48.4	32.1	8.4
70-74	11.6	35.7	45.4	7.2
75-79	12.9	23.2	57.6	6.3
80-84	14.8	13.3	66.6	5.4
85+	11.4	47.2	32.0	9.5
Total	**11.4**	**47.2**	**32.0**	**9.5**

FIGURE 1.5

The projected age distribution in 2030

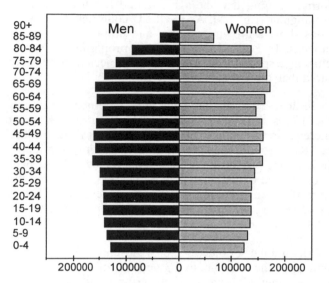

Source: Väestöliitto, 1998

FIGURE 1.6

The proportional growth of specific age groups in Finland and the EU countries 1995-2020

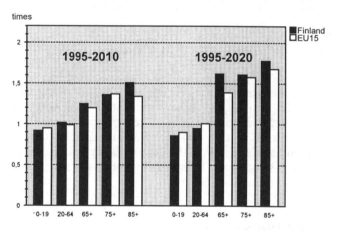

Source: Väestöliitto, 1998

able economic development. In the beginning of the 1990s deep recession transformed the economic outlook. Since the worst year, 1991, when GNP fell by seven per cent, it has again grown year by year reaching 4.2 per cent in 1994 and has been somewhat higher since (5.9 per cent in 1997). Labour productivity has increased even if it has not yet reached the level of other rich European countries. It will continue to increase as more highly educated younger cohorts enter the labour force. The high national debt, at the moment more than 60 per cent of GNP, will however force the State to thoroughly reconsider the use of public finances during the coming years.

During recent decades the age structure has been favourable with a working age population of 66-68 per cent. Simultaneously, the economically active population has declined. From 1950 to 1990 the economically active

population had fallen from 70 per cent to 50 per cent of the total population. The decrease has been especially marked in the youngest age groups and among those aged 65 or more. Among the young the reason can be found in more prolonged education. Among senior citizens the decrease has mainly been caused by the shrinking of the agricultural sector, where many older persons used to work. In 1950, 34 per cent of people aged 65 or over were still working. In 1995 the proportion was close to zero. Even individuals aged 55-64 have exhibited a continuously shrinking work participation rate, mainly as a consequence of the early pension systems established in the mid-1980s.

To these long-term changes in economic activity rates could be added the unemployment caused by the recession in the beginning of the 1990s when the unemployment rate grew to around 18 per cent of the labour force. During the last two years the unemployment rate has fallen, but remains at about 11 per cent (at the end of 1998).

As a consequence of the decrease in economically active persons, the dependency ratio has changed significantly during the 1990s. Calculated as the ratio of economically inactive population, i.e. pensioners, unemployed, students, children etc. to economically active (multiplied by 100) the dependency ratio has changed from 100 in 1990 to 152 in 1994 (i.e. 152 economically inactive/100 economically active). After that, the dependency ratio has improved somewhat but is still much higher than before the recession (fig. 1.7).

Unemployment is projected to remain high until the 2010s when the large age groups born at the end of the 1940s and in the beginning of the 1950s reach the age of retirement (Romppanen ja Leppänen, 1993). Thereafter, the working age population is projected to decline with a probable labour shortage. At the same time, the number of pensioners will increase. As the proportion of persons aged 65 and over will grow from the current 14 per cent of the population to 25 per cent in 2030, the dependency ratio will continue to be high. Social expenditure, which in 1990 constituted 26.1 per cent of GDP, is estimated to

FIGURE 1.7

Dependency ratios in 1960-1996

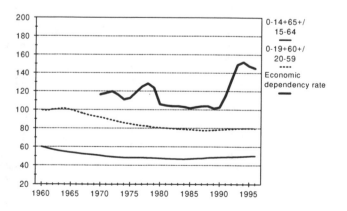

Source: Väestöliitto, 1998

reach 34 per cent by 2020 (Committee Report, 1994:9, 30). Social expenditure for elderly persons is calculated to be three times greater in 2020 than in 1994 (Committee Report, 1996:1, 34).

There is a widespread belief that there will be great difficulties in funding pension costs in the future. Several possible solutions have been suggested and discussed, including higher insurance premiums for employees, lower pensions, postponed retirement until later in life, progressively higher pensions for those who continue to work after the age of 60, etc. According to the Pension Committee (1990) the average age of retirement should be raised by one year per decade from 1990 to 2020 (Committee Report, 1991:40, 2). (In 1995 the average age of retirement was 58 years.) The proportion of the working age population would in this way remain almost unchanged until the 2020s, or about two thirds of the whole population.

Economic growth is considered to be crucial for financing the growing cost of pensions. According to a forecast made by the Government Institute for Economic Research (Romppanen-Leppänen, 1993) the yearly economic growth rate will be 3.25 per cent until 2005, which is considered high enough to keep the present system intact (Parkkinen, 1995). One must remember that while the number of the aged population increases, population growth slows, eventually becoming negative, which means that there is less need for care and education of children and the young, and even for basic investment in housing, transport or energy. It is estimated that it will be possible over the next twenty years with an annual economic growth rate of only two per cent to fund the increasing pension costs. The consensus of opinion is that over the long term there should be no difficulty maintaining that sort of growth rate because Finland enjoys sufficient means of production, including capital, natural assets, and skilled workers (Parkkinen, 1995).

Chapter Two

Living Arrangements

2.1 The pattern of living arrangements

In 1990, most aged people lived with one or several persons, men more than women (table 2.1). Eight in ten men lived with family members, relatives or others. Conversely, living alone is more common for women than men. Over one third of women aged 50 and more lived alone, compared to about one fifth of men. A small proportion of aged persons lived in institutions, women almost twice as frequently as men.

Mainly as a consequence of the difference between men and women's longevity the pattern of living arrangements changes significantly with age. The proportions of those living alone or co-residing with others are almost identical for men and women in the 50-54 age group but change markedly in the older age groups. Living alone increases more with age for women than for men. While about one in seven people aged 50-54 among both men and women lived alone, almost three-quarters of women and two fifths of men over 85, lived alone. Simultaneously, there is a corresponding decline with age in the proportions of senior citizens living with family members

or others. Among women this percentage falls from four fifths to one fifth. Among men the change is not so radical: of those over 85 half still lived with others.

In all, 1.4 per cent of older men and 2.7 per cent of older women lived in institutions. Very few people under 70 years of age lived in institutions but after that it becomes more common and the proportion increases with age. Although the average proportion is low, one in five women aged 85 or over lived in an institution, and one in eight men.

2.2 Private households

Past economic growth, leading to improved social security benefits, housing allowances, the universal pension system, etc. has resulted in greater economic independence and residential autonomy for a growing proportion of older persons. These changes are reflected in the growth in the number of private households which increased by 55 per cent from the 1960s to 1990. This increase has been most marked in the youngest and oldest

TABLE 2.1

The living arrangements of persons aged 50 and over in 1990 (*percentage*)

	Living alone	Living with others	Living in institutions
Men			
50-54	13.9	85.6	0.5
55-59	14.8	84.7	0.6
60-64	16.1	83.2	0.7
65-69	16.7	82.2	1.1
70-74	18.1	80.4	1.5
75-79	23.3	73.9	2.8
80-84	30.1	64.3	5.7
85+	38.1	48.3	13.5
All	**17.2**	**81.3**	**1.4**
Women			
50-54	15.8	83.9	0.3
55-59	21.4	78.3	0.4
60.64	28.5	71.0	0.5
65-69	38.3	60.9	0.8
70-74	49.0	49.3	1.6
75-79	57.7	38.4	4.0
80-84	61.7	29.3	9.0
85+	56.6	22.2	21.2
All	**36.5**	**60.8**	**2.7**

cohorts of senior citizens. Among those aged 75 or over, the increase has been fourfold. At the same time the average size of households has decreased: from 3.3 people in 1960 to 2.4 in 1990. The mean household size diminishes significantly with age, from 2.7 persons in the youngest cohort of aged men to 1.8 among men over age 80, and among women from 2.5 to 1.9 (fig. 2.1). Simultaneously, the number of one-person households has increased: among those aged 65 or over, from 23 per cent to 38 per cent (Lindgren, 1990).

FIGURE 2.1

Mean household size of persons aged 50 and over in 1990, by age and sex

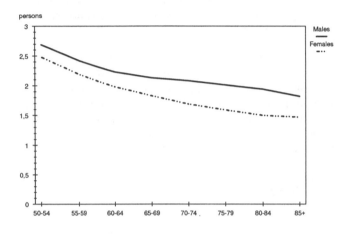

FIGURE 2.2

Proportions of households with persons aged 50 and over in 1990, by number of generations present in the household, age and sex

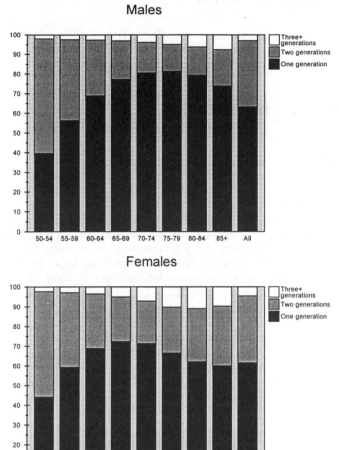

Roughly the same proportion of women and men lived with others. Nearly two thirds of senior citizens lived in a one-generation household. About one third of senior citizens, of either sex, lived in a two-generation household (fig. 2.2).

FIGURE 2.3

Distribution of persons aged 50 and over in 1990 according to generations present in the household, marital status, age and sex

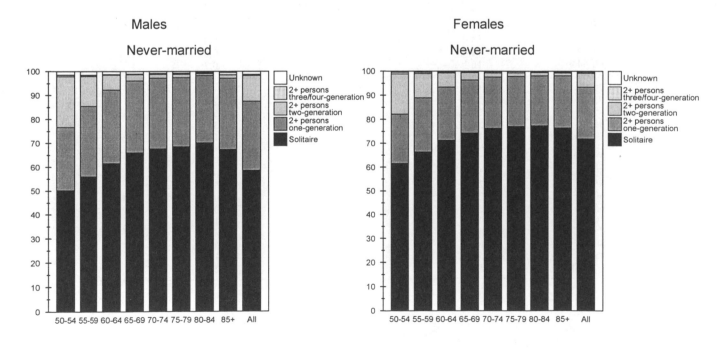

FIGURE 2.3 (*continued*)

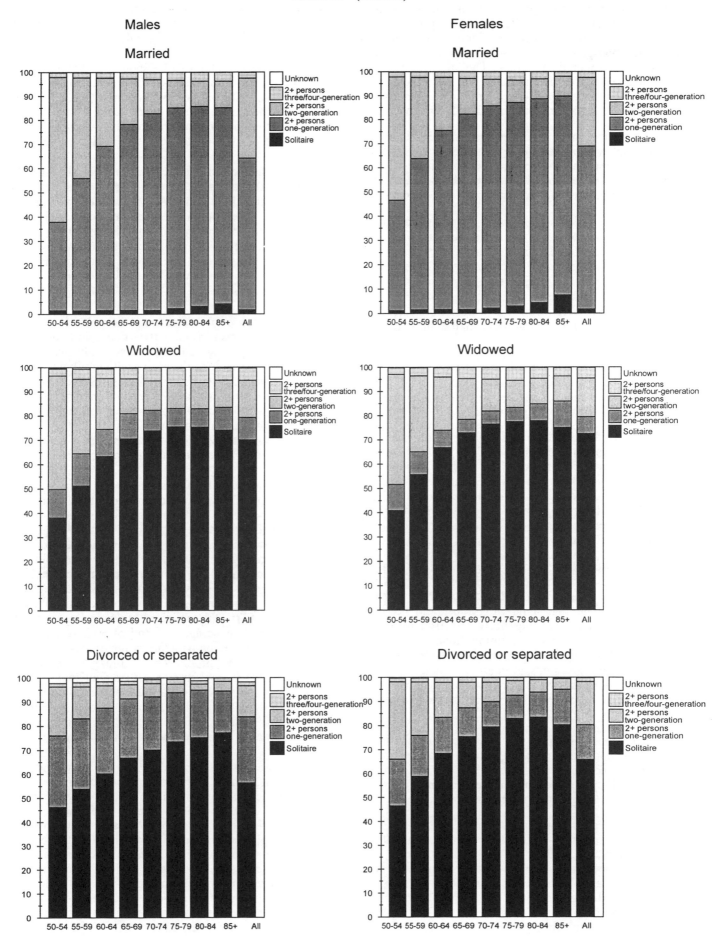

In the youngest age group, those aged 50-54, 58 per cent still lived in a two-generation household, i.e. in a conventional family with children and a spouse. In the subsequent age groups it becomes increasingly common to live in a one-generation household, in the empty nest, but more so for men than women. The proportion of men living in one-generation households reaches its peak of 81 per cent in the age group 75-79, later than the corresponding 72 per cent peak for women in the 65-69 age group.

Living with three or more generations is rather unusual. But with increasing age it does become somewhat more common. One tenth of the oldest age groups of women lived in a household with three generations present. For men this type of household is less common.

Co-residing varies significantly according to marital status. More than two thirds of married senior citizens, the largest sub-group, lived mainly in one-generation households. In the youngest age group, however, 60 per cent of men and 50 per cent of women still lived in a two-generation household. The proportions change gradually with age: among older persons only one in ten belonged to a two-generation household but more than eight in ten to a one-generation household (fig. 2.3).

Widowed, divorced or separated, as well as those who never married, co-reside less and less with age. That means the proportion of men living alone increases as well as the proportion of women.

One half of those categorized as young widowed lived in a two-generation household, evidently with their own children, while one quarter lived alone. The picture changes rapidly with age. At age 70 already three-quarters of the widowed individuals lived alone and only about one tenth lived in a two-generation household. Among the widowed, the proportion of one-generation households is small in all age groups.

In the divorced or separated category, nearly half the 50-54-year-olds lived alone. Among older persons the proportion increases to almost the same level as among the widowed. The two-generation household becomes less and less common. While fully one fifth of 50-54-year-olds lived in a two-generation household only a small proportion of the older persons lived in this way. One-generation households are more common in this category than among the widowed. Divorced men live more often in a one-generation household than divorced women.

Among people who have never married there is a small increase in individuals living alone. Two-generation households account for only a small proportion after the age of 60. The proportion of one-generation households remains almost unchanged regardless of age.

In one-generation households among men, the spouse is the most common co-resider: on average about 70 per cent of men lived with their spouse. Among women, living with the spouse is less common: only 46 per cent lived with their husband. With increasing age the spouse as co-resider diminishes gradually. While about 60 per cent in the 50-54 age group (63 per cent of males and 67 per cent of females) lived in this type of household, only 55 per cent of men aged 80 and over still live with their wife, and

a mere 13 per cent of women still with their husband. Most of those who are co-residing in a one-generation household lived with their spouses only, and only four per cent live with other relatives (fig. 2.4).

In two-generation households spouses and children are the most common co-residers. With increasing age this type of household becomes less common (fig. 2.5). Proportionally, men aged 80 and over lived more frequently with both their spouses and children than women did: of men aged 85 or over, 40 per cent lived with their spouse.

While residence in a typical nuclear family (spouse plus children) decreases with age, there is an increase in residence with children only. Among women over age 80 living in two-generation households, residence with children constitutes the only type of household; roughly eight in ten women lived with one or more children. The corresponding proportion for men is only about four in ten. Some older persons lived with other relatives, roughly ten per cent for both sexes.

The distribution of co-residers in households of three or more generations is roughly the same as in two-generation households (fig. 2.6). In these multi-generation households most senior citizens live with family members in a pattern that differs little from that observed in two-generation households. Here the proportion of senior citizens living with non-relatives is almost as small as that observed in two-generation households; non-relatives are, however, seen somewhat more frequently in these multi-generation households in the age groups below 65.

In 1990, the majority of persons aged 50 and over lived with family members, if one defines as family members parents, grandparents and parents-in-law in addition to spouse and children (table 2.2). There is, however, some variation between men and women, reflecting sex differences in longevity. The majority of men live into old age with one or several family members, and fully one half of those over age 85 or over still do. Among women this living arrangement becomes gradually less and less common after the age of 70. Only one third of women aged 75-79, and one fifth of those aged 85 and over co-reside with family members. Living with family members diminishes with age; and the proportion of those living alone increases with age more among women than among men. In the oldest age group one half of men and eight out of ten women live alone. It is unusual to live with another person who is not a family member: this arrangement accounts for only one or two per cent of each age group.

As the preceding figures show, living in two-person households is, generally speaking, the most common living arrangement. At ages 50 and above 54 per cent of men and 44 per cent of women live in such households (fig. 2.7). Two-person households (usually consisting of a married couple) become more common towards the general age of retirement. With advancing age, such households become less frequent again, a decline proportionally steeper among women than among men. Men live more often than women in a two-person household. While two-person households are rather uncommon among women aged 85 and over, among men of the same age they are as common as one-person households.

FIGURE 2.4

Distribution of persons aged 50 and over living in one-generation households in 1990, by household composition, age and sex

Males

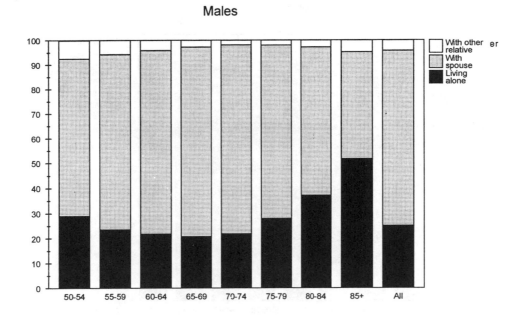

Females

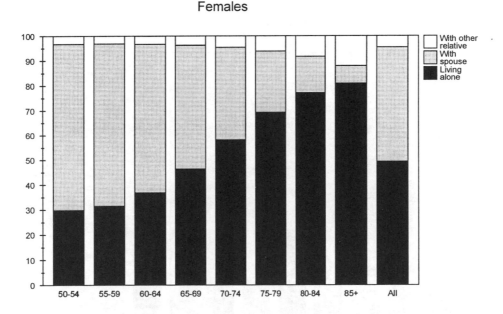

Three-person or larger households are fairly common among the youngest cohort (aged 50-54 years): a quarter of them live in this way. With increasing age this type of household becomes increasingly exceptional: it is home to only a small proportion of persons aged 80 and over (11 per cent of men and 7 per cent of women).

For women the likelihood of living alone increases rapidly with age. This is not only the case among childless women but also among mothers (fig. 2.8). The number of children born seems to affect the likelihood of a woman living alone. As expected childless women live alone more often than those with children. Above age 85, when living with children is most common, 16 per cent of mothers with one offspring live with that son or daughter, 31 per cent of mothers with two offspring live with one of them, and 34 per cent of those with three or more offspring live with one. However, at most only about ten per cent of women live with offspring.

2.3 Living with a disabled person

Around ten per cent of men and somewhat more women who are not receiving a disability pension live with a disabled person (fig. 2.9). For those who live in two-generation households, the proportion grows rather rapidly after 65. Among those aged 85 and over, 27 per cent live with a disabled person. Evidently, two-generation households mostly consist of persons living with a disabled child or with a disabled spouse.

FIGURE 2.5

**Distribution of persons aged 50 and over living in two-generation households in 1990,
by household composition, age and sex**

Males

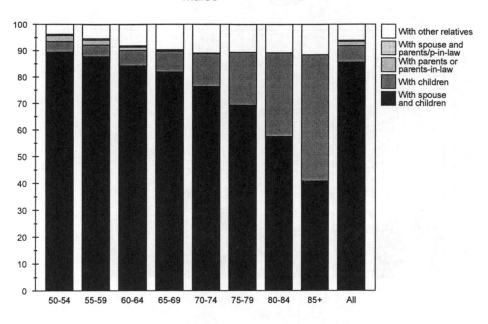

Females

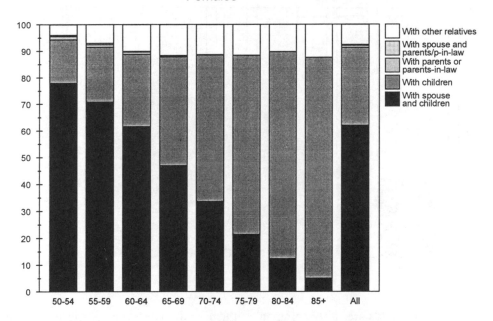

FIGURE 2.6

**Distribution of persons aged 50 and over living in households of three or more generations in 1990,
by household composition, age and sex**

Males

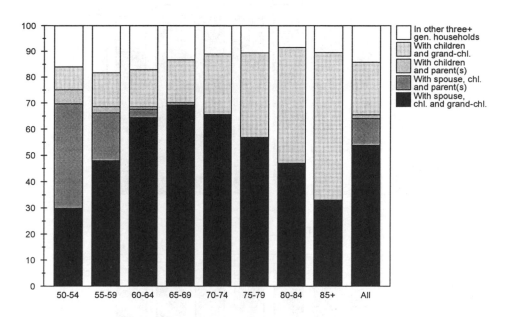

Females

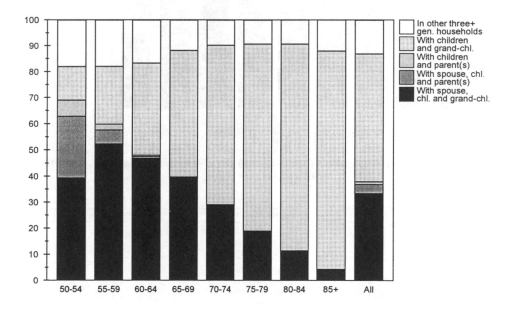

FIGURE 2.7

**Distribution of household size for persons aged 50 and over
in 1990 by age and sex**

Males

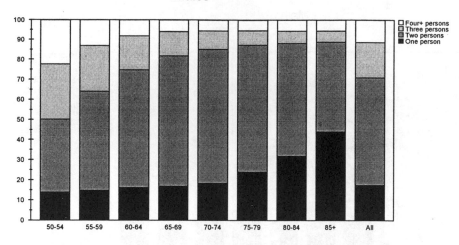

Females

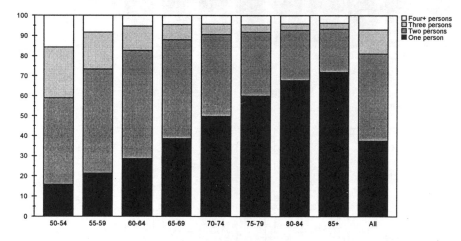

TABLE 2.2

**Distributions of non-institutionalized persons aged 50 and over by living arrangements in 1991,
by age and sex** (*percentage*)

	Living alone	*Living with family members* *	*Living with others*
Men			
50-54	14.0	80.3	5.7
55-59	14.8	79.3	5.8
60-64	16.2	78.4	5.4
65-69	16.9	79.0	4.1
70-74	18.4	78.2	3.4
75-79	24.0	72.8	3.2
80-84	31.9	64.3	3.8
85+	44.1	50.1	5.8
All	**17.5**	**77.6**	**4.9**
Women			
50-54	15.8	80.3	3.8
55-59	21.4	74.0	4.6
60-64	28.7	66.4	4.9
65-69	38.6	56.4	5.0
70-74	49.8	44.6	5.5
75-79	60.1	33.2	6.7
80-84	67.8	23.8	8.4
85+	71.9	16.0	12.1
All	**37.5**	**57.0**	**5.5**

* Spouse, child(ren), grandchild(ren), parent(s), parent(s)-in-law or grandparent(s).

FIGURE 2.8

FIGURE 2.8

The distribution of females aged 50 and over according to living arrangement, number of children ever born and age

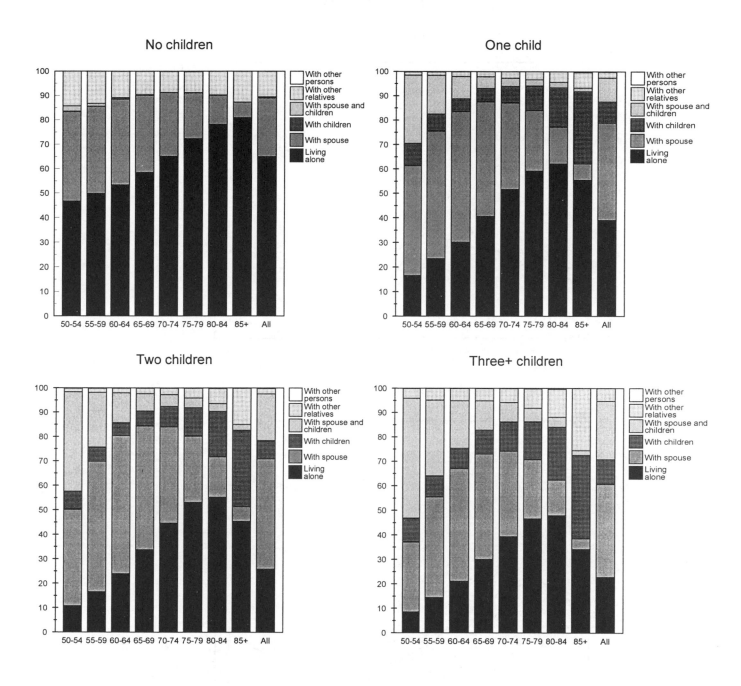

Note: With spouse includes also households where there are other persons (other than children) than the couple

The proportion of persons living in one- and three-generation households decreases rather rapidly among men over 70, and among women over 60. A slight increase in three-generation households is observed after 75. In one-generation households, a decline starts at 70 for men and 60 for women. The shrinking proportion of households with a disabled person is simply because mortality is higher than normal among the disabled.

2.4 Living in institutions

According to the Scandinavian universal welfare model, social security services are guaranteed to all. Characteristic of the Scandinavian model is the effort to diminish dependence on the family. The family's legal duty of care of parents in old age was abolished in the

FIGURE 2.9

The proportion of persons not receiving a disability pension themselves but living with a disabled person in 1990, by number of generations present in the household

Males

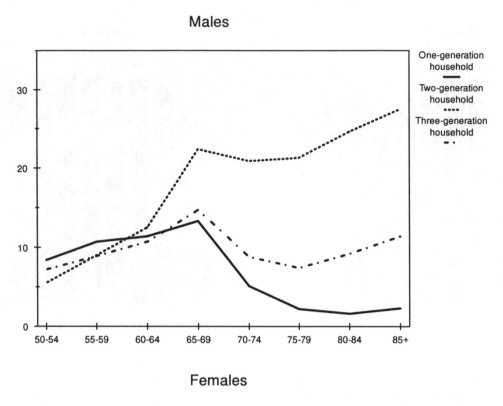

Females

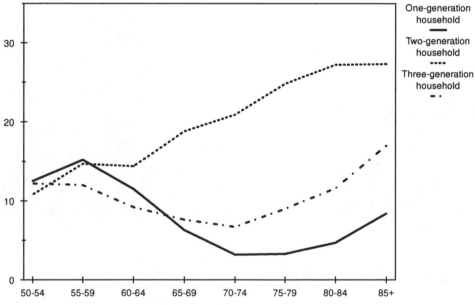

1970s. In practice, municipalities run the services for senior citizens. These include service flats and service houses, homes for senior citizens as well as nursing homes and centres where older persons can obtain auxiliary services like meals, bathing, pedicure, etc. The cost of living in service flats and homes for senior citizens is subsidized and means-tested (dependent on the resident's income).

Home help and home nursing have been intensified. Consequently, today older persons mostly live alone, or with others, for as long as possible, in an owner-occupied[1] apartment, service apartment or service house, or on the farm, with maintenance arranged for them.[2]

---

[1] A characteristic feature of the development of Finnish housing conditions has been the rising trend of owner-occupied housing. In 1990, 70 per cent of dwellings were owner-occupied, mostly in the form of housing corporations.

[2] When a farm is transmitted to the following generation payment sometimes is affected in a form of maintenance agreement. The maintenance agreement includes mostly an allowance in kind, living accommodation, different foodstuffs, clothing, etc.

FIGURE 2.10

Institutionalized persons aged 50 and over in 1990 by marital status, age and sex

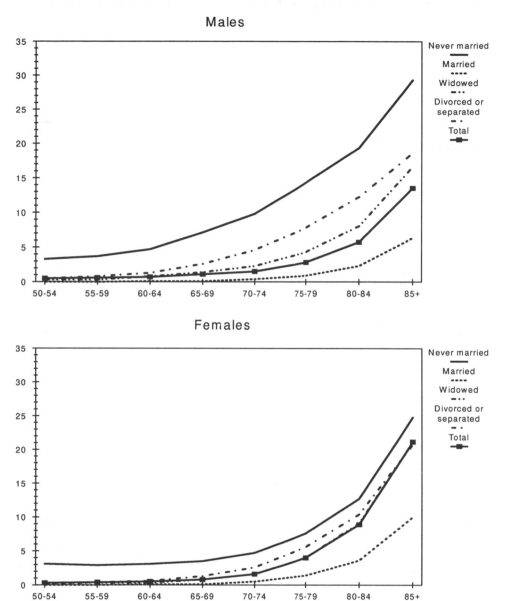

Males

Females

Institutionalized senior citizens are mainly clients in homes for senior citizens or in nursing homes or patients at hospitals and mental institutions. In 1990, five per cent of persons aged 75-84 and 19 per cent of persons aged 85 or more were institutionalized (Ministry of Social Affairs and Health, 1995).

The pattern of institutionalization varies widely according to marital status. Those who live alone, were never married, were widowed, divorced or separated are far more likely to live in an institution (fig. 2.10). Senior citizens who never married and who lived in 1990 in an institution constitute six per cent which is much higher than the total average proportion of aged persons who lived in institutions. The average proportion for men aged 50 and over was 1.4 per cent and for women 2.6 per cent.

Widows and widowers aged over 80 constitute up to five per cent. Married persons are seldom clients in institutions.

Clearly, a pension is the most common source of income for those who live in institutions regardless of gender and marital status (fig. 2.11). As the institutionalized are often sick or disabled, a pension is common even among those who have not yet reached the age of retirement. Earned income is in fact almost negligible. As with private households, other income, from property, investments, bonds, dividends, assets, sale of timber, etc. is received by those in the age groups under 65 but amounts to relatively little. Men have somewhat more income from other sources than women; and there is also some variation between men according to marital status.

FIGURE 2.11

Proportion of persons aged 50 and over living in institutions with a pension as sole source of income and with other sources (excluding pensions and wages) in 1990, by marital status, age and sex

Males

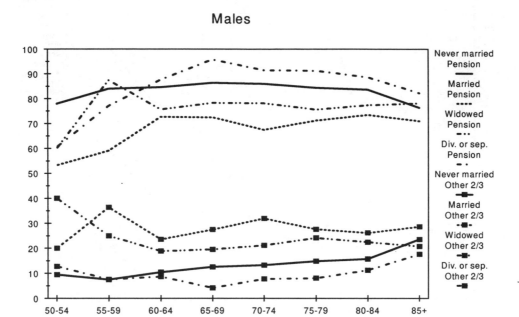

Females

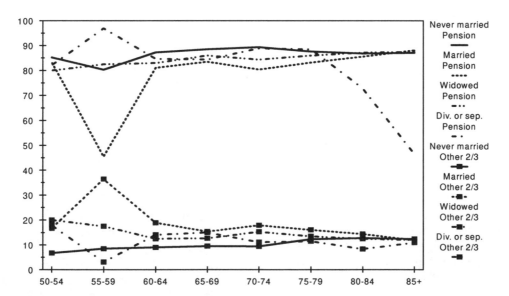

Chapter Three

Work and Retirement

3.1 Economic activity of senior citizens

In 1990 the labour force participation rate[3] was practically the same for both men and women, or almost 80 per cent among those aged 50-54 and nearly 60 per cent in the next older five-year age group (fig. 3.1). Among those aged 60-64 only 49 per cent of men and 45 per cent of women were economically active, and after 65 years of age very few individuals continue to work. The decrease of activity with age is caused not only by declining health and greater unemployment (leading to a pension) but also by a decline in the social valuation of work. The fact that an early old-age pension is easy to receive is an important incentive for declining work activity. To some extent, lower education in the older age groups has contributed as the working environment has undergone rapid changes (see below).

It is somewhat surprising to find that about half of the 60-64 age group is still economically active when, according to the *Statistical Yearbook of Pensioners in Finland* in 1995, 80 per cent of the age group were pensioners. Apparently, the explanation is that some pensioners are still working while at the same time receiving a pension. This is perfectly legal in many Finnish pension systems.

In 1990 unemployment was low, with only a few people under 60 unemployed. In the 60-64 age group unemployment had jumped to 20 per cent. The substantial unemployment rate[4] among those aged 60-64 was apparently a consequence of the pension reforms of the 1980s, which made it easier to draw a pension. Later, in the 1990s the recession forced entrepreneurs to restructure their businesses and the cost-cutting efforts hastened workers' inclination to retire. There was a desire to pension off and to be pensioned. According to a study from the beginning of the 1990s (Gould, 1993) unemployment was an important path to a pension among older workers whose activity rate was lowest. Activity rates were low in industries highly dependent on the economic cycle, especially in construction, typically employing men, and textiles, typically employing women.

Gradually, the rules governing early pensions became more rigorous. The result was that the number of persons receiving unemployment pensions diminished even though unemployment rose. In 1995, there were 30 per cent fewer pensioners in the unemployment pension system than in 1990.

Classified as "other" in the chart (fig. 3.1) are people not categorized as belonging to the workforce, i.e. neither employed nor unemployed, nor pensioners. Apparently, most of these are family members e.g. housewives. Those who have not been economically active and are not entitled to an employment pension receive a pension under the national pension system at 65.

Men and women show about the same rate of economic activity and these rates vary only slightly with marital status (fig. 3.2). Married people show the highest activity rates, particularly married men aged 50-54, of whom around 88 per cent are economically active. Divorced or separated women also show a relatively high economic activity rate, almost as high as that of married women. The activity rate among divorced or separated men is by contrast relatively low. Apparently, divorced or separated women are often lone breadwinners and work until the age of retirement.

The high economic activity rate for women is a consequence of the increasing participation of women in the labour force, especially since the 1970s. In 1970-1974, the female workforce constituted 60-65 per cent of the female population aged 15-64. During subsequent years it continued to grow, reaching 73 per cent in 1985-1989. During the recession at the beginning of the 1990s female participation in the labour force decreased somewhat, but it has since increased, reaching 70 per cent in 1995.

Men who never married show the lowest economic activity rate, proportionally lower than that of women who never married (fig. 3.3.). Evidently, the low activity rate among divorced or separated men, or men who never married, is caused by ill health, and also by the higher probability of death among men living alone. For women the variation with marital status is on the whole rather slight. The probability of death, often used as an indicator of morbidity, shows that in Finland the probability of death at the age of 50 is twice as high among men who never married, or divorced or widowed men, compared to married men. However, the difference diminishes with age and is almost non-existent at 80 (Koskinen-Martelin, 1994, 211-218).

It is widely known that unemployment hits the less educated first. Hence, in all age groups the economic activity rate increases with education (fig. 3.4). In the 50-54 age group about 80 per cent of those with the lowest

---

[3] The ratio of members of the labour force to the total working-age population.

[4] The ratio of unemployed to all members of the labour force.

FIGURE 3.1

Economic activity of persons aged 50 and over in 1990 by age and sex

Males

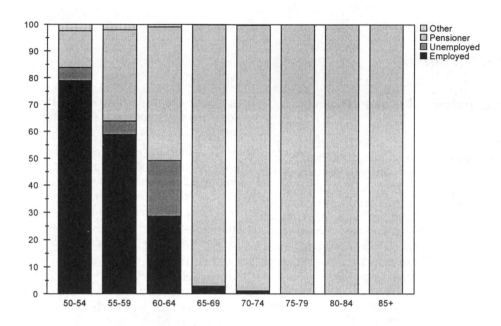

Females

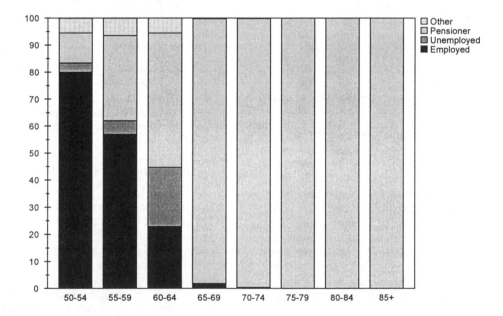

FIGURE 3.2

**Economic activity rates of persons aged 50 and over in 1990
by marital status, sex and age**

Males

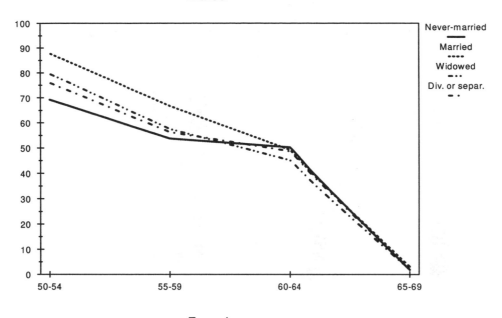

Females

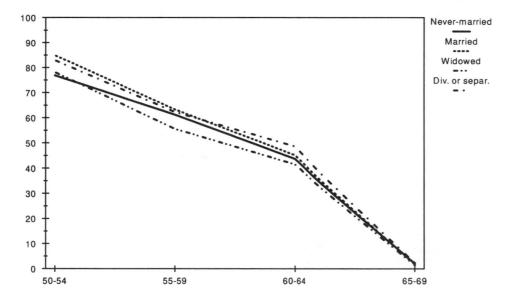

education, irrespective of gender, were economically active, whereas the activity rate was almost 94 per cent among graduates.[5] In the oldest economically active age group, 60-64 years, 47 per cent of men and 45 per cent of women with the lowest education were active compared to 67 per cent of graduate men and 57 per cent of female graduates.

On the whole, the economic activity rate varies little with gender when educational levels are factored into the equation.

Two-generation households produce the most economically active persons. The average rate of employment is 57 per cent among men and 48 per cent among women. These households obviously consist in the main of couples or single parents with children. The rates for all other household groups are between 18 and 29 per cent, except men and women living alone: 23 per cent and 14 per cent respectively.

It might seem confusing that women living alone are markedly less active economically than men. The explanation is that there are far more women than men in the oldest age groups, which skews the proportions. Actually, the activity rate for women living alone is greater or as great as that for men in the 50-64 age group, which is also evident from the rates for the age cohorts.

---

[5] The educational levels used are:

Educational level 1 and 2 = Lower and upper level of secondary education

Educational level 1 and 3 = Lowest level of higher education

Undergraduate = Undergraduate level of higher education

Graduate = Graduate and postgraduate level of higher education.

FIGURE 3.3

**The unemployment rate of persons aged 50 and over in Finland in 1990,
by marital status, sex and age**

Males

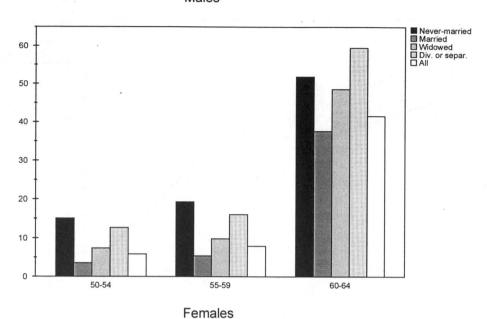

Females

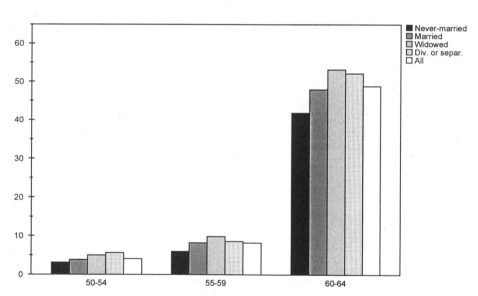

Hence a comparison of the averages by sex runs the risk of errors. The same may also be said of the other generation groups even within the same sex. One means of avoiding these pitfalls is to use age-standardization.

There is significant variation in the age-standardized economic status index according to number of generations living in the household, especially among men (fig. 3.5). For men, two-generation households exhibit the highest employment rate. Of those who live alone, i.e. those never married, the divorced, separated and widowed, there are fewer employed persons. Consequently, most of the unemployed are to be found among those liv-

ing alone and fewer in three-generation households. There is practically no variation between households in the number of pensioners, be there one, two or more generations present in the household. A rather unexpected finding is that men living alone and categorized as being outside the workforce actually show the highest rates of economic activity.

For women, the differences between household groups are small. Unlike for men, roughly the same proportion of women living alone are unemployed as women living in other household groups. Those categorized as "other" and economically inactive are few, around one or two per cent

FIGURE 3.4

**Economic activity of persons aged 50 and over in 1990
by educational level, sex and age**

Males

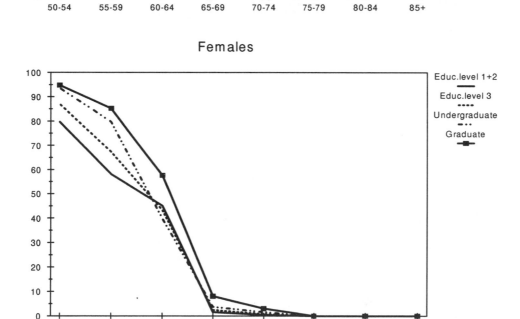

Females

or less, and apparently receive a daily allowance for sickness or some other income. Consequently they could be considered well on the road towards a pension.

3.2 Part-time work

The number of part-time workers is appreciably smaller in Finland than in other west European countries. In 1993, part-time workers accounted for only 8.6 per cent of those employed. The majority of part-time workers are women. The reason for extensive full-time working might be that full-time employment and sufficient earnings have been considered important for women's financial independence. Another reason could be the full-time work tradition, especially among men. Furthermore, the relatively high educational background of women might have con-

tributed to the fact that part-time work is less favoured (Kangasharju et al., 1995). The availability of part-time work seems to be dictated more by employers' policy rather than the employee's wish to find part-time work. This has been the case particularly among those employed in industry. Part-time workers often want full-time work (Julkunen and Nätti, 1995).

Although attitudes towards increasing the availability of part-time work have been positive, the proportion of part-time workers has remained low. During the recession voluntary part-time work was encouraged in order to share work more equally. People raising small children, studying, retiring, etc. were thought to be interested in this opportunity to reduce working hours and spend more time on other activities. However, the measure failed to boost the number of part-time workers.

FIGURE 3.5

Age-standardized index showing economic activity of persons aged 50 and over in 1990, by age, sex and number of generations present in the household

Males

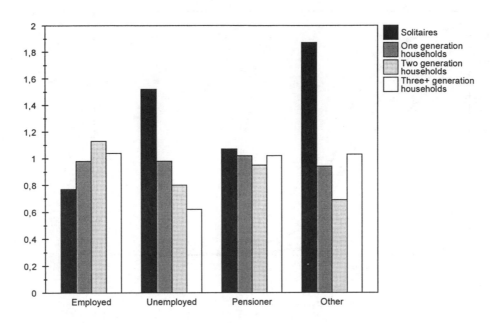

Females

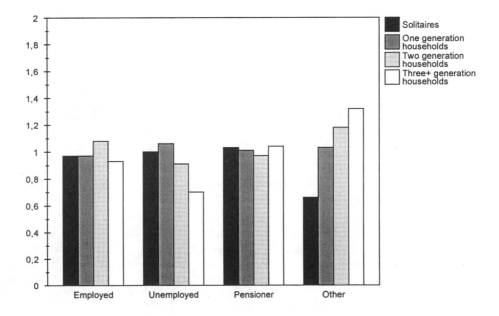

3.3 More pensioners

Over recent decades the number of pensioners has increased rapidly. Average lifespans have increased and a pension can be drawn at an earlier age than previously. The recession in the early 1990s also contributed to an increase in the number of pensioners.

In 1990, people receiving some form of pension constituted 23.2 per cent of the total Finnish population. In 1995 this proportion was 23.8 per cent (*Statistical Yearbook of Pensioners in Finland*, 1991, ditto 1996).

In the mid-1980s, the pension system was extended with two new early old-age retirement pensions (see section 3.4). There were several underlying reasons for this policy change. A lower age of retirement was desired for those who had defended the country during the war of 1939-1945. Malnutrition, war injuries and other hardships encountered during the war had affected people's long-term health and thus increased the need for an earlier retirement system. In addition, after the war a new economic era began. Agriculture became a rapidly shrinking mechanized industry that required less manual labour. In industry new methods of production gradually took over. Older workers often had difficulties in learning the new skills. Within the service sector the new information technology was presented a hurdle too high for many aged workers to overcome. Recurrent unemployment also contributed to reform the pension systems (Nurminen, 1990). Early retirement from gainful employment to a disability pension or early pension has been possible for large numbers of people. As a result, the proportion of people on a disability or early pension in Finland is high by international standards. In 1993 a male pensioner had on average a span of 17.3 years left after he had retired (Hytti, 1996). For women the corresponding life expectancy was 22.6 years.

In Finland, attitudes towards work gradually changed with the economic boom in the 1980s. Many believed that one possessed the moral right to retire as early as possible to be able to enjoy life at least a few years in fairly good health. In addition, the progressive taxation system and the opportunity to take advantage of various free social services may also have contributed to the popularity of early retirement (EVA, 1989). The pensioner's is a socially acceptable way of life in Finland (*Statistical Yearbook of Pensioners in Finland*, 1996).

The new pension system made it possible for individuals to retire at an earlier age than was the case previously. At the beginning of the 1980s, the mean age at retirement of both sexes was 60 (Lindgren 1992). In 1990, about 80 per cent of the population aged 60-64 years and 41 per cent of those aged 55-59 received some form of pension (*Statistical Yearbook of Pensioners in Finland*, 1991). The mean age at retirement fell to 58 (Hufvudstadsbladet, 1997). Subsequently, the proportion receiving a pension among those aged 60-64 years has further increased to 85 per cent in 1995 but decreased among those aged 55-59 years to 37 per cent (*Statistical Yearbook of Pensioners in Finland*, 1996).

On the whole, there is a lower proportion of individuals in the workforce aged 55-65 in Finland than in other Nordic or west European countries (Keinänen, 1993).

3.4 The Finnish pension system

There are two main pension insurance systems in Finland: the national pension system and the employment-based pension system. National insurance, which covers the entire population, is aimed at providing the security of a minimum income for all pensioners. Employment-based pensions are calculated in proportion to previous earnings and are payable to employees as well as the self-employed. The national pension and the employment-based pension systems provide pensions on the grounds of old age, disability, death of a spouse or parent, and long-term unemployment. In addition, there are also special pension systems like the war-front veteran's pension, and in agriculture the change-of-generation pension or farm closure pension.

The general age of retirement in Finland is 65 years. However, in State and municipal pension systems the age of retirement could under older contracts be 63 or even lower. In 1986-1989 a pension reform introducing flexible retirement age was enacted. It became possible to draw an old-age pension before the age of 65 by opting for an early pension payable at a permanently reduced rate. The early old-age pension is payable from age 60 in the private sector and from 58 in the public sector. In the same reform package, a special disability pension called individual early retirement pension was introduced for persons aged 55-64 with a long working career provided that their capacity to work has been so permanently impaired that they cannot be expected to continue in their present job. Normally, a disability pension (either full or partial) is awarded to an employee who has lost the capacity to work, is disabled or injured, irrespective of age. After 65 the disability pension turns into an old-age pension.

An individual who has drawn the unemployment daily allowance for the maximum period (500 days) and has reach the age of 57 before the end of this period continues to receive the unemployment daily allowance up to the age of 60. After that he has right to an unemployment pension if he has been employed at least five years during the last 15 years. The unemployment pension ends at the age of 63 when he is entitled to an old-age pension. In practice, it means that an individual who is 55 years old when he is discharged could leave the workforce if he wants. This pension system is rather popular among entrepreneurs when wanting to rejuvenate the age-structure of the enterprise.

Employment-based pensions are determined by earnings and length of working career. A full pension in the private sector is 60 per cent of salary after a 40-year period of employment, or 1.5 per cent for every year of employment. The full public sector pension, which is payable after 30 years of service, is 66 per cent of salary, or 2.2 per cent for every year. Since 1994, those aged 60 and over receive 2.5 per cent for every year of employment both in the private and public sectors. The pension scheme in the private sector was introduced in the beginning of the 1960s and the full amount, 60 per cent, will be attainable not prior to the turn of the millennium. As a consequence, in 1995 four out of five pensioners who had retired on grounds of age simultaneously drew an employment-based pension and a national pension (*Statistical Yearbook of Pensioners in Finland*, 1996). As the employment-based pension is too small to guarantee a minimum income it is completed with a national pension.

If retirement is postponed beyond 65 the size of the pension received is increased. Pension benefit levels are adjusted every year using an index calculated from the price index and the general wages index.

Chapter Four

Sources of Income

4.1 Pensioners' income

Three studies which have examined the well-being of pensioners could be mentioned. One of them, published at the end of the 1980s was based on the official household survey conducted in 1985 (Puhakka, 1988). The other two are based on the 1990 household survey (Sailas, 1994; Tennilä, 1994). The latter, which approach the topic from somewhat different angles, give information on the income of senior citizens. Because the data collected by the Population Activities Unit do not include any information on income structure or size, it would be useful to cite some results from these studies.

In 1985 pensioners' households in which the reference person[6] was 65-69 had the highest incomes—calculated in terms of consumption units[7]—while those over 80 received the lowest. The difference is mainly due to the fact that the younger age group included more recipients of the employment-based pension than the older age group, who commonly drew the smaller national pension (see section 3.4). Sixty per cent of households headed by a person aged 65-69 drew an employment-based pension compared to only 38 per cent of those aged 80 and over. Overall the employment-based pension has accounted for an increasing proportion of the gross income of pensioners since 1985, reaching on average 64 per cent in 1990 (Sailas, 1994).

According to the household survey of 1985, the income of households consisting entirely of pensioners was about twenty per cent lower than that of households without pensioners. A good two thirds of these pensioner households fell into the two lowest income quintiles. Almost 70 per cent were one-person households, and most of the remainder were two-person households (Puhakka, 1988).

The highest incomes—even higher than those of non-pensioners—were enjoyed by pensioners' households in which the reference person had the highest level of education (university degree or equivalent). In all, these households comprised only about four per cent of pensioner households. The lowest incomes were received by those households where the reference person had the lowest level of education. Those aged 80 and over were particularly well represented in this group. In 1985 income from assets was greatest among households whose members were 65 or over.

Senior citizens, aged 80 or over, saved more than other households. This is due apparently not only to the fact that people are less able to consume as they get older but also because they opt to save for a rainy day. Older generations are commonly disinclined to seek the assistance of social welfare: they attach great importance to the need to manage one's life without support from outsiders. If savings are aggregated, in 1985 pensioner households accounted for almost 20 per cent of total household savings. However, saving is negligible among persons on a low income, or among the majority of senior citizens (Puhakka, 1988).

In 1985, pensioners gave away more of their disposable income in the form of donations and gifts than households without pensioners. According to the 1990 household survey persons aged 55-64 living alone were the greatest helpers of other households. Transfers from non-pensioner households to households consisting of persons 65 and over amounted to two per cent of gross income (Sailas, 1994).

The 1990 household survey shows us that consumption was highest per capita in households of persons aged 30-34. Expenditure decreased with age, dropping to 50 per cent of the peak level by the 70-74 age group, and about 40 per cent of the peak level for people aged 80 or over (Tennilä, 1994).

Although income decreases with age, in 1985 only eight per cent of those aged 65 or over were dissatisfied with their economic circumstances, while three per cent referred to occasional financial difficulties (Tennilä, 1994). In 1994, roughly the same proportion, nine per cent, considered their pension too low. Twelve per cent said that they were fairly satisfied with their income (Ministry of Social Affairs and Health, 1994).

The household survey of 1990 shows little variation by gender of disposable income among one-person households in the age groups 55-74, whereas among persons aged 75 and over, women's incomes are ten per cent lower than men's. It is not possible, at least not from the household surveys, to get detailed information on the income or use of income of elderly persons who live in households together with younger persons (Sailas, 1994).

---

[6] The head of the household who is considered mainly responsible for providing the earnings of the household.

[7] The consumption unit for one adult is 1 and 0.7 for other adults. A household with e.g. two adults represents 1.7 consumption units.

FIGURE 4.1

**Types of source of income of persons aged 50 and over living
in one-person households in 1990, by age and sex**

Males

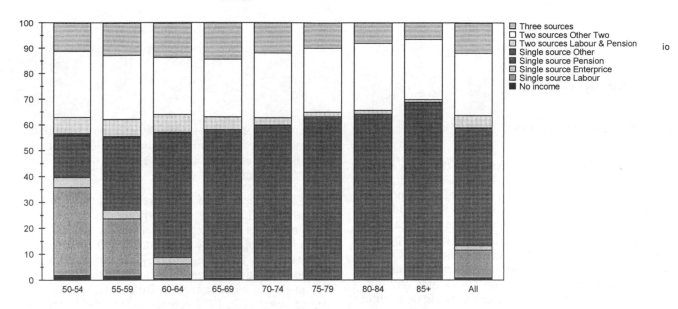

Females

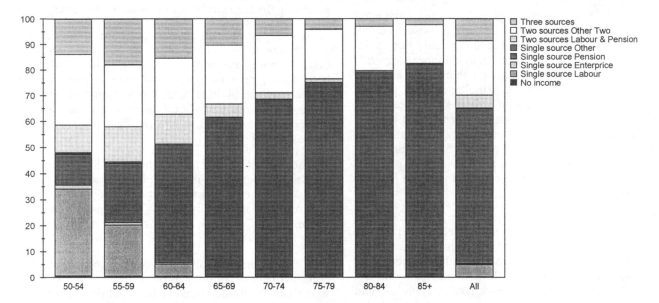

4.2   Sources of income in private households

The most important single source of income among economically active single-person households in 1990 was labour (fig. 4.1). In the age group 50-54, on average one third of men and women derived their income from work. Labour as a source of income decreases rapidly with age, and a pension is already the most important single source of income already in the age group 55-59. After 65 almost nobody derives an income from labour.

With increasing age, the old-age pension rapidly becomes the most important single source of income. A

pension is on average the only source of income for roughly six out of ten people aged 65-69 (58 per cent of men and 61 per cent of women). This is the case for 65 per cent of men, and 80 per cent of women aged 80 and over.

Although a pension is the most common single source of income among persons who have reached the general age of retirement, a significant proportion of senior citizens also has an income from other sources than work or pension. But the income from these other sources is rather small. According to the household survey of 1985, these other sources constituted on average nine per cent of the total income of pensioner households with persons aged

FIGURE 4.2.

Types of sources of income of persons aged 50 and over in 1990 living in two- or three-person households in 1990, by age and sex

Males

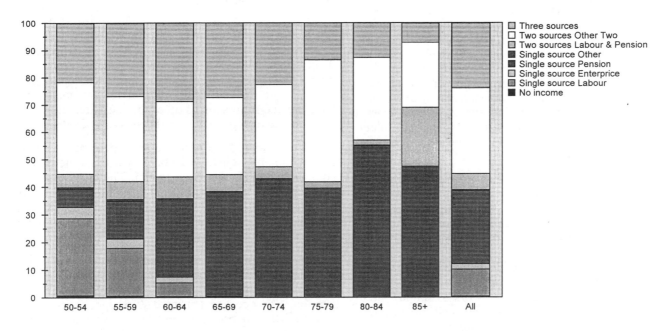

Females

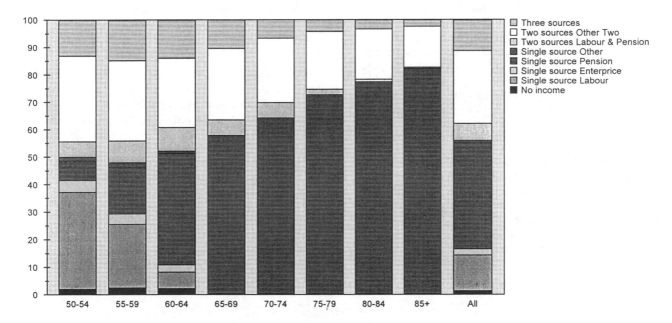

55 or over. Most of it was estimated income based on products produced or picked for own use, mostly farm and forest products (Puhakka, 1988). In 1990, among households of persons aged 65 or over, the income per consumption unit from other sources, i.e. property rental income and income from owner-occupied dwellings, was about ten per cent of disposable income (Sailas, 1994). This sort of income was almost nil in the lowest income quintiles (to which the majority of senior citizens belonged).

For men, the proportions of income from other sources are more or less unaffected by age. On average, about a quarter of men have some income from two sources other than wages or a pension. By contrast women receive less and less income from other sources with increasing age. In the 50-54 age group almost one third of women receives income from other sources; among the older women only one eighth. People classified as recipients of income from three sources are much fewer and their presence decreases rapidly after the general age of retirement, especially among women.

There is some variation by marital status in the relative magnitude of the different sources of income. Labour as a sole source of income is most common among men who have never married, who are divorced or separated men. Widowed men show the greatest proportion of recipients of a pension as sole source of income. The main reason for the high proportion of widowed men with pension as a sole source of income is the proportionally high number of widowers in the oldest age group i.e. long-lived men. Regardless of marital status, women are on average best represented amongst those living exclusively on a pension. However, the proportion receiving income solely from work in age groups 50 to 64 exceeds that of men in all marital status groups.

Those living in two- or three-person households generally show the same income distribution pattern as those living alone (fig. 4.2). However, among the former there is on average a significantly smaller proportion of people living solely on a pension. The reason is that fewer people receive a pension in the working-age age groups. Conversely, these households contain a somewhat higher proportion of people with income from several sources, especially among men. Among women work as single source of income is twice as frequent in two- and three-person households than in one-person households.

Most two- and three-person households have two income recipients (table 4.1). Regardless of sex and marital status the proportion of households with two recipients is about 80-85 per cent. Only households with married people have proportionally somewhat fewer income recipients. Between 10 and 24 per cent of households in the category of two- and three-person households contain three income recipients. From the material available, it is not possible separately to determine the number of recipients in two- and three-person households respectively.

A pension is the most important single source of income after age 60 and its significance increases with age. In one-person households, divorced and separated people constitute the largest percentages of people with a pension as sole source of income (fig. 4.3). This appears more prominently among men than women where the proportions are almost the same in all marital status groups. Twenty to thirty per cent of pensioners have income from sources other than pension and work. Other

income sources are in general more important among working-age people. Among men the proportions diminish fairly little with age, and even older men frequently receive income from sources other than a pension. Among older women this kind of income is less prevalent than in younger age groups.

In two- and three-person households the pattern is nearly the same as in one-person households (fig. 4.4). For women the proportions are much the same independently of marital status. Men, however, show a more complicated picture: the differences according to marital status are more marked. Married men, for example, often have income from sources other than pension and work; for divorced or separated men this is less often the case.

An overview of the proportions of persons with pension as the only source of income by age and household composition is shown in figure 4.5. The curve showing the proportion of men with pension as the only source of income in two- and three-person households exhibits some peculiar jumps which evidently are caused by faults in the sample material used.

The proportion of persons with a disability pension increases towards the general age of retirement (fig. 4.6). Persons living alone are most often awarded a disability pension, 40 per cent of men aged 60-64 and 30 per cent of women. The proportion of persons receiving a disability pension is almost the same in one- to three-generation households. However, men receive a disability pension somewhat more often than women. The difference between the proportion of male pensioners living alone and those living with others is also greater than among female pensioners.

A disability pension becomes an old-age pension on reaching the age of 65. Those in the 65-69 age group who still get the disability pension have for some reason not been able to receive an old-age pension at their 65th birthday.

4.3 Sources of income from persons living in institutions

A pension is the most common source of income for those who live in institutions regardless of gender or marital status (fig. 4.7). As the institutionalized are often sick or disabled a pension is common even among those

TABLE 4.1

Distribution of households according to number of income recipients among persons aged 50 and over living in two- or three-person households in Finland in 1990, by sex and marital status
(*percentage*)

	Never married	Married	Widowed	Divorced or separated
Men				
One recipient	3.2	1.3	1.7	3.1
Two recipients	81.5	74.2	83.7	82.0
Three recipients	15.1	24.4	14.6	14.8
Women				
One recipient	2.9	1.6	2.2	4.2
Two recipients	87.1	77.4	82.5	82.7
Three recipients	9.9	21.3	15.2	12.9

FIGURE 4.3

Proportion of persons aged 50 and over in 1990 in one-person households with pension as the only source of income as well as with other sources of income (excluding pension and labour), by age, sex and marital status

Males

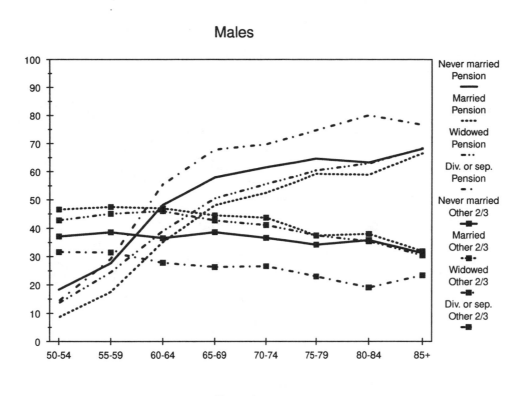

Females

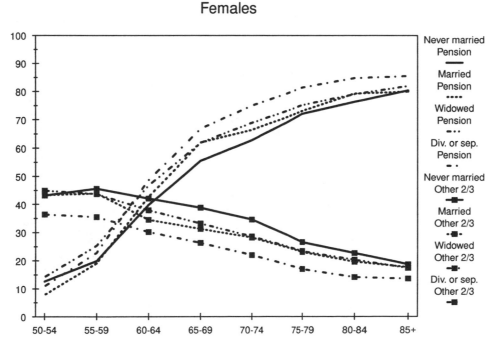

who have not yet reached the age of retirement. Earned income is in fact almost negligeable. As with private households, other income, from property investments, bonds, dividends, assets, sale of timber etc. is received by those in the age group under 65 but amounts to relatively little. Men have somewhat higher income from other sources than women and there are also some variations between men according to marital status.

FIGURE 4.4

Proportion of persons aged 50 and over in 1990 in two- or three-person households with pension as only source of income as well as with other sources of income (except pension and labour), by age, sex and marital status

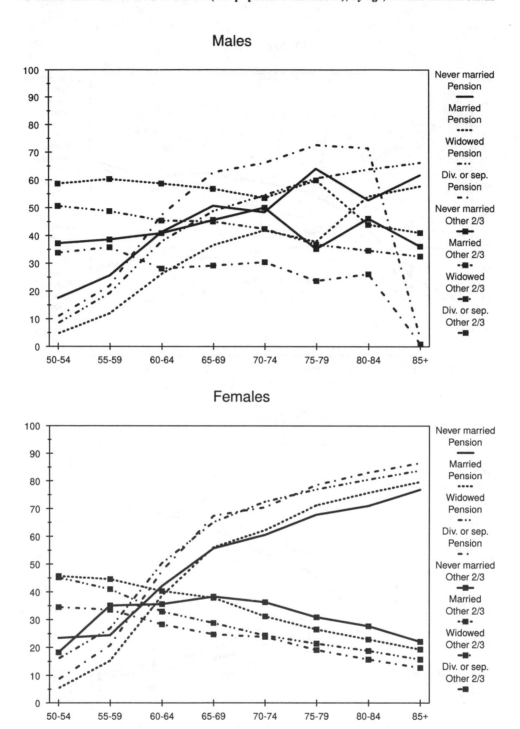

FIGURE 4.5

Proportion of persons aged 50 and over in 1990 with pension as the only source of income, by age and household composition

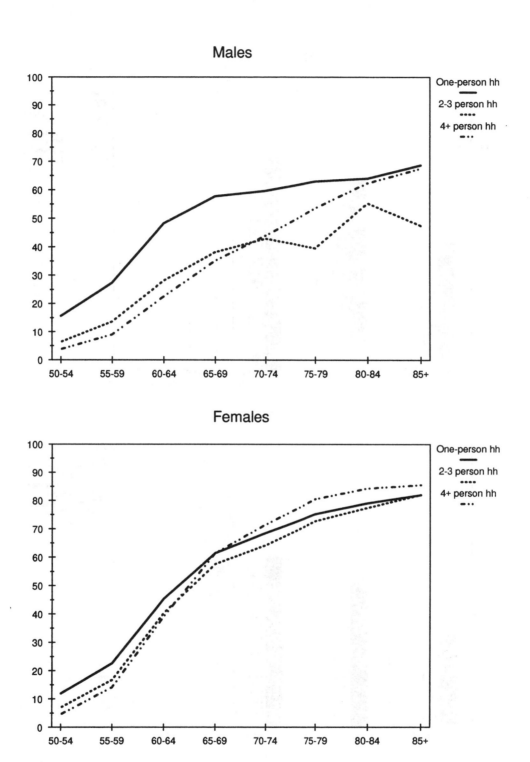

FIGURE 4.6

Proportions of persons aged 50-69 receiving disability pension in 1990, by number of generations present in the household

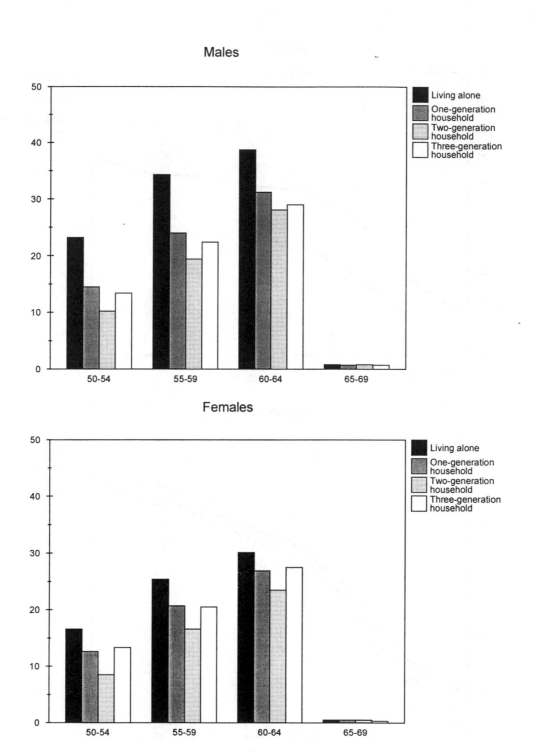

FIGURE 4.7

FIGURE 4.7

Proportion of persons aged 50 and over living in institutions with a pension as sole source of income and with other sources (excluding pensions and wages) in 1990, by marital status, age and sex

Males

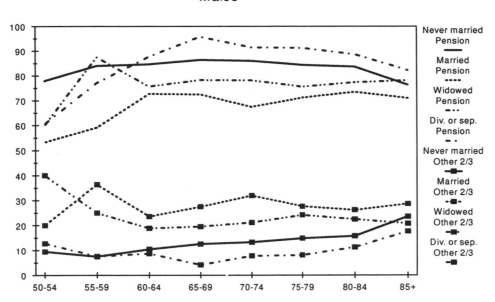

Females

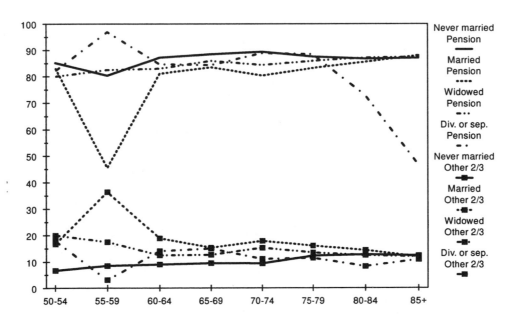

Chapter Five

Housing Conditions

5.1 From cottage to apartment

Since the Second World War, the standard of housing has improved rapidly. The number of persons per dwelling has decreased and the number of square metres per person has increased. Increasing numbers of senior citizens live in some comfort: 80 per cent of pensioners living alone in 1990 lived in an owner-occupied dwelling, as did 87 per cent of married couples (Kärkkäinen, 1994). Half of them had a one-family house and the other half an owner-occupied apartment. When individuals age many move from their family house to an apartment building with modern facilities and an elevator.

Although the standard of housing has improved considerably during recent decades, people in Finland live, on the whole, in more overcrowded dwellings than in other Scandinavian countries. This is partly because the long, harsh winter demands better, more expensive housing than in warmer countries, and partly due to the relatively late industrial take-off from a predominantly agricultural society.

5.2 Dwelling size and number of rooms

In 1990, pensioners lived in more spacious housing conditions than the average citizen. While the average national dwelling size was 31 square metres per person, for pensioners it was 43. As retirement age approaches and household size diminishes, living space grows. Although the majority of senior citizens live in spacious housing, in 1990 almost one fifth of non-institutionalized persons aged 65 or over lived in an overcrowded dwelling, as did one tenth of married pensioners aged 75 or over.[8]

Of pensioners aged 75 and over living alone, roughly a quarter lived in a dwelling consisting of one room and kitchenette. By modern standards such a dwelling is considered too small for an older person probably spending nearly all their time there (Kärkkäinen, 1994).

[8] According to the norms of Statistics Finland a dwelling is overcrowded if there is less than one room per person, kitchen not included. A person living alone is never classified as living in an overcrowded dwelling.

Among persons aged 50 and over, there is a slight tendency for the average dwelling size per person to diminish with age regardless of marital status (fig. 5.1). Widowed people had most space and married people less. The average dwelling size was somewhat larger for women (42 m²) than for men (39 m²) regardless of marital status.

The situation is the same when comparing average number of rooms. Widowed people have on average 2.4-2.5 rooms per person and married people 1.8 rooms. The other marital status groups live in dwellings consisting on average of two rooms (fig. 5.2).

The proportion of overcrowded dwellings increases markedly with increasing age. Among divorced and separated people, half the overcrowded dwellings are occupied by those aged 85 and over. The proportion is also rather high among older persons who never married (45 per cent). Fewer overcrowded dwellings are seen in the married and widowed categories (fig. 5.3).

The average dwelling size per person diminishes noticeably with the number of generations present in the household (fig. 5.4). Those living alone have the largest average dwelling area per capita (52.2-52.7 m²) while households with four or more generations have the smallest (18.6-20.0 m²). Only one-generation households show a marked diminution in dwelling size with age. This certainly follows from the fact that one-generation households mainly consist of married couples. The average number of rooms follows the same pattern as the average dwelling size. Thus those living alone have on average 2.5 rooms, compared to only 0.8 rooms per person for households with four or more generations. (Households with four or more generations are rare and therefore omitted from the figures and tables below.)

The proportion of overcrowded dwellings increases (in inverse proportion to the size of dwelling) with age and with the number of generations present in the household. One-generation households have the lowest proportion of dwellings with one room or less per person, i.e. 13 per cent, which means that couples mostly do not live in overcrowded dwellings (table 5.1). By contrast almost all households with four or more generations are overcrowded.

FIGURE 5.1

**Average dwelling size per person among persons aged 50 and over in 1990 by age,
sex and marital status**

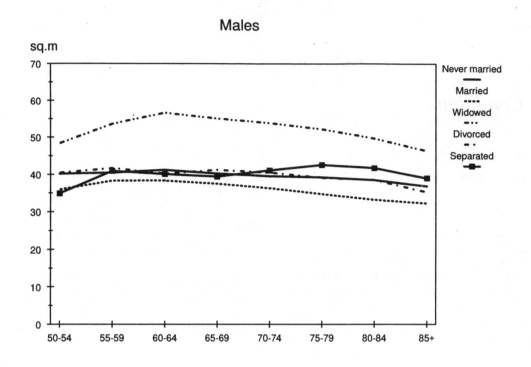

5.3 Household amenities

Dwellings with poor facilities have been a great problem for many senior citizens. The situation has however improved rapidly. In 1970, about 70 per cent of pensioners lived in poorly or very poorly equipped housing.[9] By 1992 the proportion was only 20 per cent. Nevertheless,

many older persons, 18 per cent of those aged 75 or over, live in very poorly equipped housing, mostly in rural areas. If we combine those people classified as having poor amenities and those with extremely poor amenities, then a quarter of those aged 75 or over live in substandard housing. A rather large proportion of those with poor amenities are living with their spouse or with middle-aged children, which makes it possible for them to continue to live in sub-standard housing conditions. Another group with poor housing is single men (Kärkkäinen, 1994).

---

[9] A very poorly equipped dwelling lacks drainage, a water supply or hot water, while a poorly equipped dwelling lacks central heating and/ or bathroom but does have the three aforementioned conveniences.

FIGURE 5.2

**Average number of rooms per person among persons aged 50 and over in 1990
by sex, age and marital status**

Males

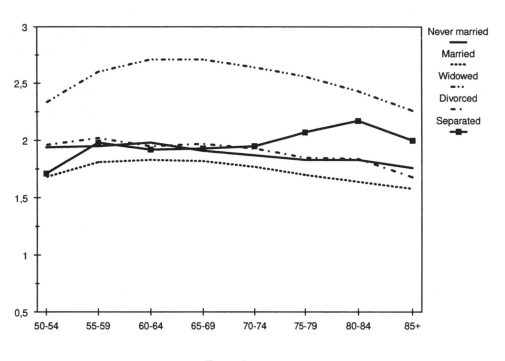

Females

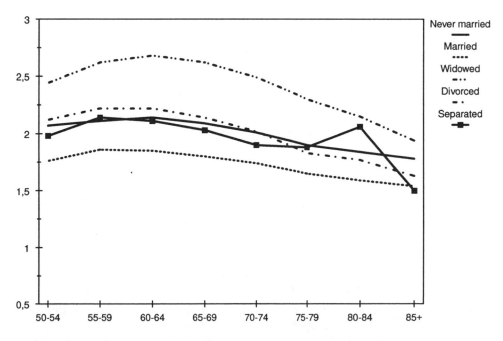

The standard of amenities varies widely with marital status. Among those aged 50 and over, men who have never married live, on average, in the worst equipped housing while married people enjoy the best standard of amenities. Women who are widowed or divorced or who never married enjoy a standard almost as high as married people.

Only a tiny percentage of housing lacks a water supply, regardless of marital status of the occupant. The exception is men who never married, of whom one fifth lacks a

water supply. A toilet is almost as common as running water. A bath, by contrast, is lacking in about twenty per cent of dwellings. Men who never married are the group most lacking in bathroom facilities: only every other man in this group has his own bath. He is more likely to have hot water than a bath, but even the former is sometimes lacking.

Generally, the proportion of badly equipped housing increases with age. Among older persons, the proportion

FIGURE 5.3

Proportion of dwellings with one room or less per person among persons aged 50 and over in 1990 by age, sex and marital status

Males

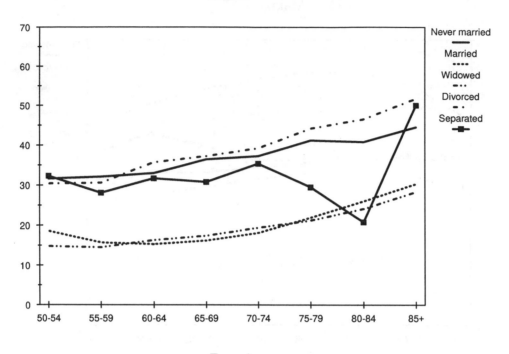

Females

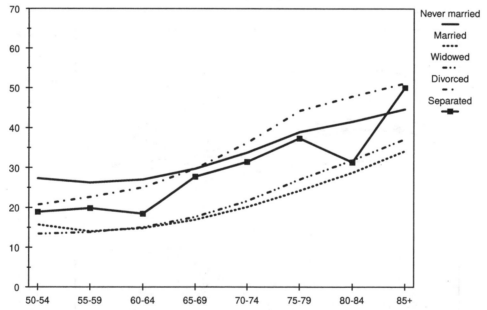

of households lacking facilities is often very different from the overall average (table 5.2, cf. also appendix table 17b showing proportions by age). The exception is again men who never married, among whom the tendency is the opposite: in this category for some reason, older persons have better equipped dwellings than younger ones.

The variation in provision of household amenities according to number of generations present is comparatively slight (table 5.3, appendix table 18b). The variation with gender is also trivial. However, men living alone are found to occupy significantly more households lacking

amenities. For men living alone (including those who never married as well as many widowed, divorced or separated) the proportion in sub-standard housing is not as high as for men who never married. Women living alone occupy sub-standard housing roughly as frequently as households with several persons present. One-generation households, which probably mainly comprise married couples, occupy sub-standard housing only slightly less frequently than married people.

The proportions lacking household amenities mostly increase with age, and with an increasing number of generations present.

FIGURE 5.4

**Average dwelling size per person among persons aged 50 and over in 1990
by age, sex and number of generations present in the household**

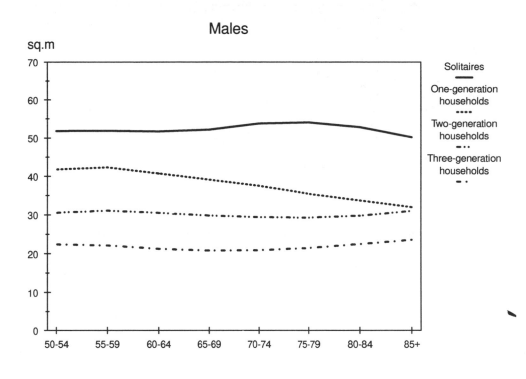

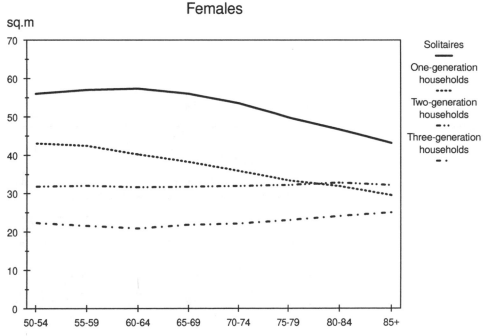

TABLE 5.1

Proportions of dwellings with one room or less per person among persons aged 50 and over in 1990 by age, sex and number of generations present in the household

Age	Living alone		One-generation		Two-generation		Three-generation	
	Men	Women	Men	Women	Men	Women	Men	Women
50-54	27.3	18.8	12.5	9.5	24.9	21.3	63.3	64.4
55-59	27.5	18.0	10.8	9.2	24.3	21.8	67.2	69.7
60-64	29.4	18.2	11.3	10.7	26.2	24.5	72.6	71.2
65-69	29.1	20.0	12.5	13.6	28.6	26.7	74.6	67.6
70-74	26.7	23.6	14.3	17.9	31.4	26.9	72.1	66.4
75-79	25.5	29.2	18.7	23.6	32.7	27.0	71.1	62.0
80-84	25.9	36.2	23.1	29.6	33.2	27.0	66.8	57.8
85+	28.5	39.7	29.0	36.7	31.3	30.3	65.9	51.4
Total	**27.7**	**24.9**	**13.4**	**13.7**	**26.0**	**23.4**	**69.7**	**65.5**

Male average 20.7   Female average 21.4

TABLE 5.2

Proportions of households which lack common household amenities among persons aged 50 and over in 1990 by sex and marital status

	Toilet		Bath		Water supply		Hot water	
	Men	Women	Men	Women	Men	Women	Men	Women
Never married								
80+	27.4	12.0	42.1	23.8	19.1	6.4	31.8	14.0
Average	29.2	9.9	44.8	21.7	19.8	6.1	34.5	12.7
Married								
80+	10.5	10.5	30.4	31.1	6.7	6.7	16.6	17.3
Average	6.3	6.3	21.4	21.9	3.7	3.7	10.1	10.1
Widowed								
80+	19.9	11.9	31.5	27.4	8.0	6.6	18.8	16.7
Average	11.9	9.8	29.6	24.1	7.3	5.9	17.2	14.2
Divorced or separeted								
80+	13.5	8.9	29.8	17.8	9.8	3.5	19.6	11.8
Average	12.1	5.5	26.0	13.7	7.8	3.2	16.7	7.7

TABLE 5.3

Proportions of households that lack common household facilities among persons aged 50 and over in 1990 by sex, age and number of generations present in the household

	Toilet		Bath		Water supply		Hot water	
	Men	Women	Men	Women	Men	Women	Men	Women
Living alone								
60+	17.7	8.0	33.2	19.8	12.1	4.8	22.5	11.4
80+	14.1	10.6	32.4	24.2	9.6	5.6	20.1	14.3
Average	18.8	7.4	34.1	18.5	12.8	4.5	23.7	10.6
One-generation								
60+	8.0	7.9	25.0	24.9	5.1	4.9	12.5	12.5
80+	10.2	11.3	29.7	29.4	6.6	6.6	16.3	17.3
Average	7.6	6.8	23.1	22.4	4.8	4.2	11.5	10.3
Two-generation								
60+	12.6	15.3	31.5	34.3	7.0	9.1	17.6	21.0
80+	22.2	21.0	45.2	41.1	13.2	13.4	29.6	28.4
Average	7.9	9.6	22.5	24.9	4.3	5.5	11.7	13.7
Three-generation								
60+	9.0	9.1	29.0	28.0	3.6	4.2	13.3	13.7
80+	9.3	8.5	28.6	25.7	3.8	3.9	13.0	13.4
Average	8.9	8.7	27.7	27.0	3.7	3.9	12.9	13.0

Chapter Six

Some Concluding Remarks

This report deals mainly with two important areas affecting the well-being of old people: their income and household arrangements. Sometimes a more detailed view of the structure of the groups used in the standard tabulations of the Population Activities Unit could have yielded interesting information; sometimes the five-year age grouping seemed too coarse for the derivation of explanations for trends; sometimes more sophisticated methods would have been needed for a comprehensive picture of living arrangements. Often it has been possible to put together a fairly complete picture of an item by using information from earlier studies.

The material on which this report is based can only give an approximate estimate of the economic situation of older persons in Finland. There are no Finnish studies which give a comprehensive picture, though some could provide useful supplementary information.

The contentment of elderly persons is highly dependent on their economic circumstances. For senior citizens, a sufficient income is undoubtedly a prerequisite for independence and personal activity. Those who feel that their economic situation is bad are also more likely to be dissatisfied with their lives. Household arrangements influence the social security of elderly persons.

Very few senior citizens consider their economic situation to be bad. The majority of pensioners think that they cope well enough with their pension but that they have to be thrifty. As older persons generally do not receive a full employment-based pension, and sometimes only the national pension, they are mostly the poorest in society. Another pensioner group with low pensions is that of people with a low level of education. The situation will change gradually at the beginning of the next millennium when new old-age pensioners receive a full employment pension.

In Finland more often than in other EU countries the next most important prerequisite for a feeling of security is good housing (Ministry of Social Affairs and Health, 1994). During recent decades, the standard of housing has improved by leaps and bounds. Now the majority of seniors live in more spacious housing than the average citizen. Nevertheless, there are more overcrowded dwellings among seniors than in other Scandinavian countries.

The standard of housing for older pensioners, especially men who never married, is noticeably lower than the average, and should be improved.

Loneliness and isolation are intimately related issues. Household arrangements are also a matter of relevance to the future care of elderly persons. Those who live with others can obviously get help and support more easily than those who live alone and mostly have to resort to municipal services for seniors. Children and other relatives are often thought to be unable or even disinclined to assist their older kin, at least over the long term. Indeed, senior citizens mostly prefer to use municipal social services rather than seek assistance from children or relatives, which is generally regarded merely as a complementary source of support (Ministry of Social Affairs and Health, 1994). On the other hand, husband and wife are each other's best support. Hence, the trend towards greater longevity among men will in the long run serve to bring down the cost of social services.

Besides a satisfactory income and good housing, senior citizens also need services for older persons, medical and health care, the latter generally more than the economically active population. If in future the universal Finnish social security policy deteriorates, with less money devoted to health care and services, as a consequence of the neo-liberal ideas increasingly prevalent in Finnish society, the present relatively comfortable position of senior citizens could deteriorate.

Although economists consider it possible to maintain the present level of social security, there is a tendency in society to think that its costs must be cut. Mindful of the deep recession of the early 1990s, and the prospect of the national debt remaining high for a long time, the conservative parties and some experts believe that it will be necessary to continue to reduce social security costs. They see the cost of social security as a burden on production, since employers fund almost half. This way of thinking is bolstered up by membership of the EU, and the tendency to adapt central European social security systems for domestic purposes. Thus the Scandinavian model of a social security system is arguably gradually losing its universal appeal (Kautto and Kärkkäinen, 1993).

45

It is imperative that the current situation be subject to analysis and discussion with a view to finding ways to maintain as far as possible the current level of social security. Cheaper alternatives to the current system have been debated. One alternative put forward is that children should be more responsible for the care of their parents in old age. However, it is admitted that it would be extremely difficult to put such a reform into effect. Internal migration has proceeded apace in recent decades, with the result that parents and children often live a considerable distance apart. Young families living in cities mostly have small apartments, which would make it difficult to have a parent living with them. Women, who would be the principal carers, work outside the home almost to the same extent as men.

Thus, a return to a system where families are responsible for the care of their old relatives does not seem very probable. It is more likely that arrangements closely related to present practice will be adopted. More privatization could be one solution. Considering that the present system is held to be working well—and that economic growth will evidently remain high enough—all the indications are that there will be little change in the short term.

This study illustrates the situation in Finland during the late 1980s and early 1990s. As the changes during the 1990s have been fairly slight, the living arrangements of senior citizens could be described as more or less the same as at the beginning of the decade. Since then, however, the income picture has changed somewhat. More senior citizens are entitled to an employee's pension and consequently one might expect that their circumstances have now improved. On the other hand, taxes are higher; pensioners pay higher sickness insurance than economically active people; the index by which the pension benefit level is annually adjusted has been reduced, etc. As for household composition, the changes have been very slight, because these are generally slow, but also because the economic recession at the beginning of the decade acted as an effective brake on social development. It is only in the past very few years that a wind of change has begun to blow.

Finally, we borrow a section from the committee report on old-age policy in Finland (*Committee Report*, 1996:1, 100-101) which gives a rather optimistic description of the situation of elderly persons when the large age groups born at the end of the 1940s reach the age of retirement. The text, here freely translated and somewhat abbreviated, depicts the situation in 2020:

The employment pension has increased somewhat since the beginning of the century. Part-time working has been more common and the income of many 60-70-year-olds consists, besides their pension, of income from work, mostly part-time work.

More people in the large age groups have obtained private pension assurance than in the earlier age groups. The property of older persons, especially real estate, has grown. In addition, income from investments has increased. Many persons have received large inheritances. The pensioners have more money to spend on goods and services and they are solvent consumers. Par-

ticularly affluent people use many different welfare services and are prepared to pay for them.

The service network has been preserved during the transition period thanks to female employment. This has given them rather a good standard of living even as pensioners. On the other hand, unemployed women who have been working in low-wage industries have rather low pensions. The high unemployment during the 1990s and the difficulties experienced by the older working-age population in finding employment, even after the employment situation had improved, is reflected in the pensions in 2020.

Although the differences in income between pensioners have increased, the more so because of differences in income from property, pensioners cannot be divided into the haves and the have-nots. This is a result of the universal pension system and of the well-run services provided by municipalities at a reasonable price to all citizens, funded mainly out of tax revenue.

Pensioners can have a decisive influence on their situation as they form an important part of the electorate. Senior citizens' professional organizations also contribute actively to the improvement of the pension system and social security.

The living conditions of elderly persons will evidently improve in the future even if social security and social services deteriorate.

Summary

Men and women's living arrangements in private households show many differences which become more noticeable with age.

The majority of senior persons live with family members, men more often than women. The younger senior citizens live most often with a spouse and children, older senior citizens with a wife or a husband. To some extent senior citizens live with parents, grandparents and grandchildren (women somewhat more than men) but few live together with children, brothers, sisters or others. In the mid-1960s half the population aged 55 and over lived with the younger generation; at the beginning of the 1990s, it was only a quarter. Although it is rather unusual to live solely with children, it is not uncommon to get assistance from a child or children living elsewhere. However, assistance from children is mostly considered a form of support complementary to public services.

Women end up living alone earlier than men. Older women are slightly less likely to live alone if they have had more children, perhaps because the last child leaves the home later in a large family than in a small one. When looking at the influence of marital status any gender variation seems less obvious. Women who are widowed, divorced or separated, or who never married, live alone more often than their male counterparts. Women living alone are often older town-dwellers, former blue- or white-collar workers. A fifth of them have never married, a quarter are childless and almost a third in poor physical health. Single men form a more hetero-geneous group, living in the countryside as well as in towns. About half of them have worked as manual labour-ers.

In general it is rare to find three generations of a family living under one roof. Men live somewhat more often with their spouse, children or grandchildren than women do.

In general it is unusual for seniors to live in an institu-tion. It only becomes more common among the older senior citizens. Men are on average less often institution-alized than women: a consequence of the greater longev-ity of women. Up to 70 years of age, men are found to be living in institutions more often than women but after that the proportion of institutionalized women increases rap-idly.

Those who never married, especially men, live in insti-tutions more often than people in the other marital status categories. Married people are less often institutionalized. A pension is the most common source of income among institutionalized persons.

Women are found to be engaged in economic activity almost as commonly as men. Married people show the highest economic activity rate, especially married men, followed by divorced and separated women. The activity rate increases with education and is highest among gradu-ates. After 60 economic activity is very low and after 65 it is almost negligible.

Unemployment was lowest among married men and women and highest among men living alone, divorced or separated. Unemployment increases with age and is larg-est in the age group 60-64.

Part-time work is rather rare in Finland.

The poorest senior citizens are those with low educa-tion. Most of the oldest pensioners belong to this group. Their pension is smaller than that of younger senior citi-zens. The situation will change gradually until the begin-ning of 2000, when a full employment pension becomes payable to all retired employees and entrepreneurs.

Logically, the most usual source of income among eco-nomically active senior citizens is earned income. How-ever, the proportion is very low by international standards even among those aged 50-54, for whom earned income provides only one third of total income, regardless of gen-der. In subsequent age groups it amounts to an even lower proportion.

From the age of 60, the old-age pension is the most important source of income for senior citizens. For most retired people it is indeed the only one. The proportion of women living solely on pension income increases more rapidly with age than that of men. Women have on aver-age a lower pension than men, and the difference increases with age.

Many senior citizens have an income other than a pen-sion, but it usually amounts to no more than a modest sup-plement. According to the 1990 household survey, income from other sources, i.e. from property and owner-occupied dwellings, constitutes on average ten per cent of total disposable income.

Two thirds of pensioner households are in the lowest income quintiles. Those aged 80 and over have the lowest incomes. They also have the lowest level of education.

With regard to housing conditions, pensioners live in more spacious quarters than the average population. While the size of the average national dwelling in 1990 was 31 square metres per person, it was 43 square metres among old-age pensioners. The average dwelling size per person diminishes slightly with age. Those who live alone and widows and widowers occupy the most spacious housing while married people occupy the least spacious. The greater the number of generations living in a house-hold, the smaller the average dwelling size.

The average dwelling size is somewhat larger for women than for men.

The proportion of overcrowded dwellings increases with age. Among the divorced and separated, one half of individuals aged 85 and over live in overcrowded dwell-ings. The proportion is almost as high among older senior citizens who never married. Less overcrowded dwellings are typical of married and widowed people.

One fifth of all pensioners lived in a badly or very badly equipped dwelling, mostly in the countryside. Men who never married live, on average, in the worst equipped dwellings while married people enjoy the highest stand-ard of facilities. Widows, divorcees and spinsters enjoy roughly the same standard as married persons. The num-ber of generations present in a household has only a slight effect on the standard of amenities.

Nearly all dwellings have a water supply and toilet. Hot water is less commonly found but more often installed than a bath. A bath is lacking in many dwellings.

The pattern of life on a disability pension is the same for men as women. People living alone draw a disability pension somewhat more often than those in other types of households, and men more often than women. House-holds where the recipient of an old-age pension lives with a disabled person, typically a child or spouse, are most often two-generation households. People younger than 65 without a disability pension living with a disabled person are seen in similar numbers in all categories of household. After 65, it becomes less common to live with a disabled person, especially in one-generation households.

Bibliography

Committee Report (1991:40). Eläkekomitean mietintö (Pension Committee). The Ministry of Social Affairs and Health, Helsinki.

———— (1994:9). Sosiaalimenotoimikunnan mietintö (The report of the committee on social costs). The Ministry of Social Affairs and Health, Helsinki.

———— (1996:1) Vanhuuspolitiikka vuoteen 2001. Suomen vanhuspoliittisen tavoite- ja strategia-toimikunnan mietintö (Old-age policy to 2001). Committee report of the commission for old-age policy aims and strategy in Finland, Helsinki.

EVA (Elinkeinoelämän Valtuuskunta) (1989). Työtä tarjolla, missä tekijät (Jobs to be had; where are the workers?). Publications of the Council of Economic Organizations (EVA). Helsinki.

Gould, Raija (1994). Työelämän takanapäin? Tutkimus ikääntyneiden työssä pysymisestä vuosina 1990-1993 (Leaving work. A study on the prevalence of remaining in work among elderly persons in 1990-1993). Eläketurvakeskus. Tutkimuksia 1994:3. Eläketurvakeskus, Helsinki.

Hufvudstadsbladet (1997). Lönsamt satsa på de äldsta (It is profitable to stake on the oldest). 4 October 1997.

Hytti, Helka (1996). Active and Retirement Life Expectancy in Finland. Yearbook of Population Research in Finland 33. Population Research Institute, Helsinki.

Julkunen, Raija and Jouko Nätti (1995). Muuttuvat työajat ja työsuhteet. Työministeriön työaikamuo-tuojen tutkimus- ja kehittämisprojektin I vaihe. (Changing working times and employment contracts). Ministry of Labour, Studies in Labour Policy No. 104. Helsinki.

Kangasharju, Riitta and Jarl Lindgren (1995). Division of paid and unpaid labour in Finland. In: Work and Family in Europe: The Role of Policies, ed., Tineke Willemsen et al., pp. 29-43. Tilburg University, Tilburg (Net).

Kärkkäinen, Sirkka-Liisa (1994). Mökistä taajamiin. Ikääntyvien asuinolot 1950-luvulta 1990-luvulle (From cottages to densely populated areas. The housing conditions of senior citizens from the 1950s to the 1990s.) In: 55+. Katsaus ikääntyvien elinoloihin (55+. An overview of the living conditions of elderly persons), pp. 95-115. Living Condition 1994:1. Statistics Finland, Helsinki.

Kautto, K. and K. Kärkkäinen (1993). Eurooppalainen hyvinvointikunta. Sosiaali- ja terveyspalvelut Alankomaissa, Iso-Britanniassa, Ranskassa ja Saksassa. (The European welfare municipality. Social and health services in Holland, Great Britain, France and Germany). Suomen Kuntaliitto, Helsinki.

Keinänen, Päivi (1993). Työelämän sinnittelijät (Unyielding workers). Hyvinvointikatsaus 1993:4. Statistics Finland, Helsinki.

Kolari, Risto (1980). Cohort Mortality in Finland from 1851. Central Statistical Office of Finland (Statistics Finland), Studies No. 57. Helsinki.

Koskinen, Seppo and Tuija Martelin (1994). Kuolleisuus (Mortality). In: Suomen väestö, ed., Koskinen et al., pp. 150-225. Gaudeamus, Helsinki.

Lindgren, Jarl (1990). Towards an Ageing Society. Some Demographic and Socio-economic Aspects of Population Ageing in Finland. The Population Research Institute, Series D 25 1990. Helsinki.

———— (1992). Demographic Trends and Pension Problems in Finland. International Institute for Applied System Analysis. Working Paper 92-30. IIASA, Laxenburg (Au).

Melkas, Tuula (1997). Muut ihmiset ikääntyvien elämässä. Ikääntyvien sosiaaliset ympäristöt (Persons around elderly persons. The social surroundings of elderly persons). In: 55+. Katsaus ikääntyvien elinoloihin (55+. An overview of the living conditions of elderly persons), pp. 123-145. Living Condition 1994:1. Statistics Finland, Helsinki.

Ministry of Social Affairs and Health (1987). Sosiaalimenot ja niiden rahoitus vuosina 1987-2030 (Social expenditure and its financing in Finland in 1987-2030). Publications 1:1987. Helsinki.

————— (1988). Vanhuspoliittinen katsaus. Vanhusten elinoloja ja vanhuspolitiikan ajankohtaisia haasteita kartoittava raportti (Old-aged policy. A report on the living conditions of elderly persons and current old-age policy challenges). Ministry of Social Affairs and Health, Helsinki.

————— (1994). Vanhuusbarometri 1994 (The old-age barometer). Ministry of Social Affairs and Health, Helsinki.

————— (1995). Sosiaaliturva Suomessa 1993 (Social security in Finland 1993). Sosiaaliturva 1995:2. Ministry of Social Affairs and Health, Helsinki.

Nurminen, Jaakko (1990). Väestönkehitys ja koulutus. (Population development and education). In: Suomalainen väestöruletti—viisi näkökulmaa Suomen väestön tulevaisuuteen (The Finnish population roulette—five visions of the future of the Finnish population). Väestöliiton kolmikanta-sarja 12. The Family Federation of Finland, Helsinki.

Palm, Heikki (1988). Sosiaalimenojen kehitykseen vaikuttavat tekijät vuosina 1960-2030. (Factors affecting social expenditure 1960-2030). Ministry of Social Affairs and Health. Planning Department. Publications 3:1988. Helsinki 1988.

Parkkinen, Pekka (1986). Harmaantuva Suomi 2030 (Greying Finland 2030). The Economic Planning Centre. Helsinki.

————— (1995). Ikääntyvän väestön taloudelliset vaikutukset (The economical implications of the ageing population). Hyvinvointikatsaus 3/95. Statistics Finland, Helsinki.

————— and Maija-Liisa Järviö (1988). Terve Suomi 2030. Terveysmenojen kehityspiirteet (A Healthy Finland in 2030. The development of health care costs). The Economic Planning Centre, Helsinki.

Puhakka, Aune (1988). Project regarding the impact of social security benefits. The pensioner household's livelihood in 1985. Ministry of Social Affairs and Health, Planning Department. Publications 6/1988. Ministry of Social Affairs and Health, Helsinki (with English summary).

Romppanen A. and S. Leppänen, eds.,(1994). Avautuva Suomi - tulevaisuuden haasteet (Finland opens out—challenges of the future). VATT-julkaisuja 11. The Government Institute for Economic Research, Helsinki.

Sailas, Raija (1997). Ansioeläkkeistä toimeentulon turva. Ikääntyvien tulojen rakenne vuosina 1966-1990 (Employees' pension, the security of livelihood. The income structure of older persons 1966-1990). In: 55+ Katsaus ikääntyvien elinoloihin (55+. An overview of the living conditions of elderly persons), p.69-82. Living Condition 1994:1. Statistics Finland, Helsinki.

Statistical Yearbook of Pensioners in Finland (1995). The Central Pension Security Institute and the Social Insurance Institution, Helsinki.

————— (1990). The Central Pension Security Institute and the Social Insurance Institution, Helsinki.

Statistics Finland (1997). Väestöennuste 1997-2030 (Population Projection 1997-2030). Statistics Finland, Helsinki, unpublished.

————— (1994). Evaluation Study of the 1990 Census. Population Census. Volume 98. Statistics Finland, Helsinki.

————— (1994). 55+ Katsaus ikääntyvien elinoloihin (55+. An overview of the living conditions of elderly persons). Living Condition 1994:1. Statistics Finland, Helsinki.

Strömmer, Aarno (1969). Väestöllinen muuntuminen Suomessa. Analyyttinen kuvausyntyvyyden, kuolevuuden ja luonnollisen kasvun tähänastisesta kehityksestä ja alueellisesta vaihtelusta (The demographic transition in Finland. An analytic description of the development and regional variation in fertility, mortality and natural increase of the Finnish population 1722-1965). The Population Research Institute, series A:13. Tornio, 1969.

Tennilä, Liisa. Viisikymmentä ja risat (Fifty and over). In: 55+ katsaus ikääntyvien elinoloihin (55+. An overview of the living conditions of elderly persons), pp. 83-94. Living Condition 1994:1. Statistics Finland, Helsinki.

Väestöliitto (1990). Suomalainen väestöruletti—viisi näkökulmaa Suomen väestön tulevaisuuteen (The Finnish population roulette—five visions on the future of the Finnish population). Väestöliiton kolmikanta-sarja 12. The Family Federation of Finland, Helsinki.

————— (1997). Suomen väestö 203—Miten, mistä ja kuinka paljon? Väestöpoliittinen raportti Suomen väestönkehityksestä vuoteen 2030. Väestöliitto, Väestöpoliittinen työryhmä (Population in Finland in 2031. How, whence and how much? Population policy report on the population development in Finland to 2030). The Family Federation in Finland; the Commission for Population Policy, Helsinki (to be published in 1998).

Sample selection and reliability of data

The sample is taken from the 1990 census, which is entirely register-based. The registers are linked using personal identification codes and domicile codes. The sample draws on the data files of all kinds of individuals including those in private households, institutions and the homeless. Everybody has the same chance of being included in the sample.

Three age categories have been used. The sample size in the categories is proportional to the population size:

In the age category 50-64 the sample size is 60 per cent;

In the age category 65-79 the sample size is 85 per cent;

In the age category 80+ the sample size is 100 per cent.

People in every age category are randomized separately for men and women. After that the sampled person is picked out. All other people living in the same dwelling as the sampled person have been linked together.

The exact number of institutionalized persons cannot be ascertained as some people living in institutions are registered as living in their usual dwelling. Some register-keepers may consider people living in private service homes for senior citizens as institutionalized. It is impossible to ascertain how many senior citizens from Finland live abroad in institutions: the resulting margin of error is however only a few per cent.

A sample-based study to measure the reliability of the 1990 census was published in 1994. The aim of the study was to maintain the same standards as the questionnaire censuses. The comparative data collected by questionnaires was compared with the register-based data of the 1990 population census. The quality of data in the registers was assessed, and discrepancies between register data and questionnaire data are closely described in the study (Statistics Finland, 1994). The evaluation study confirmed that the register data produced perfectly acceptable population statistics.

Appendix One: Annexed Tables

TABLE 1

**Household size of persons aged 50 and over in Finland in 1990 by age and sex
(Persons living in private households)**

		Males	*Females*
50-54		2.69	2.48
55-59		2.42	2.19
60-64		2.23	1.98
65-69		2.13	1.83
70-74		2.08	1.69
75-79		2.01	1.59
80-84		1.94	1.50
85+		1.82	1.47
	Total	**2.31**	**1.94**

TABLE 2

**Generations present in the households of the sampled persons in Finland in 1990
by age, sex and marital status, per cent (non-institutionalized population)**

		One generation	*Two generations*	*Three generations*	*Total*	*Number*
Males						
Never married						
50-54		54.9	43.9	1.2	100.0	8 217
55-59		69.4	29.4	1.3	100.0	6 093
60-64		82.6	16.6	0.8	100.0	4 882
65-69		91.2	8.0	0.8	100.0	2 674
70-74		93.7	5.2	1.1	100.0	1 259
75-79		93.8	4.6	1.6	100.0	826
80-84		95.7	2.7	1.6	100.0	441
85+		92.2	4.4	3.4	100.0	204
	Total	**72.2**	**26.6**	**1.2**	**100.0**	**24 595**
Married						
50-54		37.0	61.0	2.0	100.0	97 664
55-59		55.3	42.5	2.2	100.0	90 315
60-64		68.8	28.7	2.4	100.0	86 810
65-69		77.9	19.4	2.7	100.0	68 754
70-74		82.4	14.5	3.1	100.0	45 294
75-79		84.7	11.8	3.5	100.0	30 818
80-84		85.2	11.0	3.8	100.0	14 696
85+		84.5	11.6	4.0	100.0	4 373
	Total	**63.6**	**33.9**	**2.5**	**100.0**	**438 726**
Widowed						
50-54		19.2	76.1	4.7	100.0	1 134
55-59		27.5	63.9	8.5	100.0	1 430
60-64		30.8	58.0	11.2	100.0	1 744
65-69		35.5	49.3	15.2	100.0	1 924
70-74		32.5	46.7	20.7	100.0	1 939
75-79		31.2	44.4	24.5	100.0	2 221
80-84		31.1	44.0	24.9	100.0	1 954
85+		36.8	43.6	19.5	100.0	1 358
	Total	**31.1**	**51.7**	**17.2**	**100.0**	**13 704**
Divorced/separated						
50-54		58.0	39.4	2.6	100.0	9 028
55-59		66.2	29.9	3.9	100.0	5 873
60-64		71.2	24.2	4.6	100.0	4 015
65-69		77.2	18.3	4.5	100.0	1 991
70-74		75.6	18.6	5.8	100.0	918
75-79		78.9	13.6	7.6	100.0	487
80-84		83.3	10.6	6.1	100.0	180
85+		75.8	17.7	6.5	100.0	62
	Total	**65.6**	**30.7**	**3.7**	**100.0**	**22 553**

TABLE 2 (*concluded*)

		One generation	Two generations	Three generations	Total	Number
Total Males						
50-54		39.7	58.3	2.0	100.0	116 043
55-59		56.4	41.3	2.3	100.0	103 711
60-64		68.9	28.5	2.6	100.0	97 451
65-69		77.3	19.7	3.0	100.0	75 343
70-74		80.6	15.6	3.8	100.0	49 410
75-79		81.4	13.7	4.9	100.0	34 352
80-84		79.4	14.5	6.2	100.0	17 271
85+		73.8	18.6	7.5	100.0	5 997
	Total	**63.2**	**33.9**	**2.9**	**100.0**	**499 578**
Females						
Never married						
50-54		54.3	43.9	1.8	100.0	4 880
55-59		67.9	30.1	1.9	100.0	4 105
60-64		78.0	20.5	1.5	100.0	3 926
65-69		86.4	12.0	1.6	100.0	3 583
70-74		90.6	7.2	2.2	100.0	2 751
75-79		91.1	6.4	2.5	100.0	2 516
80-84		92.4	6.1	1.5	100.0	1 872
85+		93.4	5.2	1.5	100.0	1 203
	Total	**77.4**	**20.7**	**1.8**	**100.0**	**24 837**
Married						
50-54		46.0	52.0	2.1	100.0	95 786
55-59		63.3	34.3	2.4	100.0	83 982
60-64		75.0	22.6	2.4	100.0	79 790
65-69		82.0	15.1	2.9	100.0	62 204
70-74		85.4	11.4	3.2	100.0	36 863
75-79		86.7	9.7	3.7	100.0	20 602
80-84		88.1	8.7	3.2	100.0	7 921
85+		88.9	9.0	2.1	100.0	1 616
	Total	**68.4**	**29.1**	**2.6**	**100.0**	**388 763**
Widowed						
50-54		18.4	77.0	4.6	100.0	5 547
55-59		21.3	71.1	7.6	100.0	6 932
60-64		21.7	66.5	11.8	100.0	9 175
65-69		20.6	62.3	17.1	100.0	11 267
70-74		23.0	56.2	20.8	100.0	11 153
75-79		26.2	50.3	23.4	100.0	11 535
80-84		31.8	47.9	20.2	100.0	8 657
85+		44.0	42.0	13.8	100.0	5 654
	Total	**25.2**	**58.5**	**16.2**	**100.0**	**69 918**
Divorced/separated						
50-54		36.9	60.3	2.8	100.0	10 680
55-59		42.9	53.1	4.0	100.0	6 494
60-64		48.2	45.7	6.1	100.0	4 256
65-69		48.8	43.1	8.1	100.0	2 567
70-74		50.5	40.2	9.3	100.0	1 458
75-79		54.9	36.7	8.4	100.0	905
80-84		63.3	31.3	5.4	100.0	498
85+		74.8	23.0	2.2	100.0	270
	Total	**43.4**	**51.9**	**4.7**	**100.0**	**27 133**
Total Females						
50-54		44.2	53.6	2.3	100.0	116 893
55-59		59.4	37.8	2.8	100.0	101 513
60-64		68.9	27.6	3.4	100.0	97 147
65-69		72.4	22.6	5.0	100.0	79 621
70-74		71.4	21.5	7.1	100.0	52 225
75-79		66.6	23.3	10.1	100.0	35 558
80-84		62.1	26.9	10.9	100.0	18 948
85+		60.0	30.3	9.7	100.0	8 743
	Total	**61.6**	**33.9**	**4.5**	**100.0**	**510 651**

NOTE: Solitaires and Unknown have been excluded.

TABLE 3

Kin present in one- or two-generation households in Finland in 1990 by age and sex of the sampled person (*percentage*)

	One generation households without persons classified as having "other" relationship to CRP				Two generation households without persons classified as having "other" relationship to CRP						
	Individual living alone	*Individual living with spouse*	*Individual living with other relatives of the same generation*	*Total*	*Individual living with child(ren)*	*Individual living with spouse and child(ren)*	*Individual living with parent(s) or parent(s)-in-law*	*Individual living with spouse and parent(s) or parent(s)-in-law*	*Individual living with other relatives in two generation households*	*Total*	*Total number*
Males											
50-54	29.0	63.5	7.4	100.0	4.0	89.5	2.3	0.5	3.7	100.0	132 531
55-59	23.6	70.7	5.7	100.0	4.5	87.7	1.9	0.5	5.4	100.0	119 357
60-64	21.9	74.0	4.1	100.0	5.9	84.3	1.2	0.5	8.1	100.0	113 763
65-69	20.8	76.5	2.7	100.0	7.8	82.0	0.4	0.2	9.6	100.0	88 408
70-74	21.9	76.2	1.9	100.0	12.4	76.5	0.2	0.1	10.9	100.0	58 672
75-79	27.9	70.1	2.0	100.0	20.0	69.4	0.0	0.0	10.6	100.0	43 508
80-84	37.1	60.1	2.8	100.0	31.7	57.5	0.0	0.0	10.8	100.0	24 287
85+	51.7	43.5	4.8	100.0	47.6	40.9	0.0	0.0	11.6	100.0	10 275
Total	**25.1**	**70.7**	**4.2**	**100.0**	**6.3**	**85.6**	**1.7**	**0.4**	**6.1**	**100.0**	**590 802**
Females											
50-54	29.9	66.9	3.2	100.0	16.4	78.0	1.2	0.5	3.9	100.0	136 247
55-59	31.5	65.4	3.1	100.0	20.7	70.9	1.0	0.5	7.0	100.0	126 344
60-64	36.8	59.9	3.2	100.0	27.2	61.6	0.9	0.3	10.0	100.0	132 866
65-69	46.5	49.8	3.7	100.0	40.9	47.0	0.5	0.1	11.6	100.0	125 670
70-74	58.2	37.2	4.6	100.0	54.9	33.6	0.1	0.0	11.3	100.0	100 394
75-79	69.3	24.6	6.1	100.0	67.0	21.4	0.0	0.0	11.6	100.0	85 406
80-84	77.2	14.6	8.2	100.0	77.3	12.5	0.0	0.0	10.2	100.0	56 762
85+	81.0	7.0	12.0	100.0	82.6	5.1	0.0	0.0	12.4	100.0	30 229
Total	**49.4**	**46.0**	**4.6**	**100.0**	**29.3**	**62.0**	**0.8**	**0.4**	**7.5**	**100.0**	**793 918**

TABLE 4

Kin present in three- or more generation households in Finland in 1990 by age and sex of the sampled person (*percentage*)

		Individual living with child(ren) and parent(s)	*Individual living with spouse, child (ren) and parent(s)*	*Individual living with child(ren) and grandchild(ren)*	*Individual living with spouse, child(ren) and grandchild(ren)*	*Individual living in other three or more generation households*	*Total*	*Total number*
Males								
	50-54	5.4	39.9	8.9	29.9	16.0	100.0	2 337
	55-59	2.4	18.3	13.0	48.0	18.3	100.0	2 407
	60-64	0.9	3.3	14.4	64.4	17.0	100.0	2 520
	65-69	0.0	0.9	16.5	69.2	13.3	100.0	2 245
	70-74	0.0	0.3	23.4	65.4	11.0	100.0	1 879
	75-79	0.0	0.0	32.5	56.9	10.6	100.0	1 675
	80-84	0.0	0.0	44.5	47.1	8.5	100.0	1 064
	85+	0.0	0.0	56.5	33.0	10.4	100.0	451
	Total	**1.4**	**10.1**	**20.3**	**53.9**	**14.1**	**100.0**	**14 578**
Females								
	50-54	6.1	23.5	13.0	39.4	18.0	100.0	2 637
	55-59	2.3	5.3	22.2	52.3	17.9	100.0	2 872
	60-64	0.5	0.7	35.3	46.9	16.6	100.0	3 332
	65-69	0.0	0.2	48.4	39.6	11.8	100.0	4 008
	70-74	0.0	0.0	61.1	29.1	9.8	100.0	3 712
	75-79	0.0	0.0	71.7	19.1	9.3	100.0	3 601
	80-84	0.0	0.0	79.2	11.4	9.3	100.0	2 071
	85+	0.0	0.0	83.6	4.4	12.0	100.0	850
	Total	**1.1**	**3.5**	**48.9**	**33.5**	**13.0**	**100.0**	**23 082**

TABLE 5

Household size of persons aged 50 and over in Finland in 1990 by age and sex (per cent)
(persons of known family position only)

| | | Non-institutionalized population | | | | | |
		One person	Two persons	Three persons	Four + persons	Total	Number
Males							
50-54		14.0	36.3	27.5	22.3	100.0	134 888
55-59		14.8	49.3	22.8	13.1	100.0	121 785
60-64		16.2	58.6	17.0	8.1	100.0	116 288
65-69		16.9	65.0	12.3	5.9	100.0	90 660
70-74		18.4	66.8	9.3	5.4	100.0	60 554
75-79		24.0	63.4	7.3	5.3	100.0	45 185
80-84		31.9	56.4	6.2	5.6	100.0	25 354
85+		44.1	44.8	5.6	5.5	100.0	10 728
	Total	**17.5**	**53.6**	**17.7**	**11.3**	**100.0**	**605 442**
Females							
50-54		15.8	43.2	25.4	15.6	100.0	138 902
55-59		21.4	52.0	18.3	8.3	100.0	129 223
60-64		28.7	54.0	12.0	5.3	100.0	136 210
65-69		38.6	49.4	7.5	4.4	100.0	129 685
70-74		49.8	40.9	5.0	4.3	100.0	104 116
75-79		60.1	31.7	3.7	4.5	100.0	89 018
80-84		67.8	25.0	3.2	4.0	100.0	58 843
85+		71.9	21.4	2.9	3.7	100.0	31 090
	Total	**37.5**	**43.7**	**11.8**	**7.0**	**100.0**	**817 087**

TABLE 6

Women aged 50 and over living in one or two generation households in Finland in 1990 by age, sex,
and number of children ever born (per cent)

		Living alone	Living with spouse	Living with child(ren)	Living with spouse and child(ren)	Living with other relatives	Living with other persons	Total	Number
None									
50-54		46.7	36.7	0.2	2.2	14.3	0.0	100.0	19 182
55-59		49.9	35.7	0.1	1.1	13.2	0.0	100.0	19 135
60-64		53.4	35.2	0.1	0.5	10.8	0.0	100.0	24 572
65-69		58.5	31.7	0.1	0.2	9.5	0.0	100.0	30 218
70-74		65.1	26.2	0.0	0.1	8.5	0.0	100.0	33 562
75-79		72.4	18.8	0.0	0.1	8.6	0.0	100.0	39 722
80-84		78.2	12.0	0.0	0.1	9.7	0.0	100.0	34 884
85+		81.0	6.4	0.0	0.0	12.6	0.0	100.0	23 103
	Total	**65.0**	**24.1**	**0.1**	**0.4**	**10.4**	**0.0**	**100.0**	**224 378**
One									
50-54		16.6	44.8	9.2	28.0	1.3	0.0	100.0	23 785
55-59		23.5	52.0	7.1	15.9	1.4	0.0	100.0	20 455
60-64		30.2	53.4	5.3	9.1	1.9	0.0	100.0	22 562
65-69		40.7	46.9	5.6	4.8	2.0	0.0	100.0	24 507
70-74		51.7	35.5	6.8	3.4	2.6	0.0	100.0	21 816
75-79		59.3	24.8	10.1	2.6	3.3	0.0	100.0	19 956
80-84		62.2	15.1	16.2	2.2	4.3	0.1	100.0	11 954
85+		55.6	6.7	29.6	1.5	6.4	0.1	100.0	4 829
	Total	**39.2**	**39.8**	**8.7**	**9.8**	**2.4**	**0.0**	**100.0**	**149 865**
Two									
50-54		10.8	39.4	7.5	40.8	1.4	0.0	100.0	48 285
55-59		16.6	53.3	5.9	22.5	1.7	0.0	100.0	37 310
60-64		24.0	56.5	5.3	12.3	1.9	0.0	100.0	33 738
65-69		33.8	50.6	6.2	7.2	2.2	0.0	100.0	28 336
70-74		44.7	39.4	8.4	4.9	2.6	0.0	100.0	19 581
75-79		53.2	27.1	11.7	4.0	4.0	0.0	100.0	12 816
80-84		55.3	16.5	18.7	3.2	6.2	0.0	100.0	5 665
85+		45.4	6.1	31.2	2.4	14.9	0.1	100.0	1 506
	Total	**25.9**	**45.1**	**7.5**	**19.2**	**2.2**	**0.0**	**100.0**	**187 238**
Three or more									
50-54		8.6	28.6	9.8	49.0	4.0	0.0	100.0	45 013
55-59		14.5	41.1	8.6	31.0	4.8	0.0	100.0	49 452
60-64		21.2	45.9	8.3	19.6	5.0	0.0	100.0	52 007
65-69		30.1	43.0	9.8	12.1	5.0	0.0	100.0	42 615
70-74		39.4	34.9	12.0	8.0	5.7	0.0	100.0	25 444
75-79		46.7	24.1	15.6	5.5	8.0	0.0	100.0	12 921
80-84		48.0	14.5	21.7	4.1	11.5	0.0	100.0	4 269
85+		34.2	4.4	34.0	2.0	25.5	0.0	100.0	801
	Total	**22.9**	**37.9**	**10.1**	**24.0**	**5.2**	**0.0**	**100.0**	**232 522**

TABLE 7

**Number of persons aged 50 and over living in institutions in Finland
in 1990 by age, sex and marital status**

		Never marrtied	Married	Widowed	Divorce/separated	All
Males						
50-54		3.3	0.0	0.3	0.5	0.5
55-59		3.7	0.0	0.3	0.8	0.6
60-64		4.7	0.1	0.8	1.3	0.7
65-69		7.1	0.1	1.4	2.6	1.1
70-74		9.8	0.4	2.3	4.6	1.5
75-79		14.3	0.9	4.3	7.8	2.8
80-84		19.3	2.3	8.0	12.2	5.7
85+		29.3	6.3	16.6	18.6	13.5
	Total	**6.0**	**0.3**	**5.1**	**1.8**	**1.4**
Females						
50-54		3.1	0.0	0.2	0.1	0.3
55-59		2.9	0.0	0.3	0.4	0.4
60-64		3.1	0.1	0.3	0.6	0.5
65-69		3.5	0.1	0.8	1.3	0.8
70-74		4.7	0.5	1.6	2.6	1.6
75-79		7.6	1.4	4.0	5.6	4.0
80-84		12.7	3.6	9.1	10.4	8.9
85+		24.8	10.0	21.1	20.8	21.2
	Total	**6.4**	**0.3**	**5.0**	**2.0**	**2.6**

TABLE 8

**Number and type of income sources of persons aged 50 and over living in institutions
in Finland in 1990 by age, sex and marital status (per cent)**

		No Income	Single source			Multiple sources			Unknown	Total	Number
			Labour	Pension	Other	Labour and pension	Other two	Three or more			
Males											
Never married											
50-54		0.0	77.9	0.3	0.5	10.9	9.2	0.3	0.9	100.0	578
55-59		0.0	84.0	0.9	1.3	6.0	6.0	1.5	0.4	100.0	550
60-64		0.0	84.7	0.0	0.0	4.6	9.0	1.5	0.0	100.0	647
65-69		0.0	86.4	0.2	0.0	0.8	10.8	1.8	0.0	100.0	618
70-74		0.0	86.0	0.0	0.0	0.5	11.2	2.1	0.0	100.0	436
75-79		0.0	84.4	0.0	0.0	0.9	12.5	2.4	0.0	100.0	449
80-84		0.0	83.7	0.0.	0.0	0.6	12.7	3.0	0.0	100.0	361
85+		0.0	76.4	0.0	0.0	0.0	19.0	4.6	0.0	100.0	263
	Total	**0.0**	**83.3**	**0.2**	**0.3**	**3.6**	**10.6**	**1.9**	**0.2**	**100.0**	**3 903**
Married											
50-54		0.0	53.3	0.0	13.3	0.0	20.0	0.0	13.3	100.0	15
55-59		0.0	59.1	0.0	0.0	0.0	36.4	0.0	0.0	100.0	22
60-64		0.0	72.7	3.6	0.0	0.0	23.6	0.0	0.0	100.0	55
65-69		0.0	72.5	0.0	0.0	0.0	20.6	6.9	0.0	100.0	102
70-74		0.0	67.5	0.6	0.0	0.0	27.2	4.7	0.0	100.0	169
75-79		0.0	71.2	0.3	0.0	0.3	21.2	6.5	0.0	100.0	292
80-84		0.0	73.5	0.0	0.0	0.3	22.3	3.9	0.0	100.0	359
85+		0.0	71.0	0.0	0.0	0.3	22.8	5.9	0.0	100.0	307
	Total	**0.0**	**71.2**	**0.3**	**0.2**	**0.2**	**22.9**	**5.0**	**0.2**	**100.0**	**1 321**
Widowed											
50-54		0.0	60.0	0.0	0.0	0.0	40.0	0.0	0.0	100.0	5
55-59		0.0	87.5	0.0	0.0	0.0	25.0	0.0	0.0	100.0	8
60-64		0.0	75.7	0.0	5.4	0.0	13.5	5.4	0.0	100.0	37
65-69		0.0	78.3	0.0	0.0	0.0	17.4	2.2	1.1	100.0	92
70-74		0.0	78.2	0.0	0.0	0.6	18.4	2.8	0.0	100.0	179
75-79		0.0	75.6	0.0	0.0	0.2	21.5	2.7	0.0	100.0	414
80-84		0.0	77.4	0.3	0.0	0.1	19.3	3.2	0.0	100.0	694
85+		0.0	78.2	0.0	0.0	0.8	17.5	3.3	0.0	100.0	1 047
	Total	**0.0**	**77.5**	**0.1**	**0.1**	**0.4**	**18.7**	**3.1**	**0.0**	**100.0**	**2 476**
Divorced/separated											
50-54		3.2	60.6	3.2	16.0	3.2	12.8	0.0	0.0	100.0	94
55-59		0.0	77.1	4.8	7.6	0.0	7.6	0.0	1.9	100.0	105
60-64		0.0	87.7	0.0	1.4	2.2	8.7	0.0	0.0	100.0	138
65-69		0.0	95.8	0.0	0.0	0.0	4.2	0.0	0.0	100.0	165
70-74		0.0	91.5	0.0	0.0	0.7	7.2	0.7	0.0	100.0	153
75-79		0.0	91.3	0.6	0.0	0.0	8.1	0.0	0.0	100.0	160
80-84		0.0	88.7	0.0	0.0	0.0	11.3	0.0	0.0	100.0	106
85+		0.0	82.3	0.0	0.0	0.0	17.7	0.0	0.0	100.0	62
	Total	**0.3**	**86.5**	**1.0**	**2.5**	**0.7**	**8.8**	**0.1**	**0.2**	**100.0**	**982**

TABLE 8 (concluded)

	No Income	Single source			Multiple sources			Unknown	Total	Number
		Labour	Pension	Other	Labour and pension	Other two	Three or more			
Females										
Never married										
50-54	0.0	0.0	85.2	0.0	8.1	5.4	1.2	0.0	100.0	405
55-59	0.0	0.0	80.3	0.0	11.0	4.9	3.6	0.0	100.0	365
60-64	0.0	0.0	87.2	0.0	3.8	7.4	1.6	0.0	100.0	445
65-69	0.0	0.0	88.5	0.0	1.8	8.1	1.4	0.0	100.0	505
70-74	0.2	0.0	89.4	0.0	1.0	9.1	0.3	0.0	100.0	574
75-79	0.0	0.0	87.6	0.0	0.1	11.5	0.8	0.0	100.0	904
80-84	0.1	0.0	86.8	0.0	0.3	11.5	1.2	0.0	100.0	1 215
85+	0.3	0.0	87.1	0.0	0.1	11.4	1.0	0.0	100.0	1 712
Total	**0.1**	**0.0**	**87.0**	**0.0**	**1.8**	**9.9**	**1.2**	**0.0**	**100.0**	**6 124**
Married										
50-54	0.0	0	.0	83.3	0.0	0.0	16.7	0.0	100.0	12
55-59	0.0	0.0	45.5	0.0	13.6	13.6	22.7	0.0	100.0	22
60-64	0.0	0.0	81.1	0.0	0.0	18.9	0.0	0.0	100.0	53
65-69	0.0	0.0	83.5	0.0	0.0	15.4	0.0	0.0	100.0	91
70-74	0.6	0.0	80.4	0.0	0.6	17.3	0.6	0.6	100.0	179
75-79	0.0	0.0	83.2	0.0	0.3	15.4	0.7	0.0	100.0	298
80-84	0.0	0.0	85.6	0.0	0.0	13.7	0.7	0.0	100.0	306
85+	0.0	0.0	88.1	0.0	0.0	10.8	1.0	0.0	100.0	194
Total	**0.1**	**0.0**	**83.6**	**0.0**	**0.4**	**14.6**	**1.1**	**0.1**	**100.0**	**1 154**
Widowed										
50-54	0.0	0.0	80.0	0.0	0.0	20.0	0.0	0.0	100.0	15
55-59	0.0	0.0	82.5	0.0	0.0	17.5	0.0	0.0	100.0	40
60-64	0.0	0.0	83.0	0.0	3.4	9.1	3.4	0.0	100.0	88
65-69	0.0	0.0	86.0	0.0	1.3	11.4	1.3	0.3	100.0	315
70-74	0.0	0.0	84.4	0.0	0.1	12.8	2.6	0.1	100.0	782
75-79	0.0	0.0	86.0	0.0	0.6	12.4	1.1	0.0	100.0	2 159
80-84	0.1	0.0	87.2	0.0	0.2	11.5	0.9	0.0	100.0	3 906
85+	0.3	0.0	87.5	0.0	0.2	10.9	1.1	0.0	100.0	6 087
Total	**0.1**	**0.0**	**86.9**	**0.0**	**0.3**	**11.4**	**1.2**	**0.0**	**100.0**	**13 393**
Divorced/separated										
50-54	0.0	0.0	82.1	0.0	0.0	17.9	0.0	0.0	100.0	28
55-59	0.0	0.0	96.9	0.0	0.0	3.1	0.0	0.0	100.0	65
60-64	0.0	0.0	84.7	0.0	2.4	14.1	0.0	0.0	100.0	85
65-69	0.0	0.0	84.4	0.0	0.0	14.3	0.7	0.0	100.0	147
70-74	0.0	0.0	88.9	0.0	0.0	9.0	2.0	0.0	100.0	199
75-79	0.0	0.0	88.5	0.0	0.0	10.3	1.2	0.0	100.0	330
80-84	0.0	0.0	72.9	0.0	0.3	8.0	0.3	0.0	100.0	361
85+	0.0	0.0	46.6	0.3	0.0	9.8	1.1	0.0	100.0	367
Total	**0.0**	**0.0**	**89.1**	**0.1**	**0.2**	**9.9**	**0.8**	**0.0**	**100.0**	**1 581**

NOTES: Other single source = enterprise, other.

Other two sources = other two than pension and labour.

TABLE 9

Economic activity of persons aged 50 and over in Finland in 1990 by age and sex (per cent)

	Employed	Unemployed	Pensioner	Other	Total	Number
Males						
50-54	79.0	4.9	13.8	2.4	100.0	135 687
55-59	58.9	5.0	34.1	2.0	100.0	122 358
60-64	28.7	20.5	49.9	0.9	100.0	116 670
65-69	2.5	0.4	97.0	0.1	100.0	90 866
70-74	1.2	0.0	98.6	0.1	100.0	60 625
75-79	0.0	0.0	100.0	0.0	100.0	45 238
80-84	0.0	0.0	100.0	0.0	100.0	25 380
85+	0.0	0.0	100.0	0.0	100.0	10 743
Total	**35.5**	**6.1**	**57.3**	**1.1**	**100.0**	**607 566**
Females						
50-54	80.0	3.4	11.2	5.4	100.0	139 072
55-59	57.0	5.1	31.5	6.4	100.0	129 360
60-64	22.9	21.8	49.8	5.6	100.0	136 317
65-69	1.5	0.4	97.9	0.3	100.0	129 746
70-74	0.5	0.0	99.4	0.1	100.0	104 160
75-79	0.0	0.0	100.0	0.0	100.0	89 053
80-84	0.0	0.0	100.0	0.0	100.0	58 885
85+	0.0	0.0	100.0	0.0	100.0	31 140
Total	**26.7**	**5.1**	**65.3**	**2.9**	**100.0**	**817 732**

TABLE 10a

**Economically active persons aged 50 and over in Finland in 1990
by age, sex and educational level (per cent)**

		Educational level 1 or 2	Educational level 3	Undergraduate	Graduate
Males					
50-54		80.5	86.5	93.5	94.0
55-59		59.2	69.2	80.6	88.3
60-64		47.2	53.4	51.3	67.3
65-69		2.4	3.2	5.1	11.2
70-74		1.1	1.2	2.3	3.6
75-79		0.0	0.0	0.0	0.0
80-84		0.0	0.0	0.0	0.0
85+		0.0	0.0	0.0	0.0
	Total	**36.0**	**54.2**	**57.4**	**58.8**
Females					
50-54		79.7	87.1	93.6	94.8
55-59		58.1	67.4	79.7	85.2
60-64		45.1	43.3	39.8	57.6
65-69		1.6	2.5	3.7	8.0
70-74		0.4	0.8	1.6	3.0
75-79		0.0	0.0	0.0	0.0
80-84		0.0	0.0	0.0	0.0
85+		0.0	0.0	0.0	0.0
	Total	**26.8**	**46.2**	**49.1**	**55.6**

TABLE 10b

**Economically active persons (employed or unemployed) aged 50 and over
in Finland in 1990 by age, sex and marital status (per cent)**

	Never married	Married	Widowed	Divorced or separated	All
Males					
50-54	69.3	87.8	79.6	76.0	83.9
55-59	53.7	66.8	57.6	56.4	63.9
60-64	50.3	49.3	45.2	48.8	49.2
65-69	1.9	3.2	2.0	2.3	2.9
Females					
50-54	76.9	84.9	78.2	82.9	83.4
55-59	61.3	63.3	55.6	62.3	62.1
60-64	43.7	45.2	41.6	48.7	44.7
65-69	2.1	1.9	1.5	2.4	1.9

TABLE 11

**Economic activity of persons aged 50 and over in Finland in 1990 by sex
and number of generations present in the household (age-standardized index)**

	Employed	Unemployed	Pensioner	Other
Males				
Solitaires	0.77	1.52	1.07	1.87
One generation	0.98	0.98	1.02	0.94
Two generations	1.13	0.80	0.95	0.69
Three or more generations	1.04	0.62	1.02	1.03
Females				
Solitaires	0.97	1.00	1.03	0.66
One generation	0.97	1.06	1.01	1.03
Two generations	1.08	0.91	0.97	1.18
Three or more generations	0.93	0.70	1.04	1.32

TABLE 12

Number and type of income sources of persons aged 50 and over living in single-person households in Finland in 1990 by age, sex and marital status (*percentage*)

| | No Income | Single source | | | | Multiple sources | | | Unknown | Total | Total number |
		Labour	Entrep.	Pension	Other	Labour and pension	Other two	Three or more			
Males											
Never married											
50-54	1.5	30.4	3.8	18.3	0.9	4.9	26.7	10.4	3.1	100.0	8 740
55-59	1.6	20.1	3.8	27.7	0.6	5.1	26.5	12.0	2.5	100.0	8 200
60-64	0.8	5.7	3.6	48.2	0.2	4.7	24.1	12.4	0.4	100.0	8 193
65-69	0.3	0.1	0.1	57.9	0.0	2.9	24.7	14.0	0.1	100.0	5 429
70-74	0.1	0.0	0.0	61.5	0.0	1.8	25.8	10.8	0.0	100.0	2 731
75-79	0.2	0.0	0.0	64.6	0.0	1.0	25.9	8.3	0.1	100.0	1 860
80-84	0.4	0.0	0.0	63.2	0.0	0.7	28.5	7.3	0.0	100.0	1 059
85+	0.0	0.0	0.0	68.1	0.0	0.7	24.7	6.5	0.0	100.0	430
Total	**1.0**	**13.1**	**2.6**	**40.4**	**0.4**	**4.0**	**25.7**	**11.5**	**1.4**	**100.0**	**36 642**
Married											
50-54	4.0	26.9	5.3	8.6	0.6	5.3	28.3	18.3	2.7	100.0	1 568
55-59	2.5	18.6	4.6	17.5	0.9	6.7	28.5	19.0	1.6	100.0	1 412
60-64	0.7	5.8	1.6	35.1	0.6	8.3	24.9	22.1	0.9	100.0	1 417
65-69	1.4	0.2	0.2	48.1	0.2	5.2	22.1	22.4	0.2	100.0	1 134
70-74	0.1	0.0	0.1	52.5	0.3	2.9	27.1	16.6	0.3	100.0	735
75-79	0.8	0.1	0.0	59.2	0.0	2.2	24.7	12.8	0.1	100.0	721
80-84	0.6	0.0	0.0	58.9	0.2	2.3	29.5	8.5	0.0	100.0	484
85+	0.5	0.0	0.0	66.5	0.0	1.0	24.1	7.9	0.0	100.0	191
Total	**1.8**	**10.0**	**2.3**	**34.6**	**0.5**	**5.3**	**26.3**	**18.2**	**1.1**	**100.0**	**7 662**
Widowed											
50-54	0.4	27.0	3.5	13.6	0.0	11.5	25.3	17.6	1.1	100.0	712
55-59	0.8	17.9	2.4	24.5	0.1	8.5	24.8	20.3	0.8	100.0	1 538
60-64	0.2	4.0	1.5	39.0	0.0	9.0	26.1	19.9	0.4	100.0	3 073
65-69	0.1	0.0	0.0	50.5	0.0	6.6	25.2	17.5	0.0	100.0	4 655
70-74	0.0	0.0	0.0	55.6	0.0	3.3	27.3	13.8	0.0	100.0	5 501
75-79	0.1	0.0	0.1	60.4	0.0	1.9	26.5	11.0	0.0	100.0	6 901
80-84	0.1	0.0	0.0	62.9	0.0	1.6	26.8	8.6	0.0	100.0	5 976
85+	0.2	0.0	0.0	68.3	0.0	1.0	24.0	6.4	0.0	100.0	3 910
Total	**0.1**	**1.8**	**0.4**	**54.8**	**0.0**	**3.8**	**26.1**	**12.9**	**0.1**	**100.0**	**32 267**
Divorced/separated											
50-54	1.8	36.7	3.4	14.3	0.5	6.8	22.5	9.1	4.8	100.0	8 430
55-59	1.5	24.5	2.5	29.2	0.4	7.2	21.3	10.1	3.1	100.0	7 353
60-64	0.5	6.3	1.5	55.5	0.1	8.1	17.7	10.1	0.3	100.0	6 417
65-69	0.3	0.1	0.0	67.8	0.0	5.5	17.1	9.2	0.0	100.0	4 226
70-74	0.4	0.0	0.0	69.7	0.1	3.1	19.9	6.7	0.0	100.0	2 223
75-79	0.3	0.0	0.1	74.7	0.0	1.9	18.2	4.9	0.1	100.0	1 393
80-84	0.2	0.0	0.0	80.0	0.0	0.7	15.3	3.8	0.0	100.0	575
85+	0.0	0.0	0.0	76.6	0.0	0.0	17.2	6.2	0.0	100.0	209
Total	**1.0**	**17.2**	**1.9**	**42.1**	**0.3**	**6.4**	**19.9**	**9.1**	**2.1**	**100.0**	**30 825**
Total males											
50-54	1.8	32.7	3.7	15.6	0.7	6.0	25.0	10.7	3.7	100.0	19 450
55-59	1.6	21.6	3.2	27.3	0.5	6.4	24.5	12.5	2.5	100.0	18 503
60-64	0.6	5.6	2.4	48.2	0.1	6.8	22.3	13.6	0.4	100.0	19 100
65-69	0.3	0.1	0.1	57.7	0.0	4.9	22.6	14.3	0.1	100.0	15 444
70-74	0.1	0.0	0.0	59.6	0.0	2.8	25.4	11.9	0.0	100.0	11 190
75-79	0.2	0.0	0.0	62.9	0.0	1.8	25.2	9.9	0.0	100.0	10 875
80-84	0.2	0.0	0.0	63.9	0.0	1.5	26.4	8.1	0.0	100.0	8 094
85+	0.2	0.0	0.0	68.6	0.0	1.0	23.8	6.5	0.0	100.0	4 740
Total	**0.8**	**10.7**	**1.7**	**44.8**	**0.2**	**4.7**	**24.2**	**11.7**	**1.2**	**100.0**	**107 396**

TABLE 12 (*continued*)

		Single source				Multiple sources					
	No Income	Labour	Entrep.	Pension	Other	Labour and pension	Other two	Three or more	Unknown	Total	Total number
Females											
Never married											
50-54	0.7	36.3	1.2	12.6	0.6	4.4	33.5	9.7	1.1	100.0	7 937
55-59	0.5	25.0	1.2	19.9	0.9	5.7	31.9	13.7	1.2	100.0	8 210
60-64	0.5	7.8	0.9	39.8	0.3	8.2	26.6	15.5	0.3	100.0	9 848
65-69	0.1	0.1	0.1	55.5	0.0	5.3	26.6	12.2	0.0	100.0	10 513
70-74	0.1	0.0	0.0	62.8	0.0	2.5	26.6	8.0	0.0	100.0	8 924
75-79	0.1	0.0	0.0	72.1	0.0	1.2	22.2	4.4	0.0	100.0	8 522
80-84	0.1	0.0	0.0	76.4	0.0	0.8	19.6	3.1	0.0	100.0	6 461
85+	0.3	0.0	0.0	80.4	0.1	0.6	16.8	1.9	0.0	100.0	3 991
Total	**0.3**	**8.9**	**0.4**	**50.1**	**0.2**	**4.0**	**26.2**	**9.4**	**0.3**	**100.0**	**64 406**
Married											
50-54	2.7	37.0	2.9	7.8	1.0	3.7	33.2	10.1	1.5	100.0	1 215
55-59	3.3	24.5	1.5	19.1	1.7	4.4	29.9	14.0	1.7	100.0	1 320
60-64	2.7	7.1	2.9	42.7	0.9	8.8	21.6	12.9	0.4	100.0	1 303
65-69	1.4	0.1	0.4	62.0	0.0	4.6	20.9	10.5	0.2	100.0	1 002
70-74	0.9	0.0	0.3	66.4	0.0	4.0	21.9	6.3	0.3	100.0	780
75-79	0.3	0.0	0.0	73.1	0.0	3.3	19.2	3.9	0.2	100.0	636
80-84	0.8	0.0	0.0	79.3	0.0	0.3	17.1	2.5	0.0	100.0	363
85+	0.8	0.0	0.0	80.0	0.0	1.5	13.1	4.6	0.0	100.0	130
Total	**2.1**	**12.8**	**1.5**	**42.9**	**0.7**	**4.7**	**24.6**	**9.9**	**0.8**	**100.0**	**6 750**
Widowed											
50-54	0.1	3.9	0.3	14.2	0.1	36.4	10.2	34.7	0.1	100.0	3 855
55-59	0.4	2.7	0.2	25.3	0.1	27.3	13.2	30.4	0.2	100.0	8 778
60-64	0.6	0.7	0.2	46.8	0.1	13.5	20.5	17.5	0.1	100.0	18 482
65-69	0.1	0.0	0.0	61.9	0.0	4.7	23.2	10.0	0.0	100.0	30 348
70-74	0.1	0.0	0.0	68.9	0.0	2.4	22.3	6.3	0.0	100.0	36 286
75-79	0.0	0.0	0.0	75.2	0.0	1.3	19.4	4.0	0.0	100.0	39 719
80-84	0.1	0.0	0.0	79.1	0.0	0.5	17.3	3.0	0.0	100.0	30 477
85+	0.2	0.0	0.0	82.0	0.0	0.3	15.1	2.3	0.0	100.0	17 136
Total	**0.2**	**0.3**	**0.0**	**66.6**	**0.0**	**5.0**	**19.5**	**8.3**	**0.0**	**100.0**	**185 081**
Divorced/separated											
50-54	0.6	42.0	2.0	10.9	0.4	5.6	28.1	8.3	2.1	100.0	9 123
55-59	0.3	29.8	1.3	22.8	0.6	8.1	25.7	9.7	1.7	100.0	9 497
60-64	0.2	9.0	0.7	48.7	0.2	10.6	19.5	10.7	0.5	100.0	9 502
65-69	0.2	0.1	0.0	66.8	0.0	6.5	17.8	8.5	0.0	100.0	8 240
70-74	0.1	0.0	0.0	75.0	0.0	2.9	17.3	4.7	0.1	100.0	5 930
75-79	0.0	0.0	0.0	81.4	0.0	1.4	14.4	2.7	0.0	100.0	4 605
80-84	0.1	0.0	0.0	84.8	0.0	0.8	12.1	2.1	0.2	100.0	2 624
85+	0.2	0.0	0.0	85.5	0.1	0.5	12.1	1.5	0.1	100.0	1 123
Total	**0.3**	**14.9**	**0.7**	**48.7**	**0.2**	**6.1**	**20.7**	**7.6**	**0.8**	**100.0**	**50 644**
Total females											
50-54	0.7	33.1	1.5	11.9	0.5	10.4	27.2	13.5	1.3	100.0	22 130
55-59	0.6	19.5	0.9	22.6	0.6	13.3	23.8	17.6	1.1	100.0	27 805
60-64	0.5	4.7	0.6	45.4	0.2	11.3	21.8	15.2	0.3	100.0	39 135
65-69	0.1	0.1	0.0	61.4	0.0	5.1	23.0	10.2	0.0	100.0	50 103
70-74	0.1	0.0	0.0	68.5	0.0	2.5	22.5	6.4	0.0	100.0	51 920
75-79	0.0	0.0	0.0	75.2	0.0	1.3	19.4	4.0	0.0	100.0	53 482
80-84	0.1	0.0	0.0	79.0	0.0	0.6	17.3	2.9	0.0	100.0	39 925
85+	0.2	0.0	0.0	81.9	0.0	0.4	15.3	2.2	0.0	100.0	22 380
Total	**0.2**	**4.8**	**0.3**	**59.7**	**0.1**	**5.0**	**21.2**	**8.5**	**0.2**	**100.0**	**306 881**

TABLE 13

Number and type of income sources of persons aged 50 and over living
in two- or three-person households in Finland in 1990 by age, sex and marital status (per cent)

| | | No Income | Single source | | | | Multiple sources | | | Unknown | Total | Number |
			Labour	Entrep.	Pension	Other	Labour and pension	Other two	Three or more			
Males												
Never married												
	50-54	2.3	28.8	5.3	17.5	0.8	4.8	26.2	10.9	3.4	100.0	7 404
	55-59	2.8	18.6	5.7	25.6	0.9	4.9	26.2	12.4	2.9	100.0	5 541
	60-64	2.0	5.4	6.0	41.3	0.5	3.5	26.5	14.4	0.4	100.0	4 512
	65-69	0.2	0.2	0.6	50.7	0.0	2.7	27.9	17.7	0.0	100.0	2 489
	70-74	0.1	0.0	0.0	48.4	0.0	1.4	32.8	17.2	0.1	100.0	1 155
	75-79	0.0	0.0	0.0	64.0	0.0	0.6	17.6	17.6	0.2	100.0	620
	80-84	0.5	0.0	0.0	52.7	0.0	0.7	35.6	10.5	0.0	100.0	410
	85+	1.7	0.0	0.0	61.7	0.0	0.6	30.6	5.6	0.0	100.0	180
	Total	**1.9**	**15.3**	**4.4**	**31.9**	**0.6**	**3.9**	**26.8**	**13.2**	**1.9**	**100.0**	**22 311**
Married												
	50-54	0.5	26.1	3.9	4.7	0.6	4.6	35.0	23.7	1.0	100.0	69 609
	55-59	0.4	16.5	3.2	12.0	0.5	6.3	31.8	28.5	0.8	100.0	75 717
	60-64	0.2	4.9	2.0	26.2	0.1	7.8	28.2	30.4	0.2	100.0	78 317
	65-69	0.1	0.1	0.1	36.6	0.0	6.3	28.5	28.3	0.0	100.0	64 081
	70-74	0.1	0.0	0.0	41.9	0.0	4.5	30.3	23.2	0.0	100.0	42 607
	75-79	0.0	0.0	0.0	37.8	0.0	2.3	46.2	13.7	0.0	100.0	37 220
	80-84	0.1	0.0	0.0	54.1	0.0	1.9	30.7	13.2	0.0	100.0	13 830
	85+	0.1	0.0	0.0	57.7	0.0	1.2	31.3	9.7	0.0	100.0	4 105
	Total	**0.2**	**9.0**	**1.7**	**25.4**	**0.2**	**5.5**	**32.3**	**25.2**	**0.4**	**100.0**	**385 486**
Widowed												
	50-54	0.5	27.6	3.6	8.5	0.7	7.4	26.2	24.4	1.0	100.0	970
	55-59	0.6	17.8	2.5	19.3	0.4	9.8	27.3	21.5	0.7	100.0	1 247
	60-64	1.0	5.2	1.9	37.9	0.3	8.1	22.7	22.6	0.2	100.0	1 486
	65-69	0.3	0.1	0.1	48.8	0.0	5.6	25.9	19.3	0.1	100.0	1 615
	70-74	0.1	0.0	0.0	54.5	0.0	3.0	29.3	13.2	0.0	100.0	1 528
	75-79	0.0	0.0	0.0	60.5	0.0	2.7	26.1	10.7	0.0	100.0	1 675
	80-84	0.0	0.0	0.0	63.8	0.0	1.6	26.2	8.5	0.0	100.0	1 453
	85+	0.1	0.0	0.0	66.2	0.0	1.1	25.7	6.8	0.1	100.0	1 065
	Total	**0.3**	**5.1**	**0.9**	**46.7**	**0.2**	**4.8**	**26.2**	**15.6**	**0.2**	**100.0**	**11 039**
Divorced/separated												
	50-54	1.4	38.8	4.5	10.9	0.5	7.0	23.8	10.0	3.1	100.0	8 059
	55-59	1.2	26.6	2.9	21.9	0.5	8.4	23.2	12.6	2.8	100.0	5 341
	60-64	0.9	7.0	1.7	47.4	0.1	14.1	16.4	11.8	0.6	100.0	3 956
	65-69	0.4	0.1	0.1	62.7	0.0	7.3	17.8	11.4	0.2	100.0	1 853
	70-74	0.0	0.0	0.0	66.1	0.0	3.4	20.0	10.4	0.1	100.0	835
	75-79	0.0	0.0	0.0	72.6	0.0	3.7	18.3	5.5	0.0	100.0	438
	80-84	0.6	0.0	0.0	71.5	0.0	1.8	19.4	6.7	0.0	100.0	165
	85+	0.0	0.0	0.0	2.8	0.0	96.3	0.8	0.1	0.0	100.0	1 458
	Total	**1.0**	**21.8**	**2.7**	**27.7**	**0.3**	**14.3**	**20.0**	**10.3**	**1.9**	**100.0**	**22 105**
Total males												
	50-54	0.8	27.5	4.1	6.4	0.6	4.9	33.1	21.3	1.4	100.0	86 042
	55-59	0.6	17.2	3.3	13.6	0.6	6.4	30.8	26.4	1.1	100.0	87 846
	60-64	0.3	5.1	2.2	28.1	0.2	7.8	27.5	28.6	0.2	100.0	88 271
	65-69	0.1	0.1	0.1	38.1	0.0	6.2	28.1	27.3	0.0	100.0	70 038
	70-74	0.1	0.0	0.0	42.9	0.0	4.3	30.1	22.5	0.0	100.0	46 125
	75-79	0.0	0.0	0.0	39.5	0.0	2.3	44.6	13.5	0.0	100.0	39 953
	80-84	0.1	0.0	0.0	55.2	0.0	1.8	30.3	12.7	0.0	100.0	15 858
	85+	0.1	0.0	0.0	47.4	0.0	21.5	23.9	7.1	0.0	100.0	6 808
	Total	**0.4**	**9.8**	**1.9**	**26.4**	**0.3**	**5.8**	**31.2**	**23.6**	**0.6**	**100.0**	**440 941**

TABLE 13 (*concluded*)

		Single source				Multiple sources					
	No Income	Labour	Entrep.	Pension	Other	Labour and pension	Other two	Three or more	Unknown	Total	Number
Females											
Never married											
50-54	4.1	45.1	4.1	23.4	1.2	1.4	7.5	10.8	2.5	100.0	3 300
55-59	2.7	26.1	3.0	24.4	0.8	6.0	25.4	9.7	1.9	100.0	3 879
60-64	2.3	7.6	3.2	42.2	0.6	7.9	23.8	11.9	0.6	100.0	3 751
65-69	0.1	0.1	0.1	55.7	0.0	5.5	26.3	11.9	0.0	100.0	3 427
70-74	0.0	0.0	0.0	60.5	0.0	3.0	28.3	8.0	0.1	100.0	2 629
75-79	0.0	0.0	0.0	67.8	0.0	1.3	25.2	5.7	0.0	100.0	2 388
80-84	0.2	0.0	0.0	71.0	0.0	1.0	22.9	4.9	0.0	100.0	1 781
85+	0.4	0.0	0.0	76.8	0.0	0.6	18.7	3.4	0.0	100.0	1 117
Total	**1.4**	**11.9**	**1.6**	**44.8**	**0.4**	**4.5**	**25.9**	**8.7**	**0.8**	**100.0**	**23 523**
Married											
50-54	2.1	34.9	4.9	5.4	1.5	3.7	33.8	12.0	1.8	100.0	75 764
55-59	2.8	23.4	4.3	15.2	1.9	6.1	30.7	13.9	1.9	100.0	74 683
60-64	2.5	6.2	3.0	38.7	0.9	7.9	26.5	13.8	0.5	100.0	74 337
65-69	0.2	0.1	0.1	56.1	0.0	5.6	27.2	10.7	0.0	100.0	58 799
70-74	0.1	0.0	0.0	62.2	0.0	6.5	24.4	6.8	0.0	100.0	36 167
75-79	0.0	0.0	0.0	71.2	0.0	2.2	22.2	4.3	0.0	100.0	19 520
80-84	0.1	0.0	0.0	75.7	0.0	1.3	19.5	3.4	0.0	100.0	7 561
85+	0.2	0.0	0.1	79.6	0.0	0.8	17.0	2.4	0.0	100.0	1 551
Total	**1.6**	**14.0**	**2.6**	**34.7**	**0.9**	**5.2**	**28.5**	**11.4**	**0.9**	**100.0**	**347 214**
Widowed											
50-54	0.2	2.7	0.3	16.0	0.0	35.4	8.9	36.3	0.3	100.0	4 905
55-59	0.6	2.5	0.2	26.8	0.2	28.3	13.1	27.9	0.4	100.0	6 176
60-64	1.0	1.2	0.4	50.4	0.0	13.9	17.1	15.9	0.1	100.0	7 922
65-69	0.3	0.0	0.0	65.1	0.0	5.8	20.9	7.8	0.0	100.0	9 287
70-74	0.1	0.0	0.0	72.5	0.0	3.0	19.2	5.1	0.0	100.0	8 812
75-79	0.1	0.0	0.0	76.9	0.0	1.6	18.0	3.4	0.0	100.0	8 794
80-84	0.1	0.0	0.0	80.5	0.0	0.6	16.1	2.7	0.0	100.0	6 762
85+	0.2	0.0	0.0	83.8	0.0	0.4	13.6	2.1	0.0	100.0	4 663
Total	**0.3**	**0.7**	**0.1**	**61.0**	**0.0**	**9.7**	**16.6**	**11.4**	**0.1**	**100.0**	**57 321**
Divorced/separated											
50-54	1.2	44.2	2.2	8.6	0.8	6.2	26.4	8.1	2.3	100.0	10 033
55-59	1.1	31.7	1.6	20.7	0.8	8.3	23.6	9.9	2.2	100.0	6 111
60-64	0.7	10.4	1.0	47.6	0.2	11.3	18.7	9.6	0.6	100.0	3 968
65-69	0.0	0.1	0.0	67.4	0.0	7.7	16.7	8.0	0.0	100.0	2 357
70-74	0.0	0.0	0.0	70.5	0.0	5.4	17.9	6.0	0.3	100.0	1 327
75-79	0.0	0.0	0.0	78.5	0.0	2.3	15.3	3.7	0.1	100.0	828
80-84	0.2	0.0	0.0	83.0	0.0	1.1	13.8	1.9	0.0	100.0	464
85+	0.0	0.0	0.0	86.5	0.4	0.4	10.3	2.4	0.0	100.0	252
Total	**0.9**	**26.8**	**1.4**	**30.7**	**0.5**	**7.2**	**22.5**	**8.3**	**1.6**	**100.0**	**25 340**
Total females											
50-54	2.0	34.6	4.3	7.0	1.3	5.5	30.8	12.8	1.8	100.0	94 002
55-59	2.5	22.6	3.8	16.7	1.6	7.8	28.8	14.4	1.8	100.0	90 849
60-64	2.3	6.0	2:7	40.3	0.8	8.6	25.2	13.7	0.5	100.0	89 978
65-69	0.2	0.1	0.1	57.6	0.0	5.7	26.1	10.3	0.0	100.0	73 870
70-74	0.1	0.0	0.0	64.2	0.0	5.7	23.5	6.6	0.0	100.0	48 935
75-79	0.0	0.0	0.0	72.7	0.0	2.0	21.1	4.1	0.0	100.0	31 530
80-84	0.1	0.0	0.0	77.4	0.0	1.0	18.3	3.2	0.0	100.0	16 568
85+	0.2	0.0	0.0	82.0	0.0	0.5	14.9	2.3	0.0	100.0	7 583
Total	**1.4**	**12.9**	**2.2**	**38.4**	**0.8**	**6.1**	**26.3**	**11.1**	**0.8**	**100.0**	**453 315**

TABLE 14

**Number and type of income sources of persons aged 50 and over living
in four- or more person households in Finland in 1990 by age, sex and marital status (per cent)**

	No Income	Single source				Multiple sources			Unknown	Total	Number
		Labour	Entrep.	Pension	Other	Labour and pension	Other two	Three or more			
Males											
Never married											
50-54	3.8	28.6	6.9	21.2	0.9	4.0	20.3	10.5	3.8	100.0	873
55-59	6.3	20.2	4.8	30.4	0.0	5.7	20.5	10.0	2.1	100.0	619
60-64	4.0	4.7	3.0	56.2	0.0	4.2	17.6	9.8	0.5	100.0	427
65-69	0.9	0.0	0.5	75.2	0.0	2.8	15.6	5.0	0.0	100.0	218
70-74	0.0	0.0	0.0	63.5	0.0	0.9	29.6	6.1	0.0	100.0	115
75-79	0.0	0.0	0.0	72.6	0.0	0.0	24.2	3.2	0.0	100.0	62
80-84	0.0	0.0	0.0	80.6	0.0	2.8	11.1	5.6	0.0	100.0	36
85+	0.0	0.0	0.0	70.8	0.0	0.0	25.0	4.2	0.0	100.0	24
Total	**3.8**	**16.6**	**4.4**	**39.6**	**0.3**	**4.0**	**19.9**	**9.2**	**2.0**	**100.0**	**2 374**
Married											
50-54	0.3	21.0	4.5	2.9	0.6	3.6	35.2	30.8	1.1	100.0	28 094
55-59	0.4	13.1	5.0	7.3	0.5	4.5	32.1	36.3	0.7	100.0	14 624
60-64	0.4	4.2	3.3	19.1	0.1	6.4	28.2	38.1	0.1	100.0	8 514
65-69	0.2	0.1	0.1	30.7	0.0	6.0	27.5	35.3	0.1	100.0	4 685
70-74	0.1	0.0	0.0	39.9	0.0	4.1	29.8	26.2	0.0	100.0	2 690
75-79	0.2	0.0	0.0	48.7	0.0	3.4	30.3	17.4	0.0	100.0	1 749
80-84	0.0	0.0	0.0	57.8	0.0	1.5	25.5	15.2	0.0	100.0	868
85+	0.0	0.0	0.0	63.8	0.0	0.4	26.9	9.0	0.0	100.0	268
Total	**0.3**	**13.3**	**3.7**	**12.3**	**0.4**	**4.4**	**32.3**	**32.6**	**0.7**	**100.0**	**61 492**
Widowed											
50-54	2.5	15.5	6.2	8.1	0.0	9.3	28.0	29.2	1.2	100.0	161
55-59	1.1	5.3	3.7	17.0	0.0	12.2	29.3	28.7	2.7	100.0	188
60-64	0.0	1.9	2.7	34.7	0.0	11.5	26.3	22.1	0.8	100.0	262
65-69	0.0	0.0	0.0	52.6	0.0	6.1	23.4	17.9	0.0	100.0	312
70-74	0.0	0.0	0.0	58.6	0.0	4.6	24.1	12.8	0.0	100.0	415
75-79	0.0	0.0	0.0	65.7	0.0	1.3	22.6	10.4	0.0	100.0	548
80-84	0.0	0.0	0.0	67.7	0.0	2.0	24.2	6.0	0.2	100.0	504
85+	0.0	0.0	0.0	70.2	0.0	1.0	22.4	6.4	0.0	100.0	299
Total	**0.2**	**1.5**	**0.9**	**54.1**	**0.0**	**4.7**	**24.4**	**13.9**	**0.4**	**100.0**	**2 689**
Divorced/separated											
50-54	1.9	37.5	5.3	11.1	0.6	5.6	24.8	9.3	3.9	100.0	1 067
55-59	2.2	24.4	5.5	25.5	0.0	6.7	19.1	13.1	3.4	100.0	581
60-64	2.0	6.4	0.6	56.5	0.0	7.2	18.0	9.3	0.0	100.0	345
65-69	0.6	0.0	0.0	74.8	0.0	4.3	13.5	6.7	0.0	100.0	163
70-74	0.0	0.0	0.0	72.4	0.0	2.3	11.5	13.8	0.0	100.0	87
75-79	0.0	0.0	0.0	68.1	0.0	0.0	19.1	12.8	0.0	100.0	47
80-84	0.0	0.0	0.0	85.0	0.0	0.0	10.0	5.0	0.0	100.0	20
85+	0.0	0.0	0.0	75.0	0.0	0.0	12.5	12.5	0.0	100.0	8
Total	**1.8**	**24.3**	**3.9**	**30.2**	**0.3**	**5.7**	**20.8**	**10.3**	**2.7**	**100.0**	**2 318**
Total males											
50-54	0.5	21.7	4.6	3.8	0.6	3.7	34.3	29.4	1.2	100.0	30 195
55-59	0.7	13.7	5.0	9.0	0.4	4.8	31.2	34.3	0.9	100.0	16 012
60-64	0.6	4.3	3.2	22.5	0.1	6.5	27.3	35.4	0.2	100.0	9 548
65-69	0.2	0.1	0.1	35.1	0.0	5.8	26.4	32.2	0.1	100.0	5 378
70-74	0.1	0.0	0.0	43.9	0.0	4.0	28.6	23.5	0.0	100.0	3 307
75-79	0.1	0.0	0.0	53.5	0.0	2.8	28.2	15.4	0.0	100.0	2 406
80-84	0.0	0.0	0.0	62.3	0.0	1.7	24.4	11.6	0.1	100.0	1 428
85+	0.0	0.0	0.0	67.4	0.0	0.7	24.4	7.5	0.0	100.0	599
Total	**0.5**	**13.3**	**3.6**	**15.5**	**0.4**	**4.4**	**31.2**	**30.3**	**0.8**	**100.0**	**68 873**

TABLE 14 (concluded)

		Single source				Multiple sources					
	No Income	Labour	Entrep.	Pension	Other	Labour and pension	Other two	Three or more	Unknown	Total	Number
Females											
Never married											
50-54	5.2	23.7	3.8	36.1	0.6	4.3	18.5	4.9	2.9	100.0	346
55-59	6.2	15.2	3.3	39.1	0.0	4.1	21.8	6.2	4.1	100.0	243
60-64	3.2	6.4	3.7	44.7	0.0	5.3	23.9	10.6	2.1	100.0	188
65-69	0.0	0.0	0.0	66.7	0.0	8.5	19.4	5.5	0.0	100.0	165
70-74	2.4	0.0	0.0	68.3	0.0	1.6	24.6	3.2	0.0	100.0	126
75-79	1.5	0.0	0.0	72.5	0.0	0.0	21.4	4.6	0.0	100.0	131
80-84	0.0	0.0	0.0	76.3	0.0	0.0	22.6	1.1	0.0	100.0	93
85+	0.0	0.0	0.0	83.3	0.0	0.0	16.7	0.0	0.0	100.0	90
Total	**3.2**	**9.5**	**2.0**	**53.6**	**0.1**	**3.7**	**20.9**	**5.2**	**1.7**	**100.0**	**1 382**
Married											
50-54	2.6	30.6	9.4	3.5	1.3	2.4	34.1	14.5	1.7	100.0	20 042
55-59	3.0	20.2	9.5	11.8	1.1	6.4	29.9	16.2	1.9	100.0	9 312
60-64	2.9	5.3	7.7	35.0	0.8	9.8	24.9	12.8	0.6	100.0	5 464
65-69	0.1	0.1	0.2	56.6	0.0	6.8	26.6	9.6	0.0	100.0	3 411
70-74	0.2	0.0	0.0	66.0	0.0	2.8	25.3	5.7	0.0	100.0	1 872
75-79	0.0	0.0	0.0	77.7	0.0	2.4	17.8	2.0	0.0	100.0	1 082
80-84	0.0	0.0	0.0	79.7	0.0	0.8	18.9	0.6	0.0	100.0	360
85+	0.0	0.0	0.0	77.3	0.0	1.5	21.2	0.0	0.0	100.0	66
Total	**2.3**	**19.9**	**7.7**	**19.4**	**1.0**	**4.6**	**30.4**	**13.4**	**1.3**	**100.0**	**41 609**
Widowed											
50-54	0.6	2.0	0.5	18.4	0.0	28.8	12.9	36.9	0.0	100.0	643
55-59	0.9	1.6	0.4	30.5	0.3	23.3	18.0	24.8	0.3	100.0	761
60-64	0.8	0.6	0.2	52.1	0.2	11.7	19.2	15.1	0.2	100.0	1 258
65-69	0.0	0.0	0.0	68.5	0.0	5.4	19.4	6.7	0.0	100.0	1 982
70-74	0.0	0.0	0.0	75.7	0.0	2.2	18.2	3.8	0.0	100.0	2 353
75-79	0.0	0.0	0.0	82.0	0.0	1.3	13.7	2.9	0.0	100.0	2 746
80-84	0.1	0.0	0.0	85.6	0.0	0.4	12.1	1.9	0.0	100.0	1 905
85+	0.0	0.0	0.1	86.1	0.0	0.2	11.9	1.7	0.0	100.0	1 002
Total	**0.2**	**0.3**	**0.1**	**70.3**	**0.0**	**5.6**	**15.8**	**7.7**	**0.0**	**100.0**	**12 650**
Divorced/separated											
50-54	2.9	37.7	3.0	9.5	1.1	7.4	26.1	8.9	3.3	100.0	660
55-59	2.3	31.7	1.8	21.3	0.8	6.1	22.8	11.4	1.8	100.0	394
60-64	1.3	5.7	0.7	54.2	0.0	6.7	19.4	11.4	0.7	100.0	299
65-69	0.0	0.0	0.0	67.1	0.0	7.5	17.8	7.5	0.0	100.0	213
70-74	0.0	0.0	0.0	77.7	0.0	3.8	13.1	5.4	0.0	100.0	130
75-79	0.0	0.0	0.0	80.2	0.0	1.2	16.0	1.2	1.2	100.0	81
80-84	0.0	0.0	0.0	85.3	0.0	0.0	11.8	2.9	0.0	100.0	34
85+	5.6	0.0	0.0	88.9	0.0	0.0	5.6	0.0	0.0	100.0	18
Total	**1.8**	**21.4**	**1.6**	**36.2**	**0.5**	**6.3**	**21.5**	**8.9**	**1.7**	**100.0**	**1 829**
Total females											
50-54	2.6	29.8	8.8	4.6	1.2	3.4	33.0	14.9	1.7	100.0	21 691
55-59	2.9	19.2	8.4	14.1	1.0	7.5	28.6	16.4	1.8	100.0	10 710
60-64	2.5	4.5	6.0	39.1	0.6	9.9	23.7	13.1	0.6	100.0	7 209
65-69	0.1	0.0	0.1	61.4	0.0	6.4	23.6	8.4	0.0	100.0	5 771
70-74	0.1	0.0	0.0	71.5	0.0	2.5	21.2	4.6	0.0	100.0	4 481
75-79	0.1	0.0	0.0	80.5	0.0	1.5	15.1	2.7	0.0	100.0	4 040
80-84	0.1	0.0	0.0	84.3	0.0	0.4	13.5	1.7	0.0	100.0	2 392
85+	0.1	0.0	0.1	85.5	0.0	0.3	12.7	1.4	0.0	100.0	1 176
Total	**1.9**	**15.4**	**5.7**	**31.9**	**0.7**	**4.9**	**26.7**	**11.8**	**1.1**	**100.0**	**57 470**

TABLE 15

**Dwelling size and number of rooms per person aged 50 and over
in Finland in 1990 by age, sex and marital status**

	Average dwelling size (per capita)	Average number of rooms (per capita)	Proportion of dwelling units with one room or less per person
Males			
Never married			
50-54	40.2	1.9	31.6
55-59	40.5	2.0	32.1
60-64	41.2	2.0	33.0
65-69	40.3	1.9	36.5
70-74	39.6	1.9	37.3
75-79	39.3	1.8	41.2
80-84	38.5	1.8	40.8
85+	36.8	1.8	44.5
Average	40.3	1.9	33.8
Married			
50-54	35.9	1.7	18.6
55-59	38.4	1.8	15.7
60-64	38.4	1.8	15.3
65-69	37.6	1.8	16.2
70-74	36.3	1.8	18.1
75-79	34.7	1.7	21.9
80-84	33.2	1.6	26.0
85+	32.2	1.6	30.3
Average	37.0	1.8	17.5
Widowed			
50-54	48.4	2.3	14.8
55-59	53.6	2.6	14.5
60-64	56.7	2.7	16.3
65-69	55.1	2.7	17.4
70-74	53.9	2.6	19.4
75-79	52.2	2.6	21.2
80-84	49.7	2.4	24.1
85+	46.4	2.3	28.3
Average	52.2	2.6	20.4
Divorced			
50-54	40.5	2.0	30.4
55-59	41.7	2.0	30.6
60-64	40.3	2.0	35.7
65-69	41.3	2.0	37.3
70-74	40.5	1.9	39.3
75-79	39.1	1.9	44.2
80-84	38.6	1.8	46.5
85+	35.2	1.7	51.7
Average	40.7	2.0	33.6
Separated			
50-54	34.9	1.7	32.3
55-59	40.9	2.0	28.1
60-64	40.1	1.9	31.7
65-69	39.5	1.9	30.8
70-74	41.1	2.0	35.4
75-79	42.6	2.1	29.5
80-84	41.8	2.2	20.8
85+	39.0	2.0	50.0
Average	38.9	1.9	31.1
Total Male Average	**38.8**	**1.9**	**20.7**

TABLE 15 (*concluded*)

	Average dwelling size (per capita)	Average number of rooms (per capita)	Proportion of dwelling units with one room or less per person
Females			
Never married			
50-54	42.7	2.1	27.3
55-59	43.7	2.1	26.2
60-64	44.5	2.1	27.0
65-69	43.7	2.1	29.7
70-74	42.3	2.0	33.7
75-79	40.2	1.9	38.9
80-84	39.1	1.8	41.5
85+	37.5	1.8	44.6
Average	42.3	2.0	32.0
Married			
50-54	37.5	1.8	15.7
55-59	39.2	1.9	14.0
60-64	38.4	1.9	14.8
65-69	37.1	1.8	16.9
70-74	35.5	1.7	20.1
75-79	33.5	1.7	24.2
80-84	32.4	1.6	28.7
85+	31.1	1.5	34.1
Average	37.4	1.8	16.6
Widowed			
50-54	50.3	2.4	13.4
55-59	53.3	2.6	13.8
60-64	54.4	2.7	15.0
65-69	53.5	2.6	17.6
70-74	51.0	2.5	21.6
75-79	47.5	2.3	27.0
80-84	44.5	2.2	31.8
85+	40.6	1.9	37.1
Average	49.3	2.4	23.4
Divorced			
50-54	42.9	2.1	20.7
55-59	45.0	2.2	22.6
60-64	45.2	2.2	25.0
65-69	44.2	2.1	29.7
70-74	42.1	2.0	36.2
75-79	39.1	1.8	44.2
80-84	37.7	1.8	47.8
85+	35.0	1.6	51.1
Average	43.2	2.1	27.9
Separated			
50-54	40.1	2.0	18.9
55-59	43.0	2.1	19.8
60-64	42.6	2.1	18.4
65-69	42.3	2.0	27.7
70-74	41.0	1.9	31.4
75-79	39.0	1.9	37.3
80-84	43.6	2.1	31.3
85+	34.1	1.5	50.0
Average	41.8	2.1	21.7
Total Female Average	**42.2**	**2.0**	**21.4**

TABLE 16

**Dwelling size and number of rooms per person aged 50 and over
in Finland in 1990 by age, sex and number of generations present in the household**

	Average dwelling size (per capita)	Average number of rooms (per capita)	Proportion of dwelling units with one room or less per person
Males			
Solitaires			
50-54	51.9	2.5	27.3
55-59	51.9	2.5	27.5
60-64	51.7	2.5	29.4
65-69	52.2	2.5	29.1
70-74	53.8	2.6	26.7
75-79	54.1	2.6	25.5
80-84	52.8	2.6	25.9
85+	50.2	2.5	28.5
Total	**52.3**	**2.5**	**27.7**
One generation households			
50-54	41.8	2.0	12.5
55-59	42.3	2.0	10.8
60-64	40.7	2.0	11.3
65-69	39.1	1.9	12.5
70-74	37.5	1.8	14.3
75-79	35.4	1.8	18.7
80-84	33.6	1.7	23.1
85+	31.9	1.6	29.0
Total	**39.6**	**1.9**	**13.4**
Two generation households			
50-54	30.6	1.4	24.9
55-59	31.1	1.5	24.3
60-64	30.5	1.4	26.2
65-69	29.8	1.4	28.6
70-74	29.4	1.4	31.4
75-79	29.2	1.4	32.7
80-84	29.7	1.4	33.3
85+	30.9	1.5	31.3
Total	**30.5**	**1.4**	**26.0**
Three generation households			
50-54	22.4	1.0	63.3
55-59	22.1	1.0	67.2
60-64	21.2	1.0	72.6
65-69	20.8	0.9	74.6
70-74	20.9	0.9	72.1
75-79	21.4	1.0	71.1
80-84	22.4	1.0	66.8
85+	23.5	1.0	65.9
Total	**21.6**	**1.0**	**69.7**
Four and more generation households			
50-54	19.2	0.8	80.1
55-59	19.4	0.8	100.0
60-64	16.6	0.8	100.0
65-69	0.0	0.0	0.0
70-74	13.7	0.6	100.0
75-79	23.3	0.9	50.2
80-84	0.0	0.0	0.0
85+	20.9	0.9	100.0
Total	**18.6**	**0.8**	**93.9**

TABLE 16 (*concluded*)

	Average dwelling size (per capita)	Average number of rooms (per capita)	Proportion of dwelling units with one room or less per person
Females			
Solitaires			
50-54	56.0	2.7	18.8
55-59	57.0	2.8	18.0
60-64	57.4	2.8	18.2
65-69	56.0	2.7	20.0
70-74	53.5	2.6	23.6
75-79	49.8	2.4	29.2
80-84	46.7	2.2	34.2
85+	43.1	2.1	39.7
Total	**52.7**	**2.6**	**24.9**
One generation households			
50-54	43.1	2.0	9.5
55-59	42.5	2.0	9.2
60-64	40.2	2.0	10.7
65-69	38.3	1.9	13.7
70-74	35.9	1.8	17.9
75-79	33.4	1.7	23.6
80-84	31.9	1.6	29.6
85+	29.5	1.5	36.7
Total	**39.3**	**1.9**	**13.7**
Two generation households			
50-54	31.8	1.5	21.3
55-59	32.0	1.5	21.8
60-64	31.6	1.5	24.6
65-69	31.7	1.5	26.7
70-74	31.9	1.6	26.9
75-79	32.2	1.6	27.0
80-84	32.8	1.6	27.0
85+	32.1	1.6	30.3
Total	**31.9**	**1.5**	**23.4**
Three generation households			
50-54	22.3	1.0	64.4
55-59	21.6	1.0	69.7
60-64	20.9	1.0	71.2
65-69	21.8	1.0	67.6
70-74	22.1	1.0	66.4
75-79	23.0	1.0	62.0
80-84	24.1	1.1	57.8
85+	25.0	1.1	51.4
Total	**22.3**	**1.0**	**65.5**
Four and more generation households			
50-54	24.5	1.0	75.0
55-59	17.2	0.8	100.0
60-64	19.0	0.8	100.0
65-69	11.9	0.6	100.0
70-74	17.9	0.7	100.0
75-79	19.2	0.8	80.1
80-84	19.7	0.8	92.9
85+	19.6	0.8	92.3
Total	**19.7**	**0.8**	**91.1**

TABLE 17a

**Household amenities of persons aged 50 and over in Finland in 1990
by age, sex and marital status**

	Toilet		Bath		Water supply		Hot water		
	Yes	No	Yes	No	Yes	No	Yes	No	Number
Males									
Never married									
50-54	71.8	26.5	55.4	42.9	80.8	17.4	66.1	32.2	17 015
55-59	67.6	30.6	51.8	46.3	77.8	20.3	62.6	35.6	14 357
60-64	66.7	31.7	50.7	47.7	76.4	22.0	61.2	37.2	13 130
65-69	68.3	30.2	53.9	44.7	77.3	21.2	63.0	35.6	8 139
70-74	0.8	27.8	56.5	42.0	79.3	19.2	66.1	32.4	4 002
75-79	71.5	27.2	56.5	42.2	79.8	18.9	66.3	32.4	2 692
80-84	69.9	29.0	55.8	43.1	79.1	19.8	65.4	33.6	1 505
85+	74.3	23.5	58.0	39.7	80.4	17.4	70.0	27.8	634
Total	**69.2**	**29.2**	**53.5**	**44.8**	**78.5**	**19.8**	**63.8**	**34.5**	**61 474**
Married									
50-54	96.0	3.6	85.2	14.4	97.6	1.9	93.5	6.1	99 272
55-59	94.5	5.2	81.3	18.4	96.7	2.9	91.6	8.1	91 753
60-64	92.8	6.9	77.0	22.7	95.8	3.9	89.2	10.5	88 250
65-69	92.1	7.6	75.1	24.6	95.2	4.5	87.8	12.0	69 900
70-74	91.6	8.2	73.3	26.6	94.6	5.1	86.9	12.9	46 034
75-79	90.6	9.2	71.0	28.8	94.2	5.5	85.0	14.8	31 541
80-84	89.3	10.4	69.4	30.3	93.1	6.6	83.3	16.4	15 182
85+	88.5	11.2	68.3	31.3	92.1	7.5	81.9	17.7	4 564
Total	**93.3**	**6.4**	**78.3**	**21.4**	**95.9**	**3.7**	**89.6**	**10.1**	**446 496**
Widowed									
50-54	91.2	7.8	79.2	19.8	94.6	4.4	87.7	11.3	1 848
55-59	89.8	9.3	76.1	23.1	93.5	5.7	86.0	13.1	2 972
60-64	87.2	11.7	71.9	27.1	91.2	7.7	83.0	16.0	4 823
65-69	87.7	11.7	71.1	28.3	92.3	7.0	82.9	16.6	6 582
70-74	88.2	11.4	69.8	29.8	92.3	7.3	82.7	16.9	7 445
75-79	87.7	11.8	68.7	30.8	92.3	7.2	82.1	17.4	9 125
80-84	86.3	13.1	66.7	32.6	90.9	8.4	80.2	19.2	7 933
85+	84.4	14.4	64.9	33.9	90.4	8.4	78.1	20.7	5 274
Total	**87.4**	**11.9**	**69.7**	**29.6**	**91.9**	**7.4**	**82.1**	**17.2**	**46 002**
Divorced/separated									
50-54	86.3	10.8	73.4	23.7	90.2	6.8	81.8	15.3	17 552
55-59	85.6	11.9	70.9	26.5	89.2	8.1	80.4	17.0	13 277
60-64	84.0	13.8	69.7	28.2	88.7	9.0	79.2	18.6	10 467
65-69	85.1	13.0	71.3	26.8	89.4	8.6	81.0	17.1	6 245
70-74	85.3	13.4	70.7	28.0	89.2	9.4	81.5	17.2	3 144
75-79	84.7	13.9	69.5	29.2	89.6	8.9	80.7	18.0	1 880
80-84	85.4	12.9	68.7	29.6	88.6	9.7	78.9	19.3	760
85+	84.5	15.1	69.0	30.6	89.3	10.3	79.3	20.3	271
Total	**85.4**	**12.2**	**71.4**	**26.2**	**89.4**	**8.0**	**80.7**	**16.9**	**53 594**

TABLE 17a (*concluded*)

		Toilet		Bath		Water supply		Hot water		
		Yes	No	Yes	No	Yes	No	Yes	No	Number
Females										
Never married										
50-54		91.8	7.6	83.2	16.2	94.9	4.5	89.5	9.9	12 833
55-59		90.5	8.9	81.0	18.3	93.9	5.4	88.0	11.3	12 332
60-64		89.8	9.8	81.3	18.3	93.4	6.1	87.4	12.2	13 785
65-69		89.9	9.7	79.7	19.9	93.1	6.5	86.8	12.8	14 104
70-74		88.8	10.7	78.6	20.9	92.4	7.1	85.5	14.1	11 681
75-79		88.6	10.8	78.7	20.7	92.8	6.6	85.7	13.7	11 041
80-84		88.2	11.2	77.1	22.2	92.9	6.5	85.2	14.1	8 335
85+		85.2	13.2	73.2	25.3	92.2	6.2	82.7	15.8	5 198
	Total	**89.5**	**9.9**	**79.8**	**19.6**	**93.3**	**6.1**	**86.7**	**12.7**	**89 309**
Married										
50-54		95.6	4.0	83.8	15.8	97.4	2.2	93.0	6.6	97 022
55-59		94.5	5.3	80.2	19.5	96.8	2.9	91.3	8.4	85 317
60-64		93.1	6.7	76.6	23.2	95.8	3.9	89.4	10.4	81 105
65-69		92.0	7.9	74.3	25.6	95.0	4.8	87.3	12.5	63 215
70-74		91.4	8.4	72.5	27.3	94.6	5.2	86.2	13.6	37 646
75-79		90.3	9.4	70.1	29.6	93.9	5.8	84.5	15.3	21 239
80-84		89.4	10.2	68.9	30.7	92.9	6.7	83.2	16.4	8 284
85+		87.8	11.8	67.5	32.0	92.9	6.6	80.5	19.1	1 747
	Total	**93.4**	**6.3**	**77.8**	**21.9**	**96.0**	**3.7**	**89.6**	**10.1**	**395 574**
Widowed										
50-54		93.8	5.7	82.8	16.8	96.4	3.2	90.6	9.0	9 403
55-59		92.1	7.6	79.9	19.7	94.8	4.8	88.7	11.0	15 713
60-64		91.6	8.0	78.2	21.4	94.6	5.0	87.9	11.8	27 660
65-69		90.7	9.1	76.7	23.1	94.0	5.7	86.5	13.2	41 619
70-74		90.1	9.7	75.6	24.2	93.6	6.1	85.5	14.3	47 442
75-79		89.5	10.1	74.5	25.1	93.3	6.3	84.8	14.8	51 261
80-84		88.4	10.9	73.3	26.1	92.9	6.4	83.6	15.7	39 144
85+		85.4	13.4	69.7	29.1	91.8	7.0	80.8	18.0	22 801
	Total	**89.8**	**9.7**	**75.5**	**24.0**	**93.6**	**5.9**	**85.4**	**14.1**	**255 044**
Divorced/separated										
50-54		95.7	3.6	88.4	11.0	97.0	2.3	93.5	5.8	19 813
55-59		94.9	4.6	87.0	12.4	96.4	3.0	92.3	7.1	15 998
60-64		94.6	4.9	86.4	13.2	96.4	3.1	91.8	7.7	13 767
65-69		93.9	5.7	84.9	14.7	95.7	3.9	91.4	8.2	10 808
70-74		93.3	6.3	83.9	15.7	95.6	4.0	90.4	9.1	7 391
75-79		92.7	6.9	82.3	17.4	95.3	4.2	90.1	9.5	5 512
80-84		91.6	7.8	80.6	18.8	95.9	3.4	88.8	10.6	3 122
85+		87.1	11.1	74.0	24.2	94.5	3.7	84.1	14.1	1 394
	Total	**94.3**	**5.1**	**85.8**	**13.6**	**96.3**	**3.2**	**91.8**	**7.7**	**77 805**

TABLE 17b

**Proportion of households lacking common household amenities inhabited by persons
aged 50 and over in Finland in 1990 by age, sex and marital status**

	Toilet	*Bath*	*Water supply*	*Hot water*
Males				
Never married				
50-54	26.5	42.9	17.4	32.2
55-59	30.6	46.3	20.3	35.6
60-64	31.7	47.7	22.0	37.2
65-69	30.2	44.7	21.2	35.6
70-74	27.8	42.0	19.2	32.4
75-79	27.2	42.2	18.9	32.4
80-84	29.0	43.1	19.8	33.6
85+	23.5	39.7	17.4	27.8
Total	**29.2**	**44.8**	**19.8**	**34.5**
Married				
50-54	3.6	14.4	1.9	6.1
55-59	5.2	18.4	2.9	8.1
60-64	6.9	22.7	3.9	10.5
65-69	7.6	24.6	4.5	12.0
70-74	8.2	26.6	5.1	12.9
75-79	9.2	28.8	5.5	14.8
80-84	10.4	30.3	6.6	16.4
85+	11.2	31.3	7.5	17.7
Total	**6.4**	**21.4**	**3.7**	**10.1**
Widowed				
50-54	7.8	19.8	4.4	11.3
55-59	9.3	23.1	5.7	13.1
60-64	11.7	27.1	7.7	16.0
65-69	11.7	28.3	7.0	16.6
70-74	11.4	29.8	7.3	16.9
75-79	11.8	30.8	7.2	17.4
80-84	13.1	32.6	8.4	19.2
85+	14.4	33.9	8.4	20.7
Total	**11.9**	**29.6**	**7.4**	**17.2**
Divorced/separated				
50-54	10.8	23.7	6.8	15.3
55-59	11.9	26.5	8.1	17.0
60-64	13.8	28.2	9.0	18.6
65-69	13.0	26.8	8.6	17.1
70-74	13.4	28.0	9.4	17.2
75-79	13.9	29.2	8.9	18.0
80-84	12.9	29.6	9.7	19.3
85+	15.1	30.6	10.3	20.3
Total	**12.2**	**26.2**	**8.0**	**16.9**

TABLE 17b (*concluded*)

	Toilet	Bath	Water supply	Hot water
Females				
Never married				
50-54	7.6	16.2	4.5	9.9
55-59	8.9	18.3	5.4	11.3
60-64	9.8	18.3	6.1	12.2
65-69	9.7	19.9	6.5	12.8
70-74	10.7	20.9	7.1	14.1
75-79	10.8	20.7	6.6	13.7
80-84	11.2	22.2	6.5	14.1
85+	13.2	25.3	6.2	15.8
Total	**9.9**	**19.6**	**6.1**	**12.7**
Married				
50-54	4.0	15.8	2.2	6.6
55-59	5.3	19.5	2.9	8.4
60-64	6.7	23.2	3.9	10.4
65-69	7.9	25.6	4.8	12.5
70-74	8.4	27.3	5.2	13.6
75-79	9.4	29.6	5.8	15.3
80-84	10.2	30.7	6.7	16.4
85+	11.8	32.0	6.6	19.1
Total	**6.3**	**21.9**	**3.7**	**10.1**
Widowed				
50-54	5.7	16.8	3.2	9.0
55-59	7.6	19.7	4.8	11.0
60-64	8.0	21.4	5.0	11.8
65-69	9.1	23.1	5.7	13.2
70-74	9.7	24.2	6.1	14.3
75-79	10.1	25.1	6.3	14.8
80-84	10.9	26.1	6.4	15.7
85+	13.4	29.1	7.0	18.0
Total	**9.7**	**24.0**	**5.9**	**14.1**
Divorced/separated				
50-54	3.6	11.0	2.3	5.8
55-59	4.6	12.4	3.0	7.1
60-64	4.9	13.2	3.1	7.7
65-69	5.7	14.7	3.9	8.2
70-74	6.3	15.7	4.0	9.1
75-79	6.9	17.4	4.2	9.5
80-84	7.8	18.8	3.4	10.6
85+	11.1	24.2	3.7	14.1
Total	**5.1**	**13.6**	**3.2**	**7.7**

TABLE 18a

**Household amenities of persons aged 50 and over in Finland
in 1990 by age, sex and number of generations present in the household**

	Toilet		Bath		Water supply		Hot water		
	Yes	No	Yes	No	Yes	No	Yes	No	Number
Males	.								
Solitaires									
50-54	79.4	19.7	64.7	34.5	86.0	13.0	74.2	25.0	18 843
55-59	77.2	21.9	62.3	36.8	83.8	15.2	72.2	26.9	18 073
60-64	77.0	22.3	62.3	37.0	83.7	15.4	72.4	26.9	18 838
65-69	80.6	18.8	66.6	32.8	86.4	13.0	76.0	23.4	15 317
70-74	83.7	15.7	68.7	30.7	88.4	1.0	79.1	20.3	11 145
75-79	85.4	14.1	68.7	30.8	90.3	9.2	80.4	19.1	10 835
80-84	85.0	14.4	67.2	32.2	89.5	9.9	79.4	20.1	8 083
85+	85.5	13.7	66.4	32.8	90.2	9.0	79.2	20.1	4 731
Total	**80.5**	**18.8**	**65.2**	**34.1**	**86.4**	**12.8**	**75.6**	**23.7**	**105 865**
One generation households									
50-54	93.1	6.6	81.6	18.1	95.4	4.2	90.1	9.6	46 088
55-59	93.1	6.7	79.9	19.9	95.6	4.2	90.1	9.7	58 472
60-64	92.2	7.6	76.8	22.9	94.9	4.7	88.4	11.3	67 185
65-69	92.1	7.7	75.6	24.2	94.9	4.8	87.8	12.0	58 231
70-74	92.1	7.7	74.3	25.6	94.8	5.0	87.5	12.3	39 830
75-79	91.1	8.7	71.8	28.0	94.3	5.4	85.6	14.2	27 964
80-84	89.8	9.8	70.1	29.5	93.2	6.5	83.7	15.9	13 707
85+	87.9	11.2	68.8	30.3	92.1	7.0	81.7	17.4	4 428
Total	**92.2**	**7.6**	**76.7**	**23.1**	**94.9**	**4.8**	**88.2**	**11.5**	**315 904**
Two generation households									
50-54	95.1	4.7	84.0	15.8	97.3	2.5	92.4	7.4	67 620
55-59	93.0	6.7	79.1	20.7	96.1	3.6	89.5	10.2	42 832
60-64	90.0	9.8	72.9	27.0	94.6	5.2	85.9	14.0	27 745
65-69	87.6	12.2	68.6	31.2	93.0	6.8	82.3	17.5	14 867
70-74	84.7	15.2	63.6	36.3	90.9	9.0	78.9	21.0	7 701
75-79	81.8	18.0	59.0	40.8	89.2	10.6	74.9	24.9	4 712
80-84	78.8	21.1	55.7	44.2	87.5	12.3	71.3	28.6	2 500
85+	75.3	24.5	52.4	47.4	84.7	15.1	68.0	31.8	1 118
Total	**91.9**	**7.9**	**77.3**	**22.5**	**95.4**	**4.3**	**88.1**	**11.7**	**169 095**
Three and more generation households									
50-54	91.3	8.3	74.3	25.3	95.9	3.6	87.0	12.6	2 337
55-59	90.7	9.0	75.2	24.6	95.7	4.0	88.0	11.7	2 408
60-64	91.1	8.7	73.3	26.5	96.4	3.4	87.5	12.3	2 520
65-69	91.0	8.7	70.9	28.9	96.1	3.7	86.5	13.3	2 246
70-74	90.5	9.3	67.6	32.3	96.0	3.8	86.2	13.7	1 879
75-79	90.6	9.2	70.3	29.4	96.4	3.4	85.0	14.8	1 674
80-84	90.4	9.4	71.3	28.5	96.0	3.9	86.8	13.0	1 064
85+	91.1	8.9	71.2	28.8	96.2	3.8	87.1	12.9	451
Total	**90.9**	**8.9**	**72.1**	**27.7**	**96.1**	**3.7**	**86.8**	**12.9**	**14 579**

TABLE 18a (*concluded*)

	Toilet		Bath		Water supply		Hot water		
	Yes	No	Yes	No	Yes	No	Yes	No	Number
Females									
Solitaires									
50-54	96.0	3.5	89.4	10.1	97.3	2.1	94.1	5.3	22 010
55-59	94.7	4.9	86.9	12.7	96.5	3.1	92.7	6.9	27 710
60-64	93.9	5.8	84.7	15.0	96.0	3.7	91.3	8.4	39 062
65-69	93.1	6.6	82.3	17.4	95.4	4.3	90.0	9.7	50 064
70-74	92.2	7.5	80.4	19.3	94.8	4.9	88.5	11.2	51 891
75-79	91.3	8.3	78.7	20.8	94.4	5.2	87.5	12.1	53 459
80-84	89.7	9.7	76.4	22.9	93.8	5.5	86.0	13.4	39 895
85+	86.6	12.3	72.4	26.6	93.1	5.8	83.0	16.0	22 346
Total	**92.2**	**7.4**	**81.1**	**18.5**	**95.1**	**4.5**	**89.0**	**10.6**	**306 436**
One generation households									
50-54	95.1	4.6	83.4	16.4	96.8	2.8	92.4	7.3	51 640
55-59	94.4	5.3	80.9	18.8	96.5	3.2	94.5	5.3	60 243
60-64	93.5	6.2	77.9	21.9	95.9	3.8	89.9	9.8	66 963
65-69	92.3	7.6	75.4	24.5	95.0	4.8	87.8	12.1	57 650
70-74	91.5	8.4	73.3	26.5	94.4	5.4	86.3	13.6	37 264
75-79	89.8	9.9	70.7	29.0	93.4	6.3	84.0	15.7	23 675
80-84	89.0	10.5	70.2	29.3	92.9	6.5	82.7	16.8	11 772
85+	85.3	12.9	68.5	29.7	91.5	6.7	79.8	18.4	5 248
Total	**92.9**	**6.8**	**77.4**	**22.4**	**95.4**	**4.2**	**89.5**	**10.3**	**314 455**
Two generation households									
50-54	95.3	4.5	84.0	15.8	97.5	2.3	92.6	7.2	62 615
55-59	92.8	7.1	77.9	21.9	96.0	3.8	89.1	10.8	38 398
60-64	88.9	11.0	71.5	28.4	93.6	6.2	84.3	15.5	26 853
65-69	84.9	15.0	65.6	34.3	90.8	9.1	79.4	20.5	17 964
70-74	81.2	18.7	61.0	38.9	88.8	11.1	74.5	25.4	11 250
75-79	80.1	19.8	59.2	40.6	87.5	12.3	72.9	27.0	8 282
80-84	79.7	20.1	59.5	40.2	87.0	12.7	72.3	27.4	5 105
85+	77.1	22.7	57.1	42.8	85.1	14.7	69.5	30.4	2 645
Total	**90.3**	**9.6**	**75.0**	**24.9**	**94.3**	**5.5**	**86.1**	**13.7**	**173 112**
Three and more generation households									
50-54	93.0	6.6	76.5	23.1	96.8	2.8	89.3	10.3	2 617
55-59	91.5	8.0	75.1	24.4	96.6	2.9	88.3	11.3	2 847
60-64	91.7	8.1	72.2	27.6	95.7	4.1	88.2	11.6	3 323
65-69	89.9	9.9	71.2	28.6	95.2	4.6	84.5	15.4	4 006
70-74	90.1	9.7	70.4	29.4	95.7	4.1	86.1	13.7	3 708
75-79	90.6	9.3	71.8	28.1	95.5	4.4	85.9	14.0	3 595
80-84	91.5	8.4	74.1	25.9	96.5	3.4	86.3	13.7	2 057
85+	91.1	8.8	74.7	25.2	95.1	4.8	86.9	12.9	836
Total	**91.1**	**8.7**	**72.8**	**27.0**	**95.9**	**3.9**	**86.8**	**13.0**	**22 989**

TABLE 18b

Proportion of households lacking common household amenities inhabited by persons aged 50 and over in Finland in 1990 by age, sex and number of generations present in the household

		Toilet	Bath	Water supply	Hot water
Males					
Solitaires					
50-54		19.7	34.5	13.0	25.0
55-59		21.9	36.8	15.2	26.9
60-64		22.3	37.0	15.4	26.9
65-69		18.8	32.8	13.0	23.4
70-74		15.7	30.7	11.0	20.3
75-79		14.1	30.8	9.2	19.1
80-84		14.4	32.2	9.9	20.1
85+		13.7	32.8	9.0	20.1
	Total	**18.8**	**34.1**	**12.8**	**23.7**
One generation					
50-54		6.6	18.1	4.2	9.6
55-59		6.7	19.9	4.2	9.7
60-64		7.6	22.9	4.7	11.3
65-69		7.7	24.2	4.8	12.0
70-74		7.7	25.6	5.0	12.3
75-79		8.7	28.0	5.4	14.2
80-84		9.8	29.5	6.5	15.9
85+		11.2	30.3	7.0	17.4
	Total	7.6	23.1	4.8	11.5
Two generations					
50-54		4.7	15.8	2.5	7.4
55-59		6.7	20.7	3.6	10.2
60-64		9.8	27.0	5.2	14.0
65-69		12.2	31.2	6.8	17.5
70-74		15.2	36.3	9.0	21.0
75-79		18.0	40.8	10.6	24.9
80-84		21.1	44.2	12.3	28.6
85+		24.5	47.4	15.1	31.8
	Total	**7.9**	**22.5**	**4.3**	**11.7**
Three and more generations					
50-54		8.3	25.3	3.6	12.6
55-59		9.0	24.6	4.0	11.7
60-64		8.7	26.5	3.4	12.3
65-69		8.7	28.9	3.7	13.3
70-74		9.3	32.3	3.8	13.7
75-79		9.2	29.4	3.4	14.8
80-84		9.4	28.5	3.9	13.0
85+		8.9	28.8	3.8	12.9
	Total	**8.9**	**27.7**	**3.7**	**12.9**

TABLE 18b (*concluded*)

	Toilet	Bath	Water supply	Hot water
Females				
Solitaires				
50-54	3.5	10.1	2.1	5.3
55-59	4.9	12.7	3.1	6.9
60-64	5.8	15.0	3.7	8.4
65-69	6.6	17.4	4.3	9.7
70-74	7.5	19.3	4.9	11.2
75-79	8.3	20.8	5.2	12.1
80-84	9.7	22.9	5.5	13.4
85+	12.3	26.6	5.8	16.0
Total	**7.4**	**18.5**	**4.5**	**10.6**
One generation				
50-54	4.6	16.4	2.8	7.3
55-59	5.3	18.8	3.2	5.3
60-64	6.2	21.9	3.8	9.8
65-69	7.6	24.5	4.8	12.1
70-74	8.4	26.5	5.4	13.6
75-79	9.9	29.0	6.3	15.7
80-84	10.5	29.3	6.5	16.8
85+	12.9	29.7	6.7	18.4
Total	**6.8**	**22.4**	**4.2**	**10.3**
Two generations				
50-54	4.5	15.8	2.3	7.2
55-59	7.1	21.9	3.8	10.8
60-64	11.0	28.4	6.2	15.5
65-69	15.0	34.3	9.1	20.5
70-74	18.7	38.9	11.1	25.4
75-79	19.8	40.6	12.3	27.0
80-84	20.1	40.2	12.7	27.4
85+	22.7	42.8	14.7	30.4
Total	**9.6**	**24.9**	**5.5**	**13.7**
Three and more generations				
50-54	6.6	23.1	2.8	10.3
55-59	8.0	24.4	2.9	11.3
60-64	8.1	27.6	4.1	11.6
65-69	9.9	28.6	4.6	15.4
70-74	9.7	29.4	4.1	13.7
75-79	9.3	28.1	4.4	14.0
80-84	8.4	25.9	3.4	13.7
85+	8.8	25.2	4.8	12.9
Total	**8.7**	**27.0**	**3.9**	**13.0**

TABLE 19a

**Disability status of persons aged 50 and over in Finland in 1990
by age, sex, and number of generations present in the household**

	Proportion of persons receiving a disability pension	Number
Males		
Solitaires		
50-54	23.2	18 843
55-59	34.3	18 073
60-64	38.7	18 838
65-69	0.8	15 316
70-74	0.0	11 145
75-79	0.0	10 835
80-84	0.0	8 083
85+	0.0	4 731
Total	**17.0**	**105 865**
One generation households		
50-54	14.5	46 088
55-59	24.0	58 472
60-64	31.2	67 185
65-69	0.7	58 231
70-74	0.0	39 829
75-79	0.0	27 964
80-84	0.0	13 707
85+	0.0	4 428
Total	**13.3**	**315 904**
Two generation households		
50-54	10.2	67 620
55-59	19.4	42 832
60-64	28.1	27 745
65-69	0.8	14 867
70-74	0.0	7 701
75-79	0.0	4 712
80-84	0.0	2 500
85+	0.0	1 118
Total	**13.6**	**169 095**
Three generation households		
50-54	13.4	2 328
55-59	22.4	2 388
60-64	29.0	2 507
65-69	0.7	2 246
70-74	0.0	1 876
75-79	0.0	1 672
80-84	0.0	1 064
85+	0.0	449
Total	**10.9**	**14 530**

TABLE 19a (concluded)

	Proportion of persons receiving a disability pension	Number
Females		
Solitaires		
50-54	16.6	22 010
55-59	25.4	27 710
60-64	30.1	39 062
65-69	0.5	50 064
70-74	0.0	51 891
75-79	0.0	53 459
80-84	0.0	39 895
85+	0.0	22 346
Total	**7.4**	**306 436**
One generation households		
50-54	12.6	51 640
55-59	20.7	60 243
60-64	26.9	66 963
65-69	0.5	57 649
70-74	0.0	37 264
75-79	0.0	23 675
80-84	0.0	11 772
85+	0.0	5 248
Total	**11.9**	**314 455**
Two generation households		
50-54	8.5	62 615
55-59	16.6	38 398
60-64	23.5	26 853
65-69	0.5	17 964
70-74	0.0	11 249
75-79	0.0	8 282
80-84	0.0	5 105
85+	0.0	2 645
Total	**10.4**	**173 112**
Three generation households		
50-54	13.3	2 617
55-59	20.5	2 847
60-64	27.5	3 323
65-69	0.3	4 006
70-74	0.0	3 708
75-79	0.0	3 595
80-84	0.0	2 057
85+	0.0	836
Total	**8.1**	**22 989**

TABLE 19b

Proportion of persons aged 50 and over not receiving a disability pension themselves, but living with a disabled person in Finland in 1990 by age, sex, and number of generations present in the household

	Proportion of persons living with a disabled person	Number
Males		
Solitaires		
50-54	0.0	18 843
55-59	0.0	18 073
60-64	0.0	18 838
65-69	0.0	15 316
70-74	0.0	11 145
75-79	0.0	10 835
80-84	0.0	8 083
85+	0.0	4 731
Total	**0.0**	**105 865**
One generation households		
50-54	8.4	46 088
55-59	10.7	58 472
60-64	11.4	67 185
65-69	13.3	58 231
70-74	5.1	39 829
75-79	2.2	27 964
80-84	1.6	13 707
85+	2.3	4 428
Total	**9.0**	**315 904**
Two generation households		
50-54	5.5	67 620
55-59	9.0	42 832
60-64	12.5	27 745
65-69	22.4	14 867
70-74	20.9	7 701
75-79	21.3	4 712
80-84	24.6	2 500
85+	27.5	1 118
Total	**10.6**	**169 095**
Three generation households		
50-54	7.2	2 328
55-59	8.9	2 388
60-64	10.7	2 507
65-69	14.7	2 246
70-74	8.8	1 876
75-79	7.4	1 672
80-84	9.2	1 064
85+	11.4	449
Total	**9.7**	**14 530**

TABLE 19b (*concluded*)

	Proportion of persons living with a disabled person	Number
Females		
Solitaires		
50-54	0.0	22 010
55-59	0.0	27 710
60-64	0.0	39 062
65-69	0.0	50 064
70-74	0.0	51 891
75-79	0.0	53 459
80-84	0.0	39 895
85+	0.0	22 346
Total	**0.0**	**306 436**
One generation households		
50-54	12.5	51 640
55-59	15.2	60 243
60-64	11.5	66 963
65-69	6.3	57 649
70-74	3.2	37 264
75-79	3.3	23 675
80-84	4.7	11 772
85+	8.4	5 248
Total	**9.5**	**314 455**
Two generation households		
50-54	10.8	62 615
55-59	14.7	38 398
60-64	14.4	26 853
65-69	18.8	17 964
70-74	20.9	11 249
75-79	24.8	8 282
80-84	27.2	5 105
85+	27.3	2 645
Total	**15.1**	**173 112**
Three generation households		
50-54	12.2	2 617
55-59	12.0	2 847
60-64	9.2	3 323
65-69	7.6	4 006
70-74	6.7	3 708
75-79	9.0	3 595
80-84	11.6	2 057
85+	17.0	836
Total	**9.7**	**22 989**

Appendix Two: Standard Tables

TABLE 2.1

Household size of persons aged 50 and over in Finland in 1990 by age and sex

| | | | Non-institutionalized population | | | | Seven or more persons | | | |
	One person	Two persons	Three persons	Four persons	Five persons	Six persons	Number	Avg. of persons	Institutionalized population	Total
Males										
50-54	19 450	48 963	37 082	20 890	6 337	1 732	1 233	8.71	692	136 379
55-59	18 503	60 017	27 828	10 625	3 298	1 238	848	8.83	685	123 042
60-64	19 100	68 212	19 813	5 783	1 917	1 038	807	8.20	877	117 547
65-69	15 445	58 918	11 124	2 771	1 165	819	626	8.18	976	91 844
70-74	11 189	40 488	5 640	1 415	756	651	485	8.01	938	61 562
75-79	10 875	28 651	3 305	869	575	541	421	7.97	1 315	46 552
80-84	8 094	14 294	1 564	488	386	294	260	8.26	1 520	26 900
85+	4 740	4 803	601	171	180	136	112	9.36	1 67	12 422
Total	**107 397**	**324 345**	**106 957**	**43 013**	**14 614**	**6 449**	**4 792**	**8.40**	**8 682**	**616 249**
Females										
50-54	22 130	59 967	35 288	15 393	4 127	1 258	908	8.32	460	139 531
55-59	27 805	67 175	23 673	6 950	2 032	1 030	695	7.88	492	129 852
60-64	39 135	73 602	16 378	3 893	1 647	985	677	7.83	672	136 989
65-69	50 104	64 105	9 764	2 438	1 587	1 104	646	7.82	1 058	130 806
70-74	51 920	42 540	5 219	1 555	1 401	924	601	8.03	1 734	105 894
75-79	53 482	28 255	3 273	1 325	1 321	854	542	8.48	3 689	92 741
80-84	39 925	14 699	1 869	857	751	424	360	9.99	5 788	64 673
85+	22 380	6 666	918	423	329	157	267	11.62	8 360	39 500
Total	**306 881**	**357 008**	**96 382**	**32 834**	**13 194**	**6 736**	**4 696**	**8.53**	**22 253**	**839 984**

TABLE 2.1a

Household size of persons aged 50 and over in Finland in 1990 by age and sex
(persons of known family position only)

| | | | | Non-institutionalized population | | | | | |
		One person	Two persons	Three persons	Four persons	Five persons	Six persons	Seven +	Total
Males									
50-54		18 843	48 945	37 053	20 873	6 317	1 718	1 138	134 888
55-59		18 073	59 997	27 810	10 622	3 282	1 230	772	121 785
60-64		18 838	68 198	19 787	5 772	1 907	1 030	757	116 288
65-69		15 316	58 905	11 112	2 762	1 158	815	592	90 660
70-74		11 145	40 480	5 638	1 414	753	648	476	60 554
75-79		10 835	28 649	3 302	869	573	540	415	45 185
80-84		8 083	14 293	1 563	484	386	294	251	25 354
85+		4 731	4 803	599	169	180	136	110	10 728
	Total	**105 865**	**324 270**	**106 864**	**42 966**	**14 555**	**6 412**	**4 511**	**605 442**
Females									
50-54		22 010	59 965	35 273	15 393	4 122	1 253	885	138 902
55-59		27 710	67 172	23 670	6 943	2 032	1 020	677	129 223
60-64		39 062	73 600	16 373	3 890	1 643	985	657	136 210
65-69		50 064	64 096	9 759	2 435	1 587	1 104	640	129 685
70-74		51 891	42 536	5 218	1 554	1 400	921	596	104 116
75-79		53 459	28 254	3 273	1 322	1 318	854	538	89 018
80-84		39 895	14 698	1 867	854	749	424	356	58 843
85+		22 346	6 665	914	417	329	157	262	31 090
	Total	**306 436**	**356 987**	**96 347**	**32 809**	**13 179**	**6 718**	**4 610**	**817 087**

TABLE 2.2

**Generations present in the households of the sampled persons in Finland in 1990
by age, sex and marital status (non-institutionalized population)**

	Solitaires	Unknown	One generation	Two generation	Three generation	Four generation	Total
Males							
Never married							
50-54	8 555	243	4 508	3 607	102	0	17 015
55-59	8 055	208	4 227	1 788	78	0	14 357
60-64	8 092	157	4 030	812	40	0	13 130
65-69	5 384	81	2 438	215	21	0	8 139
70-74	2 714	29	1 179	66	14	0	4 002
75-79	1 848	18	775	38	13	0	2 692
80-84	1 058	6	422	12	7	0	1 505
85+	428	2	188	9	7	0	634
Total	**36 134**	**745**	**17 767**	**6 546**	**282**	**0**	**61 474**
Married							
50-54	1 468	138	36 128	59 590	1 938	8	99 272
55-59	1 343	95	49 963	38 372	1 962	18	91 753
60-64	1 387	53	59 758	24 952	2 087	13	88 250
65-69	1 115	31	53 574	13 338	1 842	0	69 900
70-74	728	12	37 326	6 560	1 407	1	46 034
75-79	718	6	26 113	3 624	1 079	2	31 541
80-84	481	5	12 527	1 609	560	0	15 182
85+	189	2	3 694	506	173	0	4 564
Total	**7 430**	**342**	**279 084**	**148 550**	**11 048**	**44**	**446 496**
Widowed							
50-54	705	8	218	863	53	0	1 848
55-59	1 525	17	393	913	122	2	2 972
60-64	3 060	20	537	1 012	195	0	4 823
65-69	4 647	11	682	949	293	0	6 582
70-74	5 499	7	631	905	402	1	7 445
75-79	6 888	16	692	985	544	0	9 125
80-84	5 973	6	608	860	486	0	7 933
85+	3 905	11	499	592	265	2	5 274
Total	**32 202**	**96**	**4 260**	**7 079**	**2 360**	**5**	**46 002**
Divorced							
50-54	7 885	392	4 975	3 327	220	0	16 798
55-59	6 902	247	3 688	1 628	220	0	2 685
60-64	6 027	143	2 590	880	165	0	9 805
65-69	4 019	80	1 366	328	86	0	5 879
70-74	2 093	21	625	151	47	0	2 936
75-79	1 333	12	346	62	33	0	1 786
80-84	558	9	140	17	11	0	735
85+	203	0	45	11	4	0	263
Total	**29 019**	**904**	**13 775**	**6 404**	**786**	**0**	**50 888**
Separated							
50-54	230	17	258	233	15	0	753
55-59	248	7	200	130	7	0	592
60-64	273	8	270	90	20	0	662
65-69	152	4	171	36	4	0	366
70-74	111	1	69	20	6	0	207
75-79	48	1	38	4	4	0	94
80-84	13	0	10	2	0	0	25
85+	6	0	2	0	0	0	8
Total	**1 081**	**38**	**1 018**	**515**	**55**	**0**	**2 707**
TOTAL	**105 866**	**2 125**	**315 904**	**169 094**	**14 531**	**49**	**607 567**

TABLE 2.2 (*concluded*)

	Solitaires	Unknown	One generation	Two generation	Three generation	Four generation	Total
Females							
Never Married							
50-54	7 913	40	2 648	2 142	90	0	12 833
55-59	8 188	38	2 788	1 237	77	3	12 332
60-64	9 828	30	3 063	803	58	2	13 785
65-69	10 502	18	3 096	431	56	0	14 104
70-74	8 916	14	2 491	198	61	1	11 681
75-79	8 518	7	2 292	162	62	0	11 041
80-84	6 454	9	1 729	115	28	0	8 335
85+	3 979	16	1 123	62	18	0	5 198
Total	**64 299**	**172**	**19 231**	**5 149**	**451**	**6**	**89 309**
Married							
50-54	1 172	65	44 030	49 767	1 972	17	97 022
55-59	1 293	42	53 195	28 787	1 983	17	85 317
60-64	1 283	32	59 852	18 008	1 925	5	81 105
65-69	993	19	50 978	9 411	1 813	2	63 215
70-74	775	7	31 467	4 202	1 192	2	37 646
75-79	633	4	17 860	1 989	753	0	21 239
80-84	360	3	6 977	691	252	1	8 284
85+	130	1	1 437	145	34	0	1 747
Total	**6 640**	**172**	**265 795**	**113 000**	**9 924**	**44**	**395 574**
Widowed							
50-54	3 848	8	1 022	4 270	255	0	9 403
55-59	8 767	15	1 477	4 925	528	2	15 713
60-64	18 468	17	1 995	6 098	1 080	2	27 660
65-69	30 338	14	2 324	7 015	1 928	0	41 619
70-74	36 275	14	2 569	6 264	2 319	1	47 442
75-79	39 706	21	3 026	5 799	2 704	6	51 261
80-84	30 460	27	2 751	4 143	1 750	13	39 144
85+	17 115	32	2 486	2 376	778	14	22 801
Total	**184 977**	**148**	**17 649**	**40 890**	**11 342**	**37**	**255 044**
Divorced							
50-54	8 887	55	3 747	6 152	290	3	19 133
55-59	9 228	40	2 558	3 267	248	3	15 345
60-64	9 280	27	1 858	1 843	248	0	13 257
65-69	8 060	11	1 128	1 065	200	0	10 464
70-74	5 835	8	676	571	134	0	7 225
75-79	4 569	4	476	325	74	0	5 448
80-84	2 611	3	308	156	27	0	3 105
85+	1 119	2	200	62	6	0	1 389
Total	**49 590**	**149**	**10 953**	**13 440**	**1 228**	**7**	**75 365**
Separated							
50-54	190	2	193	285	10	0	680
55-59	233	2	225	183	10	0	653
60-64	202	2	195	100	12	0	510
65-69	171	0	124	42	8	0	345
70-74	88	0	60	15	2	0	166
75-79	33	0	21	7	2	0	64
80-84	10	0	7	0	0	0	17
85+	3	0	2	0	0	0	5
Total	**930**	**5**	**827**	**633**	**45**	**0**	**2 439**
TOTAL	**306 436**	**646**	**314 455**	**173 112**	**22 990**	**94**	**817 731**

TABLE 2.2a

**Generations present in the households of the sampled persons in Finland in 1990
by age, sex and marital status (non-institutionalized population)**

	Solitaires	One generation w/o others	w/ others	Two generation w/o others	w/ others	Three generation w/o others	w/ others	Four generation	Unknown	Total
Males										
Never married										
50-54	8 555	1 593	2 915	3 602	5	102	0	0	243	17 015
55-59	8 055	1 448	2 778	1 783	5	75	3	0	208	14 355
60-64	8 092	1 647	2 383	812	0	35	5	0	157	13 131
65-69	5 384	1 180	1 258	215	0	19	2	0	81	8 139
70-74	2 714	658	521	66	0	14	0	0	29	4 002
75-79	1 848	482	293	38	0	13	0	0	18	2 692
80-84	1 058	260	162	12	0	7	0	0	6	1 505
85+	428	98	90	9	0	7	0	0	2	634
Total	**36 134**	**7 366**	**10 400**	**6 536**	**10**	**272**	**11**	**0**	**745**	**61 474**
Married										
50-54	1 468	35 943	185	59 588	2	1 925	13	8	138	99 270
55-59	1 343	49 773	190	38 367	5	1 940	22	18	95	91 753
60-64	1 387	59 622	137	24 952	0	2 068	18	13	53	88 250
65-69	1 115	53 486	88	13 336	1	1 839	4	0	31	69 900
70-74	728	37 266	60	6 560	0	1 406	1	1	12	46 034
75-79	718	26 073	40	3 621	2	1 079	0	2	6	31 541
80-84	481	12 496	31	1 608	1	560	0	0	5	15 182
85+	189	3 681	13	506	0	172	1	0	2	4 564
Total	**7 430**	**278 340**	**744**	**148 538**	**11**	**10 989**	**59**	**44**	**342**	**446 497**
Widowed										
50-54	705	152	7	863	0	53	0	0	8	1 848
55-59	1 525	277	117	912	2	120	2	2	17	2 974
60-64	3 060	360	177	1 012	0	195	0	0	20	4 824
65-69	4 647	441	241	949	0	293	0	0	11	6 582
70-74	5 499	396	234	902	2	402	0	1	7	7 443
75-79	6 888	361	331	985	0	539	5	0	16	9 125
80-84	5 973	242	366	858	2	480	6	0	6	7 933
85+	3 905	181	318	590	2	259	6	2	11	5 274
Total	**32 202**	**2 410**	**1 850**	**7 071**	**8**	**2 341**	**18**	**5**	**96**	**46 001**
Divorced										
50-54	7 885	3 365	1 610	3 313	13	210	10	0	392	16 798
55-59	6 902	2 455	1 233	1 622	7	220	0	0	247	12 686
60-64	6 027	1 772	818	878	2	163	2	0	143	9 805
65-69	4 019	981	385	324	5	82	4	0	80	5 880
70-74	2 093	456	168	149	1	47	0	0	21	2 935
75-79	1 333	239	107	62	0	32	1	0	12	1 786
80-84	558	88	52	17	0	11	0	0	9	735
85+	203	25	20	11	0	4	0	0	0	263
Total	**29 019**	**9 381**	**4 394**	**6 377**	**28**	**770**	**16**	**0**	**904**	**50 889**
Separated										
50-54	230	207	52	233	0	13	2	0	17	754
55-59	248	175	25	130	0	7	0	0	7	592
60-64	273	240	30	87	3	20	0	0	8	661
65-69	152	164	7	36	0	4	0	0	4	367
70-74	111	66	4	20	0	6	0	0	1	208
75-79	48	29	8	4	0	4	0	0	1	94
80-84	13	8	2	2	0	0	0	0	0	25
85+	6	2	0	0	0	0	0	0	0	8
Total	**1 081**	**890**	**127**	**512**	**3**	**53**	**2**	**0**	**38**	**2 706**
TOTAL	**105 866**	**298 387**	**17 515**	**169 034**	**60**	**14 425**	**106**	**49**	**2 125**	**60 767**

TABLE 2.2a (*concluded*)

	Solitaires	One generation w/o others	w/ others	Two generation w/o others	w/ others	Three generation w/o others	w/ others	Four generation	Unknown	Total
Females										
Never married										
50-54	7 913	1 258	1 390	2 142	0	87	3	0	40	12 833
55-59	8 188	1 128	1 660	1 237	0	70	7	3	38	12 331
60-64	9 828	1 142	1 922	798	5	57	2	2	30	13 786
65-69	10 502	942	2 154	429	1	54	2	0	18	14 102
70-74	8 916	640	1 851	198	0	58	4	1	14	11 682
75-79	8 518	469	1 822	162	0	62	0	0	7	11 040
80-84	6 454	250	1 479	115	0	28	0	0	9	8 335
85+	3 979	163	960	60	2	17	1	0	16	5 198
Total	**64 299**	**5 993**	**13 238**	**5 141**	**8**	**432**	**19**	**6**	**172**	**89 308**
Married										
50-54	1 172	43 922	108	49 755	12	1 948	23	17	65	97 022
55-59	1 293	53 095	100	28 785	2	1 977	7	17	42	85 318
60-64	1 283	59 767	85	18 008	0	1 918	7	5	32	81 105
65-69	993	50 924	54	9 411	0	1 809	4	2	19	63 216
70-74	775	31 421	46	4 202	0	1 192	0	2	7	37 645
75-79	633	17 818	42	1 989	0	753	0	0	4	21 239
80-84	360	6 949	28	691	0	251	1	1	3	8 284
85+	130	1 420	17	145	0	34	0	0	1	1 747
Total	**6 640**	**265 315**	**481**	**112 987**	**13**	**9 882**	**41**	**44**	**172**	**395 575**
Widowed										
50-54	3 848	832	190	4 268	2	252	3	0	8	9 403
55-59	8 767	1 087	390	4 922	3	523	5	2	15	15 714
60-64	18 468	1 173	822	6 093	5	1 073	7	2	17	27 660
65-69	30 338	1 044	1 280	7 011	5	1 921	7	0	14	41 620
70-74	36 275	745	1 825	6 253	11	2 308	11	1	14	47 443
75-79	39 706	564	2 462	5 791	8	2 679	25	6	21	51 262
80-84	30 460	280	2 471	4 133	10	1 732	18	13	27	39 144
85+	17 115	307	2 179	2 368	8	762	16	14	32	22 801
Total	**184 977**	**6 030**	**11 619**	**40 838**	**52**	**11 251**	**91**	**37**	**148**	**255 043**
Divorced										
50-54	8 887	3 090	657	6 147	5	283	7	3	55	19 134
55-59	9 228	1 968	590	3 262	5	245	3	3	40	15 344
60-64	9 280	1 278	580	1 842	2	243	5	0	27	13 257
65-69	8 060	661	467	1 064	1	200		0	11	10 464
70-74	5 835	280	396	571	0	133	1	0	8	7 224
75-79	4 569	139	338	324	1	73	1	0	4	5 449
80-84	2 611	58	250	156	0	27	0	0	3	3 105
85+	1 119	37	163	62	0	6	0	0	2	1 389
Total	**49 590**	**7 512**	**3 441**	**13 426**	**14**	**1 211**	**17**	**7**	**149**	**75 367**
Separated										
50-54	190	188	5	285	0	10	0	0	2	680
55-59	233	218	7	183	0	10	0	0	2	653
60-64	202	190	5	100	0	12	0	0	2	511
65-69	171	114	9	42	0	8	0	0	0	344
70-74	88	59	1	15	0	2	0	0	0	165
75-79	33	19	2	7	0	0	0	0	0	63
80-84	10	6	1	0	0	0	0	0	0	17
85+	3	2	0	0	0	0	0	0	0	5
Total	**930**	**796**	**31**	**633**	**0**	**45**	**0**	**0**	**5**	**2 440**
TOTAL	**306 436**	**285 646**	**28 810**	**173 025**	**87**	**22 821**	**168**	**94**	**646**	**817 733**

TABLE 2.3

Kin present in one- or two-generation households in Finland in 1990 by age and sex of the sampled person

	One generation households without persons classified as having "other" relationship to CRP			Two generation households without persons classified as having "other" relationship to CRP					Persons living in one or two generation households with "other" persons present
	Individual living alone	Individual living with spouse	Individual living with other relatives of the same generation	Individual living with child(ren)	Individual living with spouse and child(ren)	Individual living with parent(s) or parent(s)-in-law	Individual living with spouse and parent(s) or parent(s)-in-law	Individual living with other relatives in two generation households	
Males									
50-54	18 843	41 260	4 828	2 715	60 495	1 575	318	2 497	20
55-59	18 073	54 128	4 343	1 910	37 565	802	223	2 313	18
60-64	18 838	63 640	3 545	1 630	23 373	340	142	2 255	5
65-69	15 316	56 252	1 979	1 159	12 181	60	32	1 429	6
70-74	11 145	38 842	987	954	5 886	13	7	838	4
75-79	10 835	27 185	779	942	3 267	1	1	498	2
80-84	8 083	13 094	613	792	1 435	0	1	269	3
85+	4 731	3 987	441	531	456	0	0	129	2
Total	105 865	298 388	17 515	10 633	144 658	2 791	724	10 228	60
Females									
50-54	22 010	49 290	2 350	10 277	48 832	738	307	2 443	18
55-59	27 710	57 497	2 747	7 938	27 200	382	195	2 675	8
60-64	39 062	63 550	3 413	7 303	16 543	242	80	2 673	12
65-69	50 064	53 685	3 965	7 335	8 441	81	21	2 078	7
70-74	51 891	33 145	4 119	6 175	3 781	15	1	1 267	9
75-79	53 459	19 008	4 667	5 542	1 769	2	1	958	9
80-84	39 895	7 543	4 229	3 939	635	1	0	520.	10
85+	22 346	1 929	3 319	2 176	133	0	0	326	10
Total	306 436	285 646	28 809	50 686	107 335	1 461	605	12 940	84

TABLE 2.4

Kin present in three- or more generation households in Finland in 1990 by age and sex of the sampled person

	Individual living with child(ren) and parent(s)	Individual living with spouse, child (ren) and parent(s)	Individual living with child(ren) and grandchild(ren)	Individual living with spouse, child(ren) and grandchild(ren)	Individual living in other three or more generation households	Persons living in three- or more generation households with other persons present
Males						
50-54	127	932	207	698	348	25
55-59	58	440	313	1 155	413	28
60-64	23	82	363	1 623	402	27
65-69	1	21	371	1 554	289	9
70-74	0	5	439	1 228	206	1
75-79	0	0	545	953	171	6
80-84	0	0	473	501	85	5
85+	0	0	255	149	40	7
Total	210	1 479	2 965	7 862	1 954	108
Females						
50-54	162	620	343	1 038	437	37
55-59	65	153	637	1 503	492	22
60-64	18	22	1 177	1 562	533	20
65-69	1	7	1 940	1 587	460	13
70-74	0	0	2 268	1 081	348	15
75-79	0	0	2 581	686	308	26
80-84	0	0	1 641	237	172	21
85+	0	0	711	37	85	17
Total	246	802	11 298	7 731	2 835	170

TABLE 2.5

Number of persons aged 50 and over living in the same household in Finland in 1990 by age, sex and marital status of the sampled person (non-institutional population)

	50+			60+				70+				80+				Total
	One person	Two persons	Three +	No person	One person	Two persons	Three +	No person	One person	Two persons	Three +	No person	One person	Two persons	Three +	
Males																
Never married																
50-54	10 448	5 335	1 232	12 225	4 162	568	63	13 237	3 330	438	10	15 163	1 750	98	3	17 015
55-59	9 078	4 335	943	10 717	3 235	328	83	12 123	2 048	158	20	12 792	1 473	85	7	14 357
60-64	8 692	3 748	690	0	9 882	2 932	317	11 675	1 388	50	17	12 272	820	35	3	13 130
65-69	5 267	2 196	315	0	6 081	1 852	206	7 146	925	41	27	7 815	308	7	8	8 139
70-74	2 795	1 058	149	0	2 909	972	121	0	3 375	582	45	3 818	169	7	8	4 002
75-79	1 909	705	78	0	1 945	689	58	0	2 147	518	27	2 488	198	2	4	2 692
80-84	1 090	376	39	0	1 106	368	31	0	1 168	319	18	0	1 343	152	10	1 505
85+	438	174	22	0	457	159	18	0	473	147	14	0	528	94	12	634
Total	**40 078**	**17 927**	**3 468**	**22 942**	**29 777**	**7 868**	**897**	**44 181**	**14 854**	**2 253**	**178**	**54 348**	**6 589**	**480**	**55**	**61 474**
Married																
50-54	48 370	50 193	708	96 333	2 687	248	3	97 752	1 313	205	2	98 420	813	37	2	99 272
55-59	13 243	77 882	628	80 910	10 717	113	13	90 672	1 015	63	3	91 085	633	33	2	91 753
60-64	6 680	83 282	288	0	43 302	44 843	103	86 523	1 703	22	2	87 942	295	12	2	88 250
65-69	2 106	67 706	88	0	10 393	59 459	48	63 222	6 671	4	4	69 655	241	0	4	69 900
70-74	1 046	44 881	107	0	2 636	13 376	21	0	27 547	18 479	8	45 425	607	0	2	46 034
75-79	891	30 271	380	0	1 346	30 178	18	0	8 556	22 974	11	29 414	2 121	0	6	31 541
80-84	553	4 140	489	0	683	14 472	27	0	2 154	13 020	8	0	11 090	4 086	6	15 182
85+	210	4 095	259	0	241	4 260	63	0	500	4 058	6	0	2 051	2 507	6	4 564
Total	**73 099**	**372 450**	**2 947**	**177 243**	**72 005**	**166 949**	**296**	**338 169**	**49 459**	**58 825**	**44**	**421 941**	**17 851**	**6 675**	**30**	**446 496**
Widowed																
50-54	1 690	157	2	1 807	42	0	0	1 825	23	0	0	1 835	13	0	0	1 848
55-59	2 640	325	7	2 862	105	5	0	2 935	33	3	0	2 948	23	0	0	2 972
60-64	4 327	480	17	0	4 557	257	10	4 767	50	2	5	4 783	37	2	2	4 823
65-69	5 991	578	14	0	6 151	420	12	6 451	126	1	5	6 551	29	0	2	6 582
70-74	6 882	538	25	0	6 996	432	16	0	7 221	213	11	7 385	56	0	4	7 445
75-79	8 372	696	56	0	8 653	449	22	0	8 795	312	18	8 992	124	1	8	9 125
80-84	7 030	777	126	0	7 550	359	24	0	7 643	273	17	0	7 786	133	14	7 933
85+	4 315	786	173	0	4 748	473	53	0	5 006	244	24	0	5 080	176	18	5 274
Total	**41 247**	**4 337**	**420**	**4 669**	**38 802**	**2 395**	**137**	**15 978**	**28 897**	**1 048**	**80**	**32 494**	**13 148**	**312**	**48**	**46 002**
Divorced																
50-54	13 660	2 977	162	15 803	935	48	12	16 270	515	13	0	16 618	180	0	0	16 798
55-59	9 697	2 850	138	11 547	1 092	25	22	12 265	403	7	10	12 450	233	0	2	12 685
60-64	7 418	2 290	97	0	8 392	1 377	37	9 433	365	5	2	9 630	175	0	0	9 805
65-69	4 556	1 264	59	0	4 901	940	38	5 554	309	6	9	5 788	87	0	4	5 879
70-74	2 336	576	24	0	2 418	502	16	0	2 708	221	7	2 888	46	0	2	2 936
75-79	1 453	318	15	0	1 494	281	11	0	1 600	181	5	1 726	58	2	0	1 786
80-84	600	126	9	0	620	110	5	0	645	85	5	0	693	38	4	735
85+	215	43	5	0	223	37	3	0	232	29	2	0	242	19	2	263
Total	**39 935**	**10 444**	**509**	**27 350**	**20 075**	**3 320**	**144**	**43 522**	**6 777**	**547**	**40**	**49 100**	**1 714**	**59**	**14**	**50 887**

TABLE 2.5 (continued)

	50+			60+				70+				80+				Total
	One person	Two persons	Three +	No person	One person	Two persons	Three +	No person	One person	Two persons	Three +	No person	One person	Two persons	Three +	Total
Separated																
50-54	498	248	7	708	43	0	2	737	17	0	0	743	10	0	0	753
55-59	337	247	8	535	55	2	0	580	10	2	0	588	3	0	0	592
60-64	343	315	3	0	510	148	3	643	18	0	0	653	8	0	0	662
65-69	179	187	0	0	196	169	0	344	22	0	0	365	1	0	0	366
70-74	122	85	0	0	128	79	0	0	171	36	0	204	4	0	0	207
75-79	59	35	0	0	64	31	0	0	76	19	0	93	1	0	0	94
80-84	15	9	0	0	15	10	0	0	16	9	0	0	22	3	0	25
85+	6	2	0	0	6	2	0	0	6	2	0	0	6	2	0	8
Total	**1 559**	**1 128**	**18**	**1 243**	**1 017**	**441**	**5**	**2 304**	**336**	**68**	**0**	**2 646**	**55**	**5**	**0**	**2 707**
Total Males	**19 318**	**406 285**	**7 363**	**233 437**	**161 674**	**210 976**	**1 479**	**444 153**	**100 332**	**62 741**	**339**	**560 529**	**39 360**	**7 532**	**145**	**607 566**
Females																
Never married																
50-54	9 543	2 773	517	10 642	1 917	243	32	11 138	1 493	198	3	11 872	908	52	2	12 833
55-59	9 055	2 852	425	10 080	2 023	182	47	11 000	1 232	93	7	11 372	902	55	3	12 332
60-64	10 425	2 990	370	0	11 217	2 347	222	12 580	1 142	47	17	13 015	728	32	10	13 785
65-69	11 012	2 761	331	0	11 402	2 441	260	12 819	1 193	65	27	13 673	411	13	7	14 104
70-74	9 275	2 125	281	0	9 455	1 999	227	0	10 279	1 273	129	11 280	369	16	15	11 681
75-79	8 813	2 019	209	0	8 976	1 876	188	0	9 435	1 473	133	10 426	565	33	18	11 041
80-84	6 645	1 479	211	0	6 788	1 370	177	0	3 989	1 197	149	0	7 681	588	66	8 335
85+	4 074	956	168	0	4 156	890	152	0	4 268	794	136	0	4 552	558	88	5 198
Total	**68 842**	**17 955**	**2 512**	**20 722**	**55 934**	**11 348**	**1 305**	**47 537**	**33 031**	**5 140**	**601**	**71 638**	**16 116**	**1 347**	**209**	**89 309**
Married																
50-54	12 379	83 710	915	85 377	11 445	190	10	95 438	1 463	118	2	96 235	752	35	0	97 022
55-59	3 160	81 747	410	46 352	38 813	137	18	83 197	2 085	35	0	84 837	458	22	0	85 317
60-64	2 000	78 960	145	46 348	11 767	69 242	97	73 072	8 020	13	0	80 605	495	5	0	81 105
65-69	1 314	61 832	69	0	2 599	60 585	32	37 254	25 952	7	2	61 818	1 396	0	2	63 215
70-74	946	36 467	233	0	1 209	36 424	13	0	7 774	29 862	9	33 972	3 669	1	4	37 646
75-79	732	20 018	489	0	821	20 405	13	0	1 976	19 255	7	14 512	6 722	1	1	21 239
80-84	399	7 527	358	0	429	7 816	39	0	627	7 655	2	0	3 071	5 212	2	8 284
85+	137	1 498	112	0	146	1 563	38	0	170	1 574	3	0	394	1 351	4	1 747
Total	**21 067**	**371 759**	**2 731**	**178 077**	**67 229**	**196 362**	**260**	**288 961**	**48 067**	**58 519**	**25**	**371 979**	**16 957**	**6 627**	**13**	**395 575**
Widowed																
50-54	8 468	913	22	9 085	308	10	0	9 268	128	7	0	9 338	63	2	0	9 403
55-59	14 440	1 262	12	15 100	612	2	0	15 498	215	0	0	15 597	117	0	0	15 713
60-64	25 997	1 645	18	0	26 505	1 142	13	27 232	422	2	5	27 440	213	2	5	27 660
65-69	39 884	1 696	39	0	40 262	1 328	28	40 986	611	13	9	41 404	207	5	4	41 619
70-74	45 247	2 078	118	0	46 147	1 227	68	0	46 626	766	51	47 167	234	11	31	47 442
75-79	47 219	3 585	458	0	49 867	1 280	114	0	50 303	858	100	50 819	367	18	58	51 261
80-84	34 457	3 865	822	0	37 163	1 464	217	0	38 252	724	168	0	38 614	396	134	39 144
85+	18 341	3 517	943	0	20 195	2 252	354	0	21 839	754	208	0	22 173	452	176	22 801
Total	**234 053**	**18 561**	**2 432**	**24 185**	**221 059**	**8 705**	**794**	**92 984**	**158 396**	**3 124**	**541**	**191 765**	**61 988**	**886**	**408**	**255 043**

TABLE 2.5 (concluded)

Divorced

Age															
50-54	16 485	2 623	25	18 397	725	10	2	283	7	2	18 987	147	0	0	19 133
55-59	13 208	2 107	30	14 450	880	12	3	263	5	0	15 187	153	5	0	15 345
60-64	11 640	1 595	22	0	12 218	1 023	15	302	7	2	13 098	155	3	0	13 257
65-69	9 518	916	29	0	9 721	719	24	289	7	7	10 400	55	1	7	10 464
70-74	6 673	533	19	0	6 822	391	12	6 942	220	9	7 161	58	2	4	7 225
75-79	5 011	399	39	0	5 171	249	28	5 156	168	22	5 359	75	6	8	5 448
80-84	2 786	289	30	0	2 910	177	18	2 831	121	15	0	3 028	69	8	3 105
85+	1 152	215	22	0	1 224	152	13	1 159	76	11	0	1 332	48	9	1 389
Total	**66 473**	**8 677**	**216**	**32 847**	**39 671**	**2 733**	**115**	**17 225**	**611**	**68**	**70 192**	**5 003**	**134**	**36**	**75366**

Separated

Age															
50-54	395	285	0	643	37	0	0	7	0	0	675	5	0	0	680
55-59	388	263	0	547	107	0	0	8	0	0	653	0	0	0	653
60-64	273	233	3	0	308	198	3	23	0	0	508	2	0	0	510
65-69	212	133	0	0	222	122	0	33	0	0	344	1	0	0	345
70-74	101	65	0	0	102	64	0	124	42	0	161	5	0	0	166
75-79	42	21	0	0	44	20	0	47	16	0	60	4	0	0	64
80-84	10	7	0	0	10	7	0	12	5	0	0	15	2	0	17
85+	3	2	0	0	2	2	0	3	2	0	0	3	2	0	5
Total	**1 424**	**1 009**	**3**	**1 190**	**832**	**413**	**3**	**257**	**65**	**0**	**2 401**	**35**	**4**	**0**	**2 439**
Total Females	**391 878**	**417 960**	**7 893**	**210 668**	**385 028**	**219 559**	**2 477**	**260 413**	**67 460**	**1236**	**707 971**	**100 100**	**8 997**	**664**	**817 732**

TABLE 2.6b

Women aged 50 and over living in one or two generation households in Finland in 1990 by age, sex and number of children ever born

	One generation households without persons classified as having "other" relationship to CRP			Two generation households without persons classified as having "other" relationship to CRP					Persons living in one or two generation households with "other" persons present	Total
	Living alone	Living with spouse	Living with other relatives of the same generation	Living with child(ren)	Living with spouse and child(ren)	Living with parent(s) or parent(s)-in-law	Living with spouse and parent(s) or parent(s)-in-law	Living with other relatives in two generation households		
None										
50-54	8 953	6 950	1 478	43	413	720	85	537	2	19 182
55-59	9 543	6 800	1 760	23	207	370	33	398	0	19 135
60-64	13 125	8 620	2 157	20	133	232	22	262	2	24 572
65-69	17 687	9 576	2 696	20	53	81	13	88	2	30 218
70-74	21 848	8 802	2 826	7	49	14	1	13	1	33 562
75-79	28 775	7 487	3 404	9	39	2	0	5	1	39 722
80-84	27 278	4 177	3 391	12	19	1	0	5	1	34 884
85+	18 705	1 478	2 904	4	7	0	0	2	3	23 103
Total	**145 915**	**53 891**	**20 616**	**139**	**921**	**1 420**	**154**	**1 310**	**12**	**224 378**
One										
50-54	3 938	10 610	295	2 195	6 667	12	50	13	5	23 785
55-59	4 798	10 610	278	1 462	3 258	7	33	2	7	20 455
60-64	6 812	12 042	430	1 207	2 048	5	13	2	3	22 562
65-69	9 972	11 484	489	1 378	1 179	0	2	2	1	24 507
70-74	11 269	7 748	573	1 489	734	1	0	0	1	21 816
75-79	11 824	4 941	667	2 013	509	0	1	1	0	19 956
80-84	7 433	1 808	508	1 939	258	0	0	2	6	11 954
85+	2 684	324	311	1 430	74	0	0	0	6	4 829
Total	**58 730**	**59 567**	**3 552**	**13 112**	**14 728**	**25**	**100**	**22**	**29**	**149 865**
Two										
50-54	5 230	18 945	317	3 633	19 677	0	103	375	5	48 285
55-59	6 205	19 815	283	2 202	8 402	0	65	337	2	37 310
60-64	8 102	19 032	315	1 777	4 165	0	20	327	2	33 738
65-69	9 586	14 321	353	1 756	2 034	0	4	279	4	28 336
70-74	8 744	7 721	334	1 638	961	0	0	178	6	19 581
75-79	6 821	3 469	311	1 504	507	0	0	201	4	12 816
80-84	3 133	937	193	1 060	183	0	0	157	2	5 665
85+	683	92	72	470	36	0	0	152	1	1 506
Total	**48 503**	**84 332**	**2 178**	**14 039**	**35 965**	**0**	**192**	**2 005**	**24**	**187 238**
Three or More										
Average	**3.9**	**3.8**	**3.93**	**4.2**	**4.02**	**3.6**	**3.71**	**4.89**	**3.85**	**3.96**
50-54	3 888	12 785	260	4 405	22 075	7	68	1 518	7	45 013
55-59	7 163	20 272	425	4 252	15 333	5	63	1 938	0	49 452
60-64	11 023	23 857	512	4 300	10 197	5	25	2 083	5	52 007
65-69	12 819	18 304	426	4 181	5 175	0	2	1 708	0	42 615
70-74	10 029	8 873	386	3 041	2 036	0	0	1 076	1	25 444
75-79	6 039	3 111	286	2 016	714	0	0	751	5	12 921
80-84	2 051	621	137	928	175	0	0	356	1	4 269
85+	274	35	32	272	16	0	0	172	0	801
Total	**53 287**	**87 856**	**2 463**	**23 395**	**55 722**	**17**	**159**	**9 603**	**19**	**232 522**

TABLE 2.7b

Women aged 50 and over living in three or more generation households in Finland in 1990 by age, sex and number of children ever born

	Living with child(ren) and parent(s)	Living with spouse, children and parent(s)	Living with child(ren) and grandchild(ren)	Living with spouse, child(ren) and grandchild(ren)	Living in other three or more generation households without "others"	Living in three or more generation households with "other" persons present	Total
None							
50-54	7	7	0	3	40	0	57
55-59	3	5	0	7	32	3	50
60-64	0	2	0	2	10	2	15
65-69	0	0	0	6	2	1	9
70-74	0	0	0	11	6	5	21
75-79	0	0	0	15	4	1	20
80-84	0	0	0	7	3	2	12
85+	0	0	0	3	7	1	11
Total	**10**	**14**	**0**	**54**	**104**	**15**	**195**
One							
50-54	50	108	40	137	22	5	362
55-59	17	48	115	185	18	7	390
60-64	8	3	245	225	8	5	495
65-69	0	1	451	288	4	4	747
70-74	0	0	660	242	7	2	912
75-79	0	0	976	224	9	13	1 222
80-84	0	0	790	102	13	12	917
85+	0	0	435	23	13	10	481
Total	**75**	**160**	**3 712**	**1 426**	**94**	**58**	**5 526**
Two							
50-54	38	215	113	347	77	12	802
55-59	8	30	162	435	63	0	698
60-64	2	3	303	440	73	3	825
65-69	0	1	495	451	76	1	1 025
70-74	0	0	615	281	56	5	958
75-79	0	0	689	172	92	4	956
80-84	0	0	441	65	72	4	582
85+	0	0	176	6	35	3	220
Total	**48**	**250**	**2 994**	**2 197**	**544**	**32**	**6 066**
Three or More							
Average	**4.25**	**3.94**	**4.19**	**4.14**	**4.70**	**4.06**	**4.26**
50-54	67	290	190	552	298	20	1 417
55-59	37	70	360	877	378	12	1 733
60-64	8	13	628	895	442	10	1 997
65-69	1	5	994	842	378	7	2 227
70-74	0	0	993	547	279	4	1 822
75-79	0	0	915	275	204	8	1 402
80-84	0	0	410	63	84	3	560
85+	0	0	100	5	30	3	138
Total	**113**	**378**	**4 591**	**4 056**	**2 092**	**66**	**11 296**

TABLE 2.7c

Women aged 50 and over living in three or more generation households in Finland in 1990 by age, sex and number of children ever born (in per cent)

		Living with child(ren) and parent(s)	Living with spouse, children and parent(s)	Living with child(ren) and grandchild(ren)	Living with spouse, child(ren) and grandchild(ren)	Living in other three or more generation households without "others"	Living in three or more generation households with "other" persons present	Total
None								
50-54		4.3	1.1	0.0	0.3	9.2	0.0	2.2
55-59		4.6	3.3	0.0	0.5	6.5	13.6	1.7
60-64		0.0	9.5	0.0	0.1	1.9	10.0	0.5
65-69		0.0	0.0	0.0	0.4	0.4	7.7	0.2
70-74		0.0	0.0	0.0	1.0	1.7	31.3	0.6
75-79		0.0	0.0	0.0	2.2	1.3	3.8	0.6
80-84		0.0	0.0	0.0	3.0	1.7	9.5	0.6
85+		0.0	0.0	0.0	8.1	8.2	5.9	1.3
	Total	**4.1**	**1.7**	**0.0**	**0.7**	**3.7**	**8.8**	**0.8**
One								
50-54		30.9	17.4	11.7	13.2	5.0	13.5	13.7
55-59		26.2	31.4	18.1	12.3	3.7	31.8	13.6
60-64		44.4	14.3	20.8	14.4	1.5	25.0	14.9
65-69		0.0	14.3	23.2	18.1	0.9	30.8	18.6
70-74		0.0	0.0	29.1	22.4	2.0	12.5	24.6
75-79		0.0	0.0	37.8	32.7	2.9	50.0	33.9
80-84		0.0	0.0	48.1	43.0	7.6	57.1	44.3
85+		0.0	0.0	61.2	62.2	15.3	58.8	56.6
	Total	**30.5**	**20.0**	**32.9**	**18.4**	**3.3**	**33.9**	**23.9**
Two								
50-54		23.5	34.7	32.9	33.4	17.6	32.4	30.4
55-59		12.3	19.6	25.4	28.9	12.8	0.0	24.3
60-64		11.1	14.3	25.8	28.2	13.7	15.0	24.8
65-69		0.0	14.3	25.5	28.4	16.5	7.7	25.6
70-74		0.0	0.0	27.1	26.0	16.1	31.3	25.8
75-79		0.0	0.0	26.7	25.1	29.8	15.4	26.6
80-84		0.0	0.0	26.9	27.4	41.9	19.0	28.1
85+		0.0	0.0	24.8	16.2	41.2	17.6	25.9
	Total	**19.5**	**31.2**	**26.5**	**28.4**	**19.2**	**18.7**	**26.3**
Three or More								
50-54		41.4	46.8	55.4	53.1	68.2	54.1	53.7
55-59		56.9	45.8	56.5	58.3	77.0	54.5	60.4
60-64		44.4	61.9	53.4	57.3	82.9	50.0	59.9
65-69		100.0	71.4	51.2	53.1	82.2	53.8	55.6
70-74		0.0	0.0	43.8	50.6	80.2	25.0	49.1
75-79		0.0	0.0	35.5	40.1	66.0	30.8	38.9
80-84		0.0	0.0	25.0	26.6	48.8	14.3	27.0
85+		0.0	0.0	14.1	13.5	35.3	17.6	16.2
	Total	**45.9**	**47.1**	**40.6**	**52.5**	**73.8**	**38.6**	**48.9**

TABLE 3.1

**Number of persons aged 50 and over in Finland in 1990 by age,
sex, marital status and institutionalization status**

		Institutionalized	*Not institutionalized*	*Total*
Males				
Never married				
50-54		578	17 015	17 593
55-59		550	14 357	14 907
60-64		647	13 130	13 777
65-69		618	8 139	8 757
70-74		436	4 002	4 438
75-79		449	2 692	3 141
80-84		361	1 505	1 866
85+		263	634	897
	Total	**3 903**	**61 474**	**65 377**
Married				
50-54		15	99 272	99 287
55-59		22	91 753	91 775
60-64		55	88 250	88 305
65-69		102	69 900	70 002
70-74		169	46 034	46 203
75-79		292	31 541	31 833
80-84		359	15 182	15 541
85+		307	4 564	4 871
	Total	**1 321**	**446 496**	**447 817**
Widowed				
50-54		5	1 848	1 853
55-59		8	2 972	2 980
60-64		37	4 823	4 860
65-69		92	6 582	6 674
70-74		179	7 445	7 624
75-79		414	9 125	9 539
80-84		694	7 933	8 627
85+		1 047	5 274	6 321
	Total	**2 476**	**46 002**	**48 478**
Divorced				
50-54		92	16 798	16 890
55-59		102	12 685	12 787
60-64		133	9 805	9 938
65-69		160	5 879	6 039
70-74		145	2 936	3 081
75-79		153	1 786	1 939
80-84		102	735	837
85+		61	263	324
	Total	**947**	**50 888**	**51 835**
Separated				
50-54		2	753	755
55-59		3	592	595
60-64		5	662	667
65-69		5	366	371
70-74		8	207	215
75-79		7	94	101
80-84		4	25	29
85+		1	8	9
	Total	**35**	**2 707**	**2 742**
Total Males		**8 682**	**607 567**	**616 249**

TABLE 3.1 (*concluded*)

	Institutionalized	Not institutionalized	Total
Females			
Never married			
50-54	405	12 833	13 238
55-59	365	12 332	12 697
60-64	445	13 785	14 230
65-69	505	14 104	14 609
70-74	574	11 681	12 255
75-79	904	11 041	11 945
80-84	1 215	8 335	9 550
85+	1 712	5 198	6 910
Total	**6 124**	**89 309**	**95 433**
Married			
50-54	12	97 022	97 034
55-59	22	85 317	85 339
60-64	53	81 105	81 158
65-69	91	63 215	63 306
70-74	179	37 646	37 825
75-79	298	21 239	21 537
80-84	306	8 284	8 590
85+	194	1 747	1 941
Total	**1 154**	**395 574**	**396 728**
Widowed			
50-54	15	9 403	9 418
55-59	40	15 713	15 753
60-64	88	27 660	27 748
65-69	315	41 619	41 934
70-74	782	47 442	48 224
75-79	2 159	51 261	53 420
80-84	3 906	39 144	43 050
85+	6 087	22 801	28 888
Total	**13 393**	**255 044**	**268 437**
Divorced			
50-54	28	19 133	19 161
55-59	65	15 345	15 410
60-64	85	13 257	13 342
65-69	145	10 464	10 609
70-74	198	7 225	7 423
75-79	325	5 448	5 773
80-84	360	3 105	3 465
85+	367	1 389	1 756
Total	**1 572**	**75 365**	**76 937**
Separated			
50-54	0	680	680
55-59	0	653	653
60-64	0	510	510
65-69	2	345	347
70-74	1	166	167
75-79	5	64	69
80-84	1	17	18
85+	0	5	5
Total	**9**	**2 439**	**2 448**
Total Females	**22 253**	**817 731**	**839 984**

TABLE 3.2

**Number and type of income sources of persons aged 50 and over living in institutions
in Finland in 1990 by age, sex and marital status**

		Single source				Multiple sources				
	No income	Labour	Entrep.	Pension	Other	Labour and pension	Other two	Three or more	Unknown	Total
Males										
Never married										
50-54	2	3	0	450	0	63	53	2	5	578
55-59	5	7	0	462	0	33	33	8	2	550
60-64	0	0	0	548	0	30	58	10	0	647
65-69	1	0	0	534	0	5	67	11	0	618
70-74	0	0	0	375	0	2	49	9	0	436
75-79	0	0	0	379	0	4	56	11	0	449
80-84	0	0	0	302	0	2	46	11	0	361
85+	0	0	0	201	0	0	50	12	0	263
Total	**8**	**10**	**0**	**3 251**	**0**	**139**	**412**	**74**	**7**	**3 903**
Married										
50-54	0	2	0	8	0	0	3	0	2	15
55-59	0	0	0	13	0	0	8	0	0	22
60-64	2	0	0	40	0	0	13	0	0	55
65-69	0	0	0	74	0	0	21	7	0	102
70-74	1	0	0	114	0	0	46	8	0	169
75-79	1	0	0	208	0	1	62	19	0	292
80-84	0	0	0	264	0	1	80	14	0	359
85+	0	0	0	218	0	1	70	18	0	307
Total	**4**	**2**	**0**	**940**	**0**	**3**	**303**	**66**	**2**	**1 321**
Widowed										
50-54	0	0	0	3	0	0	2	0	0	5
55-59	0	0	0	7	0	0	2	0	0	8
60-64	0	2	0	28	0	0	5	2	0	37
65-69	0	0	0	72	0	0	16	2	1	92
70-74	0	0	0	140	0	1	33	5	0	179
75-79	0	0	0	313	0	1	89	11	0	414
80-84	2	0	0	537	0	1	134	22	0	694
85+	0	0	0	819	0	8	183	35	0	1 047
Total	**2**	**2**	**0**	**1 919**	**0**	**11**	**464**	**76**	**1**	**2 476**
Divorced										
50-54	3	15	3	55	0	3	12	0	0	92
55-59	5	8	0	78	0	0	8	0	2	102
60-64	0	2	0	118	0	3	10	0	0	133
65-69	0	0	0	153	0	0	7	0	0	160
70-74	0	0	0	132	0	1	11	1	0	145
75-79	1	0	0	141	0	0	11	0	0	153
80-84	0	0	0	90	0	0	12	0	0	102
85+	0	0	0	50	0	0	11	0	0	161
Total	**10**	**25**	**3**	**818**	**0**	**7**	**82**	**1**	**2**	**947**
Separated										
50-54	0	0	0	2	0	0	0	0	0	2
55-59	0	0	0	3	0	0	0	0	0	3
60-64	0	0	0	3	0	0	2	0	0	5
65-69	0	0	0	5	0	0	0	0	0	5
70-74	0	0	0	8	0	0	0	0	0	8
75-79	0	0	0	5	0	0	2	0	0	7
80-84	0	0	0	4	0	0	0	0	0	4
85+	0	0	0	1	0	0	0	0	0	1
Total	**0**	**0**	**0**	**31**	**0**	**0**	**4**	**0**	**0**	**35**
Total Males	**23**	**38**	**3**	**6 959**	**0**	**162**	**1 268**	**217**	**11**	**8 682**

TABLE 3.2 (*concluded*)

	No income	Single source				Multiple sources			Unknown	Total
		Labour	Entrep.	Pension	Other	Labour and pension	Other two	Three or more		
Females										
Never married										
50-54	0	0	0	345	0	33	22	5	0	405
55-59	0	0	0	293	0	40	18	13	0	365
60-64	0	0	0	388	0	17	33	7	0	445
65-69	0	0	0	447	0	9	41	7	0	505
70-74	1	0	0	513	0	6	52	2	0	574
75-79	0	0	0	792	0	1	104	7	0	904
80-84	1	0	0	1 055	0	4	140	15	0	1 215
85+	5	0	0	1 492	0	2	196	17	0	1 712
Total	**7**	**0**	**0**	**5 325**	**0**	**112**	**606**	**73**	**0**	**6 124**
Married										
50-54	0	0	0	10	0	0	2	0	0	12
55-59	0	0	0	10	0	3	3	5	0	22
60-64	0	0	0	43	0	0	10	0	0	53
65-69	0	0	0	76	0	0	14	0	0	91
70-74	1	0	0	144	0	1	31	1	1	179
75-79	0	0	0	248	0	1	46	2	0	298
80-84	0	0	0	262	0	0	42	2	0	306
85+	0	0	0	171	0	0	21	2	0	194
Total	**1**	**0**	**0**	**965**	**0**	**5**	**169**	**13**	**1**	**1 154**
Widowed										
50-54	0	0	0	12	0	0	3	0	0	15
55-59	0	0	0	33	0	0	7	0	0	40
60-64	0	0	0	73	0	3	8	3	0	88
65-69	0	0	0	271	0	4	36	4	1	315
70-74	0	0	0	660	0	1	100	20	1	782
75-79	0	0	0	1 856	0	12	267	24	0	2 159
80-84	3	0	0	3 407	0	8	450	37	1	3 906
85+	17	0	1	5 325	0	11	662	70	1	6 087
Total	**20**	**0**	**1**	**11 637**	**0**	**39**	**1 533**	**157**	**4**	**13 393**
Divorced										
50-54	0	0	0	23	0	0	5	0	0	28
55-59	0	0	0	63	0	0	2	0	0	65
60-64	0	0	0	72	0	2	12	0	0	85
65-69	0	0	0	122	0	0	21	1	0	145
70-74	0	0	0	176	0	0	18	4	0	198
75-79	0	0	0	287	0	0	34	4	0	325
80-84	0	0	0	262	0	1	29	1	0	360
85+	0	0	0	171	1	0	36	4	0	367
Total	**0**	**0**	**0**	**1 399**	**1**	**3**	**157**	**13**	**0**	**1 572**
Separated										
50-54	0	0	0	0	0	0	0	0	0	0
55-59	0	0	0	0	0	0	0	0	0	0
60-64	0	0	0	0	0	0	0	0	0	0
65-69	0	0	0	2	0	0	0	0	0	2
70-74	0	0	0	1	0	0	0	0	0	1
75-79	0	0	0	5	0	0	0	0	0	5
80-84	0	0	0	1	0	0	0	0	0	1
85+	0	0	0	0	0	0	0	0	0	0
Total	**0**	**0**	**0**	**9**	**0**	**0**	**0**	**0**	**0**	**9**
Total Females	**28**	**0**	**1**	**19 336**	**1**	**160**	**2 465**	**257**	**6**	**22 253**

TABLE 4.1

**Economic activity of persons aged 50 and over in Finland in 1990
by age, sex and marital status**

		Economically active		Economically inactive		
		Employed	Unemployed	Pensioner	Other	Total
Males						
Never married						
50-54		10 017	1 772	4 375	852	17 015
55-59		6 227	1 488	5 938	703	14 357
60-64		3 182	3 422	6 272	255	13 130
65-69		118	38	7 967	17	8 139
70-74		27	0	3 971	5	4 002
75-79		0	0	2 692	0	2 692
80-84		0	0	1 505	0	1 505
85+		0	0	634	0	634
	Total	**19 570**	**6 719**	**33 353**	**1 831**	**61 474**
Married						
50-54		84 130	3 062	10 638	1 442	99 272
55-59		57 958	3 298	29 367	1 130	91 753
60-64		27 138	16 368	44 177	567	88 250
65-69		1 977	225	67 612	87	69 900
70-74		613	0	45 368	53	46 034
75-79		0	0	31 541	0	31 541
80-84		0	0	15 182	0	15 182
85+		0	0	4 564	0	4 564
	Total	**171 816**	**22 953**	**248 449**	**3 278**	**446 496**
Widowed						
50-54		1 363	108	337	40	1 848
55-59		1 543	168	1 215	45	2 972
60-64		1 122	1 060	2 595	47	4 823
65-69		106	22	6 445	9	6 582
70-74		81	0	7 358	6	7 445
75-79		0	0	9 125	0	9 125
80-84		0	0	7 933	0	7 933
85+		0	0	5 274	0	5 274
	Total	**4 215**	**1 359**	**40 281**	**147**	**46 002**
Divorced						
50-54		11 158	1 608	3 163	868	16 798
55-59		5 993	1 162	5 012	518	12 685
60-64		1 915	2 887	4 873	130	9 805
65-69		94	33	5 735	17	5 879
70-74		31	0	2 900	6	2 937
75-79		0	0	1 786	0	1 786
80-84		0	0	735	0	735
85+		0	0	263	0	263
	Total	**19 191**	**5 690**	**24 468**	**1 539**	**50 888**
Separated						
50-54		493	82	155	23	753
55-59		287	40	238	27	592
60-64		155	150	352	5	662
65-69		12	2	351	1	366
70-74		2	0	205	0	207
75-79		0	0	94	0	94
80-84		0	0	25	0	25
85+		0	0	8	0	8
	Total	**949**	**274**	**1 427**	**56**	**2 707**
	Total Males	**215 742**	**36 995**	**347 978**	**6 852**	**607 566**

TABLE 4.1 (*continued*)

| | | Economically active | | Economically inactive | | |
		Employed	Unemployed	Pensioner	Other	Total
Females						
Never married						
50-54		9 560	307	2 548	418	12 833
55-59		7 105	448	4 402	377	12 332
60-64		3 503	2 522	7 488	272	13 785
65-69		247	52	13 779	26	14 104
70-74		78	0	11 591	13	11 681
75-79		0	0	11 041	0	11 041
80-84		0	0	8 335	0	8 335
85+		0	0	5 198	0	5 198
	Total	**20 493**	**3 328**	**64 382**	**1 106**	**89 309**
Married						
50-54		79 245	3 135	8 768	5 873	97 022
55-59		49 598	4 427	25 105	6 187	85 317
60-64		19 097	17 572	40 315	4 122	81 105
65-69		941	278	61 841	155	63 215
70-74		217	0	37 404	26	37 646
75-79		0	0	21 239	0	21 239
80-84		0	0	8 284	0	8 284
85+		0	0	1 747	0	1 747
	Total	**149 098**	**25 411**	**204 703**	**16 363**	**395 574**
Widowed						
50-54		6 982	368	1 487	567	9 403
55-59		7 880	858	5 630	1 345	15 713
60-64		5 388	6 110	13 108	3 053	27 660
65-69		507	122	40 866	124	41 619
70-74		232	0	47 182	28	47 442
75-79		0	0	51 261	0	51 261
80-84		0	0	39 144	0	39 144
85+		0	0	22 801	0	22 801
	Total	**20 989**	**7 459**	**221 479**	**5 117**	**255 044**
Divorced						
50-54		14 968	892	2 692	582	19 133
55-59		8 707	828	5 425	385	15 345
60-64		3 068	3 398	6 647	143	13 257
65-69		199	52	10 195	18	10 464
70-74		39	0	7 172	14	7 225
75-79		0	0	5 448	0	5 448
80-84		0	0	3 105	0	3 105
85+		0	0	1 389	0	1 389
	Total	**26 981**	**5 170**	**42 073**	**1 142**	**75 366**
Separated						
50-54		540	30	78	32	680
55-59		400	28	205	20	653
60-64		137	95	267	12	510
65-69		9	2	333	0	345
70-74		1	0	165	0	166
75-79		0	0	64	0	64
80-84		0	0	17	0	17
85+		0	0	5	0	5
	Total	**1 087**	**156**	**1 133**	**63**	**2 440**
Total Females		**218 648**	**41 524**	**533 770**	**23 790**	**817 732**

TABLE 4.2

**Economic activity of persons aged 50 and over in Finland in 1990
by age, sex and educational level**

| | Economically active | | Economically inactive | | |
	Employed	Unemployed	Pensioner	Other	Total
Males					
Educ.Level 1+2					
50-54	58 790	4 412	13 123	2 187	78 512
55-59	44 028	4 667	31 787	1 773	82 255
60-64	21 860	19 237	45 145	763	87 005
65-69	1 379	282	68 518	106	70 285
70-74	518	0	46 745	57	47 319
75-79	0	0	36 279	0	36 279
80-84	0	0	20 647	0	20 647
85+	0	0	8 870	0	8 870
Total	**126 575**	**28 597**	**271 113**	**4 886**	**431 171**
Educ. Level 3					
50-54	33 978	2 047	4 802	805	41 632
55-59	18 283	1 347	8 258	478	28 367
60-64	6 947	4 047	9 423	170	20 587
65-69	424	32	13 813	8	14 277
70-74	113	0	9 012	6	9 131
75-79	0	0	6 033	0	6 033
80-84	0	0	2 942	0	2 942
85+	0	0	1 151	0	1 151
Total	**59 745**	**7 472**	**55 434**	**1 467**	**124 118**
Undergraduate					
50-54	7 720	110	422	125	8 377
55-59	5 342	92	1 220	92	6 745
60-64	2 148	413	2 405	30	4 997
65-69	159	4	3 029	4	3 195
70-74	47	0	2 012	1	2 060
75-79	0	0	1 348	0	1 348
80-84	0	0	867	0	867
85+	0	0	335	0	335
Total	**15 416**	**619**	**11 638**	**251**	**27 924**
Graduate					
50-54	6 673	63	322	108	7 167
55-59	4 355	52	505	80	4 992
60-64	2 557	190	1 295	40	4 082
65-69	345	2	2 749	13	3 109
70-74	76	0	2 033	6	2 115
75-79	0	0	1 578	0	1 578
80-84	0	0	924	0	924
85+	0	0	387	0	387
Total	**14 006**	**307**	**9 793**	**247**	**24 353**
Total Males	**215 742**	**36 995**	**347 978**	**6 852**	**607 566**

TABLE 4.2 (*concluded*)

| | Economically active | | Economically inactive | | |
	Employed	Unemployed	Pensioner	Other	Total
Females					
Educ.Level 1+2					
50-54	61 437	3 338	11 465	5 020	81 260
55-59	46 440	5 260	31 053	6 200	88 953
60-64	21 282	25 463	50 845	6 175	103 765
65-69	1 181	452	102 175	262	104 071
70-74	369	0	85 357	75	85 801
75-79	0	0	75 478	0	75 478
80-84	0	0	50 613	0	50 613
85+	0	0	26 959	0	26 959
Total	**130 709**	**34 513**	**433 945**	**17 733**	**616 900**
Educ. Level 3					
50-54	37 363	1 325	3 708	2 040	44 437
55-59	19 265	1 255	8 187	1 755	30 462
60-64	6 622	4 003	12 793	1 150	24 568
65-69	440	53	19 395	31	19 919
70-74	121	0	14 352	1	14 474
75-79	0	0	10 308	0	10 308
80-84	0	0	5 710	0	5710
85+	0	0	2 720	0	2 720
Total	**63 811**	**6 636**	**77 174**	**4 977**	**152 598**
Undergraduate					
50-54	8 735	57	293	312	9 397
55-59	5 937	50	1 242	283	7 512
60-64	2 223	190	3 450	198	6 062
65-69	153	1	3 977	14	4 145
70-74	47	0	2 893	1	2 941
75-79	0	0	2 409	0	2 409
80-84	0	0	1 823	0	1 823
85+	0	0	1 160	0	1 160
Total	**17 095**	**298**	**17 247**	**809**	**35 448**
Graduate					
50-54	3 760	12	107	100	3 978
55-59	2 048	25	285	75	2 433
60-64	1 067	40	737	78	1 922
65-69	129	0	1 467	15	1 612
70-74	28	0	912	4	944
75-79	0	0	858	0	858
80-84	0	0	739	0	739
85+	0	0	301	0	301
Total	**7 033**	**77**	**5 405**	**272**	**12 786**
Total Females	**218 648**	**41 524**	**533 770**	**23 790**	**817 732**

TABLE 4.3

**Economic activity of persons aged 50 and over in Finland in 1990
by age, sex and number of generations present in the household**

| | Economically active | | Economically inactive | | |
	Employed	Unemployed	Pensioner	Other	Total
Males					
Solitaires					
50-54	11 752	1 870	4 315	907	18 843
55-59	8 115	1 698	7 587	673	18 073
60-64	4 115	4 993	9 495	235	18 838
65-69	234	75	14 973	34	15 317
70-74	100	0	11 028	17	11 145
75-79	0	0	10 835	0	10 835
80-84	0	0	8 083	0	8 083
85+	0	0	4 731	0	4 731
Total	**24 316**	**8 637**	**71 047**	**1 866**	**105 866**
One Generation Households					
50-54	35 827	2 327	6 813	1 122	46 088
55-59	33 680	2 698	21 098	995	58 472
60-64	18 418	13 608	34 648	510	67 185
65-69	1 522	194	56 438	77	58 231
70-74	486	0	39 299	45	39 829
75-79	0	0	27 964	0	27 964
80-84	0	0	13 707	0	13 707
85+	0	0	4 428	0	4 428
Total	**89 933**	**18 828**	**204 395**	**2 748**	**315 904**
Two Generation Households					
50-54	57 413	2 225	7 015	967	67 620
55-59	28 567	1 610	12 027	628	42 832
60-64	10 160	4 843	12 527	215	27 745
65-69	480	48	14 328	11	14 867
70-74	128	0	7 567	6	7 701
75-79	0	0	4 712	0	4 712
80-84	0	0	2 500	0	2 500
85+	0	0	1 118	0	1 118
Total	**96 748**	**8 727**	**61 793**	**1 827**	**169 095**
Three or More Generation Households					
50-54	1 872	95	312	58	2 337
55-59	1 475	78	808	47	2 408
60-64	772	288	1 437	23	2 520
65-69	67	2	2 177	2	2 246
70-74	40	0	1 837	2	1 879
75-79	0	0	1 674	0	1 674
80-84	0	0	1 086	2	1 064
85+	0	0	449	0	451
Total	**4 225**	**464**	**9 735**	**131**	**14 579**
Unknown					
50-54	298	115	213	172	798
55-59	172	72	250	80	573
60-64	47	153	162	20	382
65-69	2	0	197	7	206
70-74	0	0	71	0	71
75-79	0	0	53	0	53
80-84	0	0	26	0	26
85+	0	0	15	0	15
Total	**519**	**340**	**986**	**279**	**2 124**
Total Males	**215 742**	**36 995**	**347 978**	**6 852**	**607 566**

TABLE 4.3 (*concluded*)

	Economically active		Economically inactive		
	Employed	Unemployed	Pensioner	Other	Total
Females					
Solitaires					
50-54	17 152	712	3 537	610	22 010
55-59	15 522	1 270	9 900	1 018	27 710
60-64	8 482	8 783	19 862	1 935	39 062
65-69	751	171	49 024	119	50 064
70-74	277	0	51 578	37	51 891
75-79	0	0	53 459	0	53 459
80-84	0	0	39 895	0	39 895
85+	0	0	22 346	0	22 346
Total	**42 182**	**10 936**	**249 599**	**3 719**	**306 436**
One Generation Households					
50-54	40 243	1 968	6 403	3 025	51 640
55-59	33 052	3 355	19 588	4 248	60 243
60-64	14 523	15 207	33 933	3 300	66 963
65-69	818	246	56 444	142	57 649
70-74	208	0	37 020	35	37 264
75-79	0	0	23 675	0	23 675
80-84	0	0	11 772	0	11 772
85+	0	0	5 248	0	5 248
Total	**88 844**	**20 776**	**194 084**	**10 751**	**314 455**
Two Generation Households					
50-54	51 798	1 962	5 232	3 623	62 615
55-59	23 638	1 853	10 108	2 798	38 398
60-64	7 470	5 217	12 132	2 035	26 853
65-69	287	78	17 549	49	17 964
70-74	64	0	11 184	2	11 249
75-79	0	0	8 282	0	8 282
80-84	0	0	5 105	0	5 105
85+	0	0	2 645	0	2 645
Total	**83 257**	**9 109**	**72 237**	**8 508**	**173 112**
Three or More Generation Households					
50-54	2 040	85	348	163	2 637
55-59	1 438	102	1 115	217	2 872
60-64	698	478	1 843	312	3 332
65-69	47	12	3 941	8	4 008
70-74	18	0	3 692	4	3 713
75-79	0	0	3 601	0	3 601
80-84	0	0	2 071	0	2 071
85+	0	0	850	0	850
Total	**4 241**	**677**	**17 462**	**703**	**23 083**
Unknown					
50-54	62	5	53	50	170
55-59	40	10	55	32	137
60-64	20	12	55	20	107
65-69	1	0	57	4	61
70-74	0	0	40	4	44
75-79	0	0	35	0	35
80-84	0	0	42	0	42
85+	0	0	51	0	51
Total	**123**	**27**	**388**	**109**	**646**
Total Females	**218 648**	**41 524**	**533 770**	**23 790**	**817 732**

TABLE 5.1

**Dwelling size and number of rooms per person aged 50 and over
in Finland in 1990 by age, sex and marital status**

	Average dwelling size (per capita)	Average number of rooms (per capita)	Proportion of dwelling units with one room or less per person
Males			
Never married			
50-54	40.17	1.94	31.64
55-59	40.52	1.95	32.11
60-64	41.23	1.98	33.04
65-69	40.30	1.91	36.48
70-74	39.56	1.87	37.26
75-79	39.25	1.83	41.21
80-84	38.51	1.83	40.78
85+	36.82	1.76	44.48
Average	**40.34**	**1.93**	**33.82**
Married			
50-54	35.94	1.68	18.64
55-59	38.36	1.81	15.70
60-64	38.37	1.83	15.34
65-69	37.55	1.82	16.16
70-74	36.33	1.77	18.10
75-79	34.73	1.70	21.93
80-84	33.22	1.64	26.01
85+	32.23	1.58	30.26
Average	**36.99**	**1.77**	**17.54**
Widowed			
50-54	48.35	2.33	14.82
55-59	53.63	2.60	14.51
60-64	56.67	2.71	16.27
65-69	55.11	2.71	17.41
70-74	53.90	2.64	19.42
75-79	52.22	2.56	21.17
80-84	49.74	2.43	24.11
85+	46.37	2.26	28.33
Average	**52.23**	**2.55**	**20.45**
Divorced			
50-54	40.47	1.96	30.41
55-59	41.71	2.02	30.57
60-64	40.27	1.95	35.65
65-69	41.29	1.97	37.34
70-74	40.52	1.93	39.25
75-79	39.14	1.85	44.21
80-84	38.58	1.84	46.51
85+	35.24	1.68	51.65
Average	**40.74**	**1.96**	**33.61**
Separated			
50-54	34.88	1.71	32.33
55-59	40.94	1.98	28.12
60-64	40.13	1.92	31.69
65-69	39.47	1.93	30.79
70-74	41.10	1.95	35.43
75-79	42.57	2.07	29.49
80-84	41.75	2.17	20.83
85+	39.00	2.00	50.00
Average	**38.94**	**1.89**	**31.13**
Total Male Average	**38.78**	**1.86**	**20.73**

TABLE 5.1 (*concluded*)

		Average dwelling size (per capita)	Average number of rooms (per capita)	Proportion of dwelling units with one room or less per person
Females				
Never married				
50-54		42.70	2.07	27.34
55-59		43.65	2.11	26.15
60-64		44.52	2.14	27.04
65-69		43.74	2.09	29.70
70-74		42.25	2.01	33.75
75-79		40.20	1.90	38.89
80-84		39.07	1.84	41.50
85+		37.53	1.78	44.63
	Average	**42.30**	**2.02**	**32.00**
Married				
50-54		37.53	1.76	15.70
55-59		39.15	1.86	14.03
60-64		38.41	1.85	14.78
65-69		37.13	1.80	16.90
70-74		35.45	1.74	20.08
75-79		33.45	1.65	24.19
80-84		32.44	1.59	28.71
85+		31.08	1.54	34.08
	Average	**37.44**	**1.79**	**16.57**
Widowed				
50-54		50.32	2.44	13.45
55-59		53.28	2.62	13.78
60-64		54.42	2.68	15.04
65-69		53.48	2.62	17.59
70-74		50.99	2.49	21.65
75-79		47.45	2.30	27.00
80-84		44.49	2.15	31.76
85+		40.63	1.94	37.09
	Average	**49.30**	**2.40**	**23.39**
Divorced				
50-54		42.89	2.12	20.71
55-59		44.96	2.22	22.61
60-64		45.24	2.22	24.98
65-69		44.16	2.14	29.71
70-74		42.05	2.02	36.18
75-79		39.06	1.83	44.18
80-84		37.68	1.77	47.84
85+		35.03	1.63	51.13
	Average	**43.21**	**2.11**	**27.87**
Separated				
50-54		40.11	1.98	18.86
55-59		42.99	2.14	19.79
60-64		42.55	2.11	18.42
65-69		42.28	2.03	27.74
70-74		41.00	1.90	31.42
75-79		38.98	1.88	37.25
80-84		43.59	2.06	31.25
85+		34.13	1.50	50.00
	Average	**41.75**	**2.05**	**21.74**
Total Female Average		**42.20**	**2.04**	**21.41**

TABLE 5.2

**Dwelling size and number of rooms per person aged 50 and over
in Finland in 1990 by age, sex and number of generations present in the household**

	Average dwelling size (per capita)	Average number of rooms (per capita)	Proportion of dwelling units with one room or less per person
Males			
Solitaires			
50-54	51.85	2.50	27.30
55-59	51.90	2.49	27.53
60-64	51.72	2.47	29.39
65-69	52.16	2.51	29.07
70-74	53.79	2.59	26.69
75-79	54.08	2.62	25.52
80-84	52.83	2.57	25.90
85+	50.17	2.45	28.52
Total	**52.32**	**2.52**	**27.67**
One Generation Households			
50-54	41.81	1.98	12.54
55-59	42.32	2.02	10.77
60-64	40.73	1.96	11.30
65-69	39.12	1.90	12.46
70-74	37.50	1.84	14.32
75-79	35.43	1.75	18.75
80-84	33.64	1.67	23.07
85+	31.92	1.58	28.99
Total	**39.58**	**1.91**	**13.39**
Two Generation Households			
50-54	30.56	1.42	24.91
55-59	31.08	1.45	24.29
60-64	30.52	1.44	26.17
65-69	29.80	1.42	28.56
70-74	29.38	1.41	31.36
75-79	29.24	1.41	32.71
80-84	29.72	1.43	33.25
85+	30.94	1.50	31.30
Total	**30.52**	**1.43**	**25.96**
Three Generation Households			
50-54	22.39	1.00	63.26
55-59	22.12	1.00	67.23
60-64	21.24	0.95	72.58
65-69	20.81	0.93	74.60
70-74	20.87	0.94	72.08
75-79	21.42	0.96	71.10
80-84	22.42	0.99	66.82
85+	23.48	1.01	65.92
Total	**21.63**	**0.97**	**69.66**
Four and More Generation Households			
50-54	19.24	0.79	80.07
55-59	19.40	0.81	100.00
60-64	16.60	0.75	100.00
65-69	0.00	0.00	0.00
70-74	13.67	0.58	100.00
75-79	23.29	0.93	50.21
80-84	0.00	0.00	0.00
85+	20.92	0.92	100.00
Total	**18.64**	**0.79**	**93.90**
Unknown			
50-54	14.54	0.76	50.15
55-59	16.60	1.00	100.00
60-64	64.00	2.50	0.00
65-69	46.77	2.03	20.07
70-74	28.33	1.67	0.00
75-79	60.00	2.00	0.00
80-84	28.63	1.14	50.00
85+	0.00	0.00	0.00
Total	**35.61**	**1.60**	**28.62**
Total Male Average	**38.78**	**1.86**	**20.73**

TABLE 5.2 (*concluded*)

	Average dwelling size (per capita)	Average number of rooms (per capita)	Proportion of dwelling units with one room or less per person
Females			
Solitaires			
50-54	56.01	2.73	18.77
55-59	57.02	2.79	18.03
60-64	57.36	2.80	18.20
65-69	56.00	2.73	19.96
70-74	53.54	2.60	23.61
75-79	49.82	2.40	29.17
80-84	46.67	2.24	34.24
85+	43.14	2.05	39.75
Total	**52.68**	**2.56**	**24.90**
One Generation Households			
50-54	43.07	2.04	9.48
55-59	42.46	2.03	9.21
60-64	40.22	1.95	10.71
65-69	38.25	1.87	13.65
70-74	35.92	1.77	17.88
75-79	33.39	1.65	23.64
80-84	31.88	1.56	29.58
85+	29.52	1.45	36.69
Total	**39.25**	**1.90**	**13.69**
Two Generation Households			
50-54	31.78	1.49	21.29
55-59	32.02	1.52	21.81
60-64	31.63	1.52	24.55
65-69	31.73	1.54	26.66
70-74	31.94	1.56	26.88
75-79	32.19	1.58	27.01
80-84	32.79	1.59	27.04
85+	32.14	1.55	30.32
Total	**31.87**	**1.52**	**23.41**
Three Generation Households			
50-54	22.33	1.01	64.38
55-59	21.56	0.97	69.66
60-64	20.89	0.96	71.19
65-69	21.82	0.99	67.61
70-74	22.14	1.00	66.41
75-79	23.01	1.03	61.95
80-84	24.07	1.07	57.80
85+	25.01	1.12	51.38
Total	**22.27**	**1.01**	**65.46**
Four and More Generation Households			
50-54	24.51	0.95	75.00
55-59	17.21	0.75	100.00
60-64	19.01	0.84	100.00
65-69	11.94	0.61	100.00
70-74	17.93	0.65	100.00
75-79	19.20	0.76	80.10
80-84	19.65	0.84	92.86
85+	19.63	0.83	92.31
Total	**19.68**	**0.81**	**91.07**
Unknown			
50-54	36.00	1.67	0.00
55-59	18.29	0.96	50.15
60-64	34.92	1.38	50.15
65-69	46.83	1.79	25.05
70-74	30.75	1.50	50.21
75-79	26.50	1.18	33.43
80-84	21.71	0.86	100.00
85+	36.93	1.68	50.00
Total	**32.81**	**1.41**	**40.42**
Total Female Average	**42.20**	**2.04**	**21.41**

TABLE 5.3

Household amenities of persons aged 50 and over in Finland in 1990 by age, sex and marital status

	Toilet			Bath			Water Supply			Hot Water		
	Yes	No	Missing	Yes	No	Missing	Yes	No	Missing	Yes	No	Missing
Males												
Never married												
50-54	12 213	4 503	298	9 422	7 297	297	13 755	2 955	305	11 240	5 478	297
55-59	9 703	4 387	267	7 440	6 652	265	11 172	2 918	267	8 985	5 107	265
60-64	8 763	4 160	207	6 660	6 265	205	10 035	2 883	212	8 038	4 887	205
65-69	5 562	2 459	118	4 387	3 634	118	6 293	1 724	122	5 125	2 897	118
70-74	2 832	1 112	59	2 261	1 682	59	3 174	767	61	2 646	1 298	59
75-79	1 925	732	35	1 521	1 135	35	2 147	509	35	1 785	872	35
80-84	1 052	436	17	840	649	16	1 191	298	16	984	505	16
85+	471	149	14	368	252	14	510	110	14	444	176	14
Total	**42 522**	**17 937**	**1 014**	**32 899**	**27 566**	**1 008**	**48 277**	**12 165**	**1 032**	**39 247**	**21 219**	**1 008**
Married												
50-54	95 285	3 575	412	84 570	14 292	410	96 887	1 912	473	92 837	6 025	410
55-59	86 693	4 735	325	74 590	16 838	325	88 732	2 655	367	84 015	7 413	325
60-64	81 927	6 053	270	67 962	20 020	268	84 505	3 420	325	78 745	9 237	268
65-69	64 405	5 332	164	52 520	17 218	162	66 546	3 165	189	61 344	8 394	162
70-74	42 164	3 791	80	33 724	12 232	79	43 569	2 371	94	40 020	5 935	79
75-79	28 577	2 904	61	22 389	9 091	61	29 724	1 747	71	26 813	4 667	61
80-84	13 562	1 572	48	10 538	4 596	48	14 135	997	50	12 650	2 484	48
85+	4 037	509	18	3 119	1 427	18	4 204	342	18	3 736	810	18
Total	**416 649**	**28 470**	**1 377**	**349 412**	**95 713**	**1 372**	**428 301**	**16 608**	**1 587**	**400 159**	**44 966**	**1 372**
Widowed												
50-54	1 685	145	18	1 463	367	18	1 748	82	18	1 622	208	18
55-59	2 668	275	28	2 262	685	25	2 778	168	25	2 557	390	25
60-64	4 208	567	48	3 468	1 307	48	4 400	370	53	4 003	772	48
65-69	5 773	773	37	4 682	1 864	37	6 078	464	41	5 455	1 091	37
70-74	6 567	848	29	5 200	2 215	29	6 873	540	32	6 157	1 259	29
75-79	8 001	1 077	47	6 267	2 811	47	8 424	653	48	7 488	1 589	47
80-84	6 844	1 039	50	5 295	2 588	50	7 213	668	52	6 360	1 523	50
85+	4 453	758	63	3 422	1 790	62	4 769	442	63	4 121	1 091	62
Total	**40 200**	**5 481**	**321**	**32 060**	**13 626**	**317**	**42 283**	**3 387**	**333**	**37 763**	**7 923**	**317**
Divorced												
50-54	14 465	1 833	500	12 297	4 002	500	15 130	1 147	522	13 710	2 588	500
55-59	10 822	1 535	328	8 950	3 407	328	11 285	1 050	350	10 163	2 193	328
60-64	8 217	1 375	213	6 792	2 800	213	8 672	903	230	7 727	1 865	213
65-69	4 987	774	118	4 177	1 586	117	5 249	511	119	4 748	1 014	117
70-74	2 493	402	41	2 054	841	41	2 613	281	42	2 385	511	41
75-79	1 505	257	25	1 232	531	24	1 597	164	26	1 432	331	24
80-84	626	96	13	501	221	13	649	73	13	577	145	13
85+	221	41	1	180	82	1	234	28	1	207	55	1
Total	**43 335**	**6 313**	**1 239**	**36 182**	**13 469**	**1 237**	**45 429**	**4 156**	**1 303**	**40 949**	**8 702**	**1 237**
Separated												
50-54	673	63	17	580	157	17	698	38	17	642	95	17
55-59	540	42	10	465	117	10	555	25	12	513	68	10
60-64	577	73	12	500	150	12	610	40	12	567	83	12
65-69	325	35	6	275	85	6	334	26	6	308	52	6
70-74	188	18	1	167	39	1	191	15	1	177	29	1
75-79	88	5	1	74	19	1	88	5	1	85	8	1
80-84	23	2	0	21	4	0	24	1	0	23	2	0
85+	8	0	0	7	1	0	8	0	0	8	0	0
Total	**2 422**	**238**	**47**	**2 090**	**571**	**47**	**2 508**	**150**	**48**	**2 322**	**338**	**47**
Total Males	**545 128**	**58 440**	**3 999**	**452 642**	**150 945**	**3 980**	**566 798**	**36 466**	**4 303**	**520 439**	**83 147**	**3 980**

TABLE 5.3 (*concluded*)

	Toilet			Bath			Water Supply			Hot Water		
	Yes	No	Missing	Yes	No	Missing	Yes	No	Missing	Yes	No	Missing
Females												
Never married												
50-54	11 782	972	80	10 682	2 073	78	12 173	580	80	11 487	1 268	78
55-59	11 157	1 092	83	9 993	2 255	83	11 578	663	90	10 855	1 393	83
60-64	12 383	1 345	57	11 210	2 518	57	12 877	840	68	12 048	1 680	57
65-69	12 675	1 373	55	11 247	2 801	55	13 128	917	59	12 237	1 812	55
70-74	10 377	1 249	55	9 179	2 447	55	10 797	827	58	9 982	1 644	55
75-79	779	1 198	65	8 689	2 287	65	10 247	728	66	9 460	1 517	65
80-84	7 350	932	53	6 430	1 852	53	7 744	538	53	7 103	1 179	53
85+	4 431	686	81	3 803	1 315	80	4 795	323	80	4 298	820	80
Total	**79 933**	**8 846**	**529**	**71 233**	**17 549**	**527**	**83 339**	**5 416**	**554**	**77 470**	**11 312**	**527**
Married												
50-54	92 785	3 915	322	81 342	15 360	320	94 542	2 100	380	90 253	6 448	320
55-59	80 582	4 498	237	68 438	16 642	237	82 587	2 447	283	77 877	7 203	237
60-64	75 502	5 400	203	62 112	18 790	203	77 730	3 142	233	72 488	8 413	203
65-69	58 133	4 972	111	46 946	16 160	109	60 078	3 013	125	55 206	7 900	109
70-74	34 397	3 179	71	27 288	10 288	69	35 607	1 959	80	32 441	5 135	69
75-79	19 185	2 000	54	14 897	6 288	54	19 940	1 235	64	17 937	3 248	54
80-84	7 409	844	31	5 706	2 547	31	7 697	555	32	6 894	1 359	31
85+	1 533	206	8	1 180	559	8	1 623	116	8	1 406	333	8
Total	**369 525**	**25 014**	**1 036**	**307 908**	**86 634**	**1 032**	**379 803**	**14 566**	**1 205**	**354 502**	**40 041**	**1 032**
Widowed												
50-54	8 823	538	42	7 782	1 580	42	9 062	297	45	8 520	842	42
55-59	14 465	1 195	53	12 562	3 100	52	14 903	748	62	13 938	1 723	52
60-64	25 342	2 220	98	21 642	5 920	98	26 175	1 378	107	24 308	3 253	98
65-69	37 735	3 771	113	31 904	9 604	112	39 126	2 375	118	35 995	5 512	112
70-74	42 724	4 604	115	35 869	11 458	115	44 422	2 899	121	40 558	6 769	115
75-79	45 880	5 172	209	38 207	12 845	209	47 819	3 218	225	43 448	7 604	209
80-84	34 610	4 276	258	28 687	10 200	257	36 383	2 494	267	32 736	6 151	257
85+	19 470	3 057	274	15 898	6 629	274	20 936	1 589	276	18 430	4 097	274
Total	**229 049**	**24 832**	**1 163**	**192 550**	**61 335**	**1 159**	**238 826**	**14 998**	**1 220**	**217 934**	**35 951**	**1 159**
Divorced												
50-54	18 323	680	130	16 927	2 077	130	18 570	432	132	17 903	1 100	130
55-59	14 568	697	80	13 357	1 908	80	14 798	453	93	14 170	1 095	80
60-64	12 550	650	57	11 462	1 738	57	12 782	412	63	12 178	1 022	57
65-69	9 828	598	38	8 889	1 537	38	10 021	402	40	9 573	853	38
70-74	6 738	457	31	6 060	1 134	31	6 902	288	34	6 531	664	31
75-79	5 053	377	19	4 486	944	19	5 193	229	26	4 914	515	19
80-84	2 845	242	18	2 503	584	18	2 979	106	20	2 757	330	18
85+	1 210	154	25	1 028	336	25	1 312	52	25	1 168	196	25
Total	**71 116**	**3 853**	**397**	**64 711**	**10 258**	**397**	**72 558**	**2 375**	**433**	**69 194**	**5 774**	**397**
Separated												
50-54	638	38	3	583	93	3	653	23	3	632	45	3
55-59	615	32	7	563	83	7	623	22	8	600	47	7
60-64	478	30	2	433	75	2	492	17	2	463	45	2
65-69	322	22	0	289	55	0	325	20	0	309	35	0
70-74	158	7	1	140	25	1	160	5	1	154	11	1
75-79	58	6	0	49	14	0	61	1	1	54	9	0
80-84	15	2	0	14	3	0	16	1	0	15	2	0
85+	4	1	0	4	1	0	5	0	0	4	1	0
Total	**2 288**	**138**	**13**	**2 077**	**350**	**13**	**2 335**	**89**	**16**	**2 232**	**195**	**13**
Total Females	**751 910**	**62 684**	**3 138**	**638 480**	**176 125**	**3 127**	**776 861**	**37 444**	**3 428**	**721 332**	**93 273**	**3 127**

TABLE 5.4

**Household amenities of persons aged 50 and over in Finland
in 1990 by age, sex and number of generations present in the household**

	Toilet			Bath			Water Supply			Hot Water		
	Yes	No	Missing	Yes	No	Missing	Yes	No	Missing	Yes	No	Missing
Males												
Solitaires												
50-54	14 968	3 717	158	12 185	6 502	157	16 212	2 455	177	13 985	4 702	157
55-59	13 947	3 965	162	11 263	6 650	160	15 153	2 747	173	13 052	4 862	160
60-64	14 503	4 203	132	11 730	6 978	130	15 777	2 908	153	13 643	5 065	130
65-69	12 351	2 874	92	10 201	5 024	92	13 227	1 986	104	11 646	3 579	92
70-74	9 331	1 753	61	7 658	3 426	61	9 849	1 229	66	8 820	2 264	61
75-79	9 254	1 527	54	7 441	3 340	54	9 781	998	57	8 715	2 066	54
80-84	6 870	1 166	47	5 434	2 602	47	7 232	803	48	6 414	1 622	47
85+	4 047	647	37	3 143	1 551	37	4 265	428	38	3 745	949	37
Total	**85 271**	**19 852**	**743**	**69 055**	**36 072**	**738**	**91 496**	**13 554**	**815**	**80 020**	**25 108**	**738**
One Generation Households												
50-54	42 925	3 027	137	37 607	8 345	137	43 990	1 918	180	41 543	4 408	137
55-59	54 443	3 905	123	46 738	11 612	122	55 883	2 428	160	52 707	5 643	122
60-64	61 915	5 080	190	51 582	15 413	190	63 757	3 188	240	59 408	7 587	190
65-69	53 628	4 482	120	44 039	14 074	118	55 277	2 812	142	51 150	6 964	118
70-74	36 687	3 071	72	29 575	10 182	72	37 765	1 979	86	34 866	4 892	72
75-79	25 467	2 445	52	20 082	7 831	51	26 378	1 524	62	23 932	3 981	51
80-84	12 305	1 350	52	9 608	4 048	51	12 770	885	52	11 473	2 183	51
85+	3 890	496	42	3 046	1 341	41	4 079	308	41	3 618	769	41
Total	**291 261**	**23 855**	**788**	**242 277**	**72 846**	**780**	**299 898**	**15 042**	**964**	**278 696**	**36 427**	**780**
Two Generation Households												
50-54	64 292	3 182	147	56 800	10 675	145	65 772	1 677	172	62 485	4 990	145
55-59	39 852	2 887	93	33 893	8 845	93	41 178	1 545	108	38 353	4 385	93
60-64	24 975	2 727	43	20 220	7 483	42	26 257	1 435	53	23 822	3 882	42
65-69	13 022	1 820	25	10 204	4 639	25	13 832	1 008	27	12 237	2 606	25
70-74	6 524	1 171	7	4 901	2 793	7	7 000	693	8	6 077	1 618	7
75-79	3 857	847	8	2 781	1 922	8	4 205	499	8	3 531	1 173	8
80-84	1 969	528	3	1 393	1 104	3	2 188	307	5	1 782	715	3
85+	842	274	2	586	530	2	947	169	2	760	356	2
Total	**155 332**	**13 435**	**328**	**130 778**	**37 992**	**325**	**161 378**	**7 333**	**384**	**149 046**	**19 724**	**325**
Three Generation Households												
50-54	2 125	195	8	1 730	590	8	2 233	83	12	2 027	293	8
55-59	2 163	217	8	1 790	592	7	2 285	97	7	2 100	282	7
60-64	2 287	217	3	1 842	662	3	2 418	85	3	2 195	308	3
65-69	2 045	197	5	1 592	649	5	2 159	82	5	1 942	299	5
70-74	1 698	175	4	1 267	607	2	1 801	72	4	1 617	258	2
75-79	1 515	153	4	1 177	492	4	1 612	58	2	1 422	246	4
80-84	962	100	2	759	303	2	1 021	41	2	924	138	2
85+	409	40	0	319	130	0	432	17	0	391	58	0
Total	**13 204**	**1 293**	**34**	**10 475**	**4 025**	**31**	**13 961**	**535**	**34**	**12 618**	**1 882**	**31**
Four and More Generation Households												
50-54	8	0	0	7	2	0	8	0	0	7	2	0
55-59	20	0	0	20	0	0	20	0	0	20	0	0
60-64	10	2	2	7	5	2	12	0	2	10	2	2
65-69	0	0	0	0	0	0	0	0	0	0	0	0
70-74	2	0	0	2	0	0	2	0	0	2	0	0
75-79	1	1	0	1	1	0	2	0	0	1	1	0
80-84	0	0	0	0	0	0	0	0	0	0	0	0
85+	2	0	0	2	0	0	2	0	0	2	0	0
Total	**44**	**3**	**2**	**39**	**8**	**2**	**47**	**0**	**2**	**42**	**5**	**2**
Unknown												
50-54	3	0	795	3	0	795	3	0	795	3	0	795
55-59	2	0	572	2	0	572	2	0	572	2	0	572
60-64	2	0	380	2	0	380	2	0	380	2	0	380
65-69	6	0	200	6	0	200	6	0	200	6	0	200
70-74	2	1	67	2	1	67	2	1	67	2	1	67
75-79	1	0	52	1	0	52	1	0	52	1	0	52
80-84	1	1	24	1	1	24	1	1	24	1	1	24
85+	0	0	15	0	0	15	0	0	15	0	0	15
Total	**17**	**2**	**2 105**	**17**	**2**	**2 105**	**17**	**2**	**2 105**	**17**	**2**	**2 105**
Total Males	**545 128**	**58 440**	**3 999**	**452 642**	**150 945**	**3 980**	**566 798**	**36 466**	**4 303**	**520 439**	**83 147**	**3 980**

TABLE 5.4 (concluded)

	Toilet			Bath			Water Supply			Hot Water		
	Yes	No	Missing	Yes	No	Missing	Yes	No	Missing	Yes	No	Missing
Females												
Solitaires												
50-54	21 120	767	123	19 667	2 222	122	21 418	467	125	20 713	1 175	122
55-59	26 252	1 357	102	24 083	3 527	100	26 728	862	120	25 688	1 922	100
60-64	36 698	2 247	117	33 083	5 862	117	37 498	1 427	137	35 680	3 265	117
65-69	46 632	3 280	152	41 189	8 724	151	47 777	2 129	158	45 054	4 859	151
70-74	47 827	3 913	151	41 745	9 995	151	49 169	2 561	160	45 940	5 800	151
75-79	48 789	4 440	229	42 099	11 131	229	50 458	2 754	247	46 782	6 447	229
80-84	35 790	3 859	246	30 496	9 154	245	37 435	2 206	254	34 290	5 360	245
85+	19 354	2 751	241	16 173	5 933	240	20 807	1 298	241	18 538	3 568	240
Total	**282 462**	**22 613**	**1 360**	**248 535**	**56 546**	**1 354**	**291 291**	**13 704**	**1 441**	**272 686**	**32 396**	**1 354**
One Generation Households												
50-54	49 128	2 367	145	43 043	8 453	143	50 002	1 448	190	47 730	3 767	143
55-59	56 882	3 208	153	48 753	11 337	153	58 112	1 937	195	55 018	3 072	153
60-64	62 630	4 178	155	52 168	14 640	155	64 220	2 560	183	60 217	6 592	155
65-69	53 197	4 372	81	43 448	14 120	81	54 766	2 785	99	50 618	6 951	81
70-74	34 079	3 122	62	27 313	9 889	61	35 173	2 018	73	32 151	5 052	61
75-79	21 262	2 341	72	16 734	6 869	72	22 111	1 484	81	19 897	3 707	72
80-84	10 475	1 239	58	8 269	3 445	58	10 942	770	60	9 737	1 977	58
85+	4 478	677	93	3 594	1 561	93	4 802	353	93	4 189	966	93
Total	**292 131**	**21 505**	**820**	**243 323**	**70 315**	**817**	**300 127**	**13 354**	**974**	**279 557**	**32 084**	**816**
Two Generation Households												
50-54	59 648	2 837	130	52 585	9 900	130	61 025	1 443	147	57 995	4 490	130
55-59	35 622	2 717	60	29 917	8 422	60	36 872	1 452	75	34 195	4 143	60
60-64	23 867	2 952	35	19 198	7 620	35	25 143	1 667	43	22 648	4 170	35
65-69	15 257	2 687	20	11 779	6 165	20	16 313	1 628	22	14 257	3 687	20
70-74	9 137	2 101	12	6 861	4 377	12	9 991	1 246	13	8 377	2 861	12
75-79	6 635	1 637	11	4 906	3 366	11	7 251	1 017	15	6 039	2 233	11
80-84	4 067	1 024	14	3 040	2 051	14	4 443	647	15	3 690	1 401	14
85+	2 040	601	4	1 509	1 132	4	2 252	388	5	1 838	803	4
Total	**156 272**	**16 555**	**285**	**129 795**	**43 032**	**285**	**163 289**	**9 487**	**336**	**149 038**	**23 789**	**285**
Three Generation Households												
50-54	2 433	173	10	2 003	603	10	2 533	73	10	2 337	270	10
55-59	2 607	227	13	2 137	697	13	2 748	83	15	2 513	320	13
60-64	3 052	267	5	2 400	918	5	3 183	135	5	2 933	385	5
65-69	3 604	395	7	2 853	1 147	6	3 815	185	6	3 386	614	6
70-74	3 342	359	7	2 612	1 089	7	3 548	153	7	3 192	509	7
75-79	3 258	334	4	2 582	1 009	4	3 432	158	6	3 086	506	4
80-84	1 883	173	1	1 523	533	1	1 984	71	2	1 775	281	1
85+	763	73	0	625	211	0	795	41	0	728	108	0
Total	**20 941**	**2 001**	**47**	**16 735**	**6 208**	**46**	**22 039**	**899**	**51**	**19 950**	**2 993**	**46**
Four and More Generation Households												
50-54	20	0	0	15	5	0	20	0	0	18	2	0
55-59	22	3	0	20	5	0	25	0	0	22	3	0
60-64	5	2	2	5	2	2	7	0	2	5	2	2
65-69	1	1	0	1	1	0	2	0	0	1	1	0
70-74	5	0	0	4	1	0	5	0	0	5	0	0
75-79	6	0	0	5	1	0	6	0	0	6	0	0
80-84	13	1	0	11	3	0	14	0	0	12	2	0
85+	11	2	1	10	3	1	13	0	1	11	2	1
Total	**82**	**9**	**3**	**70**	**21**	**3**	**92**	**0**	**3**	**80**	**12**	**3**
Unknown												
50-54	2	0	168	2	0	168	2	0	168	2	0	168
55-59	3	2	132	3	2	132	5	0	132	3	2	132
60-64	3	0	103	3	0	103	3	0	103	3	0	103
65-69	5	0	57	5	0	57	5	0	57	5	0	57
70-74	2	0	41	2	0	41	2	0	41	2	0	41
75-79	4	0	32	2	1	32	4	0	32	4	0	32
80-84	1	0	41	1	0	41	1	0	41	1	0	41
85+	2	0	49	2	0	49	2	0	49	2	0	49
Total	**22**	**2**	**623**	**21**	**3**	**623**	**24**	**0**	**623**	**22**	**2**	**623**
Total Females	**751 910**	**62 684**	**3 138**	**638 480**	**176 125**	**3 127**	**776 861**	**37 444**	**3 428**	**721 332**	**93 273**	**3 127**

TABLE 6.1

Number and type of income sources of persons aged 50 and over living in single-person households in Finland in 1990 by age, sex and marital status

| | | | Single source | | | | Multiple sources | | | | |
		No income	Labour	Entrep.	Pension	Other	Labour and pension	Other two	Three or more	Unknown sources	Total
Males											
Never married											
50-54		130	2 660	330	1 603	77	427	2 337	905	272	8 740
55-59		135	1 648	310	2 273	50	420	2 175	987	202	8 200
60-64		67	470	292	3 947	13	385	1 972	1 017	32	8 193
65-69		16	4	6	3 145	0	158	1 339	759	4	5 429
70-74		4	0	0	1 679	0	48	704	296	0	2 731
75-79		4	0	0	1 201	0	18	481	155	1	1 860
80-84		4	0	0	669	0	7	302	77	0	1 059
85+		0	0	0	293	0	3	106	28	0	430
	Total	**359**	**4 782**	**938**	**14 810**	**140**	**1 466**	**9 416**	**4 224**	**510**	**36 642**
Married											
50-54		63	422	83	135	10	83	443	287	42	1 568
55-59		35	262	65	247	13	95	403	268	23	1 412
60-64		10	82	22	497	8	118	353	313	13	1 417
65-69		16	2	2	545	2	59	251	254	2	1 134
70-74		1	0	1	386	2	21	199	122	2	735
75-79		6	1	0	427	0	16	178	92	1	721
80-84		3	0	0	285	1	11	143	41	0	484
85+		1	0	0	127	0	2	46	15	0	191
	Total	**136**	**769**	**174**	**2 648**	**37**	**405**	**2 016**	**1 393**	**84**	**7 662**
Widowed											
50-54		3	192	25	97	0	82	180	125	8	712
55-59		13	275	37	377	2	130	382	312	12	1 538
60-64		5	122	45	1 197	0	277	803	612	13	3 073
65-69		5	2	2	2 351	0	305	1 174	814	2	4 655
70-74		1	0	0	3 059	0	179	1 501	761	0	5 501
75-79		6	0	4	4 169	0	132	1 828	761	1	6 901
80-84		6	0	1	3 757	0	96	1 602	513	1	5 976
85+		8	0	1	2 671	0	41	938	251	0	3 910
	Total	**47**	**591**	**115**	**17 677**	**2**	**1 242**	**8 408**	**4 149**	**38**	**32 267**
Divorced											
50-54		150	3 010	278	1 160	45	557	1 853	737	393	8 183
55-59		102	1 740	180	2 070	32	518	1 517	723	218	7 100
60-64		28	380	97	3 423	5	500	1 078	612	13	6 137
65-69		12	6	0	2 772	0	218	680	382	2	4 072
70-74		8	1	0	1 473	2	62	424	140	0	2 111
75-79		4	0	1	1 005	0	24	244	66	1	1 344
80-84		1	0	0	451	0	4	85	21	0	562
85+		0	0	0	156	0	0	34	13	0	203
	Total	**305**	**5 137**	**556**	**12 510**	**84**	**1 883**	**5 915**	**2 694**	**629**	**29 711**
Separated											
50-54		3	80	12	45	0	20	47	27	13	247
55-59		7	65	7	77	0	15	52	23	8	253
60-64		2	22	2	137	0	20	57	37	5	280
65-69		0	0	0	92	0	14	41	7	0	154
70-74		0	0	0	76	0	8	19	8	0	112
75-79		0	0	0	35	0	2	9	2	0	49
80-84		0	0	0	9	0	0	3	1	0	13
85+		0	0	0	4	0	0	2	0	0	6
	Total	**12**	**167**	**20**	**475**	**0**	**79**	**230**	**105**	**27**	**1 114**
Total Males		**859**	**11 445**	**1 802**	**48 119**	**263**	**5 074**	**25 983**	**12 565**	**1 287**	**107 397**

TABLE 6.1 (*concluded*)

		Single source				Multiple sources				
	No income	Labour	Entrep.	Pension	Other	Labour and pension	Other two	Three or more	Unknown sources	Total
Females										
Never married										
50-54	53	2 883	93	997	48	347	2 658	770	87	7 937
55-59	45	2 050	95	1 632	75	470	2 623	1 123	97	8 210
60-64	50	767	87	3 923	27	812	2 620	1 530	33	9 848
65-69	15	12	7	5 839	0	555	2 800	1 281	4	10 513
70-74	7	0	2	5 600	0	222	2 375	715	1	8 924
75-79	6	0	1	6 145	0	105	1 888	375	2	8 522
80-84	7	0	0	4 937	1	50	1 268	198	0	6 461
85+	12	0	1	3 207	2	22	672	74	1	3 991
Total	196	5 712	287	32 279	153	2 583	16 904	6 067	225	64 406
Married										
50-54	33	450	35	95	12	45	403	123	18	1 215
55-59	43	323	20	252	22	58	395	185	22	1 320
60-64	35	92	38	557	12	115	282	168	5	1 303
65-69	14	1	4	621	0	46	209	105	2	1 002
70-74	7	0	2	518	0	31	171	49	2	780
75-79	2	0	0	465	0	21	122	25	1	636
80-84	3	0	0	288	0	1	62	9	0	363
85+	1	0	0	104	0	2	17	6	0	130
Total	139	866	99	2 899	45	319	1 661	670	51	6 750
Widowed										
50-54	5	152	12	547	5	1 405	392	1 337	2	3 855
55-59	38	235	20	2 222	13	2 400	1 163	2 670	17	8 778
60-64	113	128	43	8 650	18	2 502	3 782	3 228	17	18 482
65-69	20	6	2	18 785	1	1 440	7 055	3 024	15	30 348
70-74	26	0	5	25 002	1	864	8 094	2 285	9	36 286
75-79	16	0	1	29 884	0	502	7 704	1 607	5	39 719
80-84	23	1	2	24 105	1	167	5 264	909	5	30 477
85+	40	1	0	14 053	3	57	2 589	390	3	17 136
Total	282	523	85	123 247	43	9 337	36 043	15 449	72	185 081
Divorced										
50-54	55	3 743	182	982	38	498	2 505	745	185	8 933
55-59	32	2 750	122	2 127	52	752	2 385	892	152	9 262
60-64	17	822	63	4 545	20	987	1 817	990	40	9 300
65-69	13	11	0	5 382	2	529	1 440	691	1	8 069
70-74	7	0	0	4 381	0	166	1 011	272	6	5 842
75-79	2	0	0	3 726	0	65	654	122	2	4 572
80-84	2	0	0	2 218	0	21	315	54	4	2 614
85+	2	0	0	957	1	6	136	17	1	1 120
Total	130	7 326	367	24 318	113	3 024	10 263	3 782	391	49 713
Separated										
50-54	2	88	2	12	2	13	55	12	5	190
55-59	0	77	2	38	2	20	60	32	5	235
60-64	0	30	2	82	0	23	38	23	3	202
65-69	0	0	0	125	0	6	28	11	1	171
70-74	0	0	0	65	0	5	15	4	0	88
75-79	0	0	0	24	0	0	7	2	0	33
80-84	0	0	0	8	0	0	2	0	0	10
85+	0	0	0	3	0	0	0	0	0	3
Total	2	195	5	356	3	67	205	83	15	931
Total Females	748	14 621	843	183 098	358	15 329	65 077	26 052	754	306 881

TABLE 6.2

Number and type of income sources of persons aged 50 and over living in two- or three-person households in Finland in 1990 by age, sex, marital status and number of household income recipients

	No income	Single source				Multiple sources			Unknown sources	Total
		Labour	Entrep.	Pension	Other	Labour and pension	Other two	Three or more		
Males										
Never married										
50-54										
No Recipient	10	0	0	0	0	0	0	0	0	10
One Recipient	127	42	15	20	2	2	28	7	5	248
Two Recipients	30	1 750	293	983	47	287	1 467	618	182	5 657
Three or More	0	342	83	293	7	67	447	185	65	1 489
55-59										
No Recipient	18	0	0	0	0	0	0	0	0	18
One Recipient	115	28	2	23	2	5	22	10	7	214
Two Recipients	22	832	240	1 187	42	238	1 172	548	135	4 416
Three or More	0	172	72	210	7	30	258	127	17	893
60-64										
No Recipient	8	0	0	0	0	0	0	0	0	8
One Recipient	65	8	2	47	2	5	22	7	0	158
Two Recipients	15	205	225	1 568	17	142	1 027	567	15	3 781
Three or More	0	30	42	248	3	13	147	77	5	565
65-69										
No Recipient	1	0	0	0	0	0	0	0	0	1
One Recipient	4	0	2	32	0	5	14	5	0	62
Two Recipients	1	2	12	1 096	0	55	614	395	1	2 176
Three or More	0	2	0	135	0	6	67	40	0	250
70-74										
No Recipient	0	0	0	0	0	0	0	0	0	0
One Recipient	1	0	0	7	0	1	4	2	0	15
Two Recipients	0	0	0	494	0	13	348	189	1	1 045
Three or More	0	0	0	58	0	2	27	8	0	95
75-79										
No Recipient	0	0	0	0	0	0	0	0	0	0
One Recipient	0	0	0	0	0	2	1	1	0	4
Two Recipients	0	0	0	355	0	0	104	104	1	564
Three or More	0	0	0	42	0	2	4	4	0	52
80-84										
No Recipient	0	0	0	0	0	0	0	0	0	0
One Recipient	2	0	0	2	0	0	0	0	0	4
Two Recipients	0	0	0	201	0	2	139	40	0	382
Three or More	0	0	0	13	0	1	7	3	0	24
85+										
No Recipient	0	0	0	0	0	0	0	0	0	0
One Recipient	3	0	0	0	0	0	1	0	0	4
Two Recipients	0	0	0	101	0	1	51	10	0	163
Three or More	0	0	0	10	0	0	3	0	0	13
Total	**422**	**3 413**	**988**	**7 125**	**129**	**879**	**5 974**	**2 947**	**434**	**22 311**
Married										
50-54										
No Recipient	80	0	0	0	0	0	0	0	0	80
One Recipient	203	345	78	48	5	33	273	112	17	1 114
Two Recipients	95	11 208	1 553	2 182	272	2 032	14 305	8 975	488	41 110
Three or More	0	6 592	1 065	1 007	140	1 137	9 762	7 377	225	27 305
55-59										
No Recipient	52	0	0	0	0	0	0	0	0	52
One Recipient	178	325	67	148	2	82	342	195	27	1 366
Two Recipients	43	8 653	1 473	6 732	307	3 458	16 480	14 180	430	51 756
Three or More	0	3 500	868	2 205	97	1 228	7 237	7 228	180	22 543
60-64										
No Recipient	37	0	0	0	0	0	0	0	0	37
One Recipient	92	155	60	368	3	93	375	235	13	1 394
Two Recipients	27	2 848	1 010	16 340	75	4 745	16 925	17 958	90	60 018
Three or More	0	863	463	3 803	28	1 232	4 818	5 628	33	16 868
65-69										
No Recipient	32	0	0	0	0	0	0	0	0	32
One Recipient	21	4	8	300	0	55	191	139	1	719
Two Recipients	2	31	33	19 853	4	3 426	15 318	14 811	19	53 497
Three or More	0	7	9	3 321	0	569	2 754	3 173	0	9 833
70-74										
No Recipient	15	0	0	0	0	0	0	0	0	15
One Recipient	13	1	6	86	0	7	60	34	0	207
Two Recipients	0	1	5	15 800	2	1 693	11 269	8 602	20	37 392
Three or More	0	0	0	1 960	0	201	1 578	1 253	1	4 993

TABLE 6.2 (*continued*)

	No income	Single source				Multiple sources			Unknown sources	Total
		Labour	Entrep.	Pension	Other	Labour and pension	Other two	Three or more		
75-79										
No Recipient	7	0	0	0	0	0	0	0	0	7
One Recipient	7	0	0	29	0	2	26	12	1	77
Two Recipients	0	0	2	12 713	0	801	8 124	4 544	6	26 190
Three or More	0	0	0	1 316	0	61	9 041	528	0	10 946
80-84										
No Recipient	3	0	0	0	0	0		0	0	3
One Recipient	4	0	0	10	0	0	8	1	0	23
Two Recipients	0	0	0	6 850	1	246	3 832	1 637	1	12 567
Three or More	0	0	0	625	0	16	402	194	0	1 237
85+										
No Recipient	3	0	0	0	0	0	0	0	0	3
One Recipient	1	0	0	3	0	0	3	4	0	11
Two Recipients	0	0	0	2 135	0	48	1 150	360	1	3 694
Three or More	0	0	0	230	0	2	130	35	0	397
Total	**915**	**34 533**	**6 700**	**98 064**	**936**	**21 167**	**124 403**	**97 215**	**1 553**	**385 486**
Widowed										
50-54										
No Recipient	0	0	0	0	0	0	0	0	0	0
One Recipient	3	5	2	2	0	0	0	0	0	12
Two Recipients	2	195	25	63	5	52	187	167	10	706
Three or More	0	68	8	17	2	20	67	70	0	252
55-59										
No Recipient	3	0	0	0	0	0		0	0	3
One Recipient	3	3	0	7	0	3	3	0	0	19
Two Recipients	2	177	23	192	5	102	260	198	7	966
Three or More	0	42	8	42	0	17	78	70	2	259
60-64										
No Recipient	0	0	0	0	0	0	0	0	0	0
One Recipient	12	2	0	8	0	0	3	5	0	30
Two Recipients	3	67	25	482	5	98	280	288	3	1 251
Three or More	0	8	3	73	0	23	55	43	0	205
65-69										
No Recipient	1	0	0	0	0	0	0	0	0	1
One Recipient	4	0	0	9	0	4	5	2	0	24
Two Recipients	0	1	1	679	0	72	354	274	1	1 382
Three or More	0	0	0	100	0	14	59	35	0	208
70-74										
No Recipient	0	0	0	0	0	0	0	0	0	0
One Recipient	1	0	0	14	0	0	9	0	0	24
Two Recipients	0	0	0	720	0	41	374	181	0	1 316
Three or More	0	0	0	99	0	5	64	20	0	188
75-79										
No Recipient	0	0	0	0	0	0	0	0	0	0
One Recipient	0	0	0	16	0	0	8	0	0	24
Two Recipients	0	0	0	853	0	44	362	155	0	1 414
Three or More	0	0	0	144	0	1	68	24	0	237
80-84										
No Recipient	0	0	0	0	0	0	0	0	0	0
One Recipient	0	0	0	13	0	1	8	5	0	27
Two Recipients	0	0	0	778	0	18	318	97	0	1 211
Three or More	0	0	0	136	0	4	54	21	0	215
85+										
No Recipient	0	0	0	0	0	0	0	0	0	0
One Recipient	1	0	0	17	0	0	7	0	0	25
Two Recipients	0	0	0	587	0	9	224	64	1	885
Three or More	0	0	0	101	0	3	43	8	0	155
Total	**35**	**568**	**95**	**5 152**	**17**	**531**	**2 890**	**1 727**	**24**	**11 039**
Divorced										
50-54										
No Recipient	8	0	0	0	0	0	0	0	0	8
One Recipient	92	80	15	30	0	8	70	22	12	329
Two Recipients	13	2 420	267	710	30	445	1 397	595	202	6 079
Three or More	0	450	62	83	8	87	358	147	27	1 222
55-59										
No Recipient	2	0	0	0	0	0	0	0	0	2
One Recipient	58	45	2	25	0	10	27	17	2	186
Two Recipients	3	1 120	120	940	20	343	1 003	515	128	4 192
Three or More	0	185	20	135	3	75	142	97	13	670
60-64										
No Recipient	2	0	0	0	0	0	0	0	0	2
One Recipient	28	2	5	15	0	2	13	5	2	72
Two Recipients	7	215	55	1 510	3	248	483	353	18	2 892
Three or More	0	35	2	202	0	278	83	40	5	645

TABLE 6.2 (*continued*)

	No income	Single source				Multiple sources			Unknown sources	Total
		Labour	Entrep.	Pension	Other	Labour and pension	Other two	Three or more		
65-69										
No Recipient	1	0	0	0	0	0	0	0	0	1
One Recipient	6	0	0	24	0	0	5	4	0	39
Two Recipients	1	2	2	942	0	101	258	155	4	1 465
Three or More	0	0	0	94	0	16	21	16	0	147
70-74										
No Recipient	0	0	0	0	0	0	0	0	0	0
One Recipient	0	0	0	2	0	0	1	0	0	3
Two Recipients	0	0	0	458	0	21	139	65	1	684
Three or More	0	0	0	47	0	1	13	6	0	67
75-79										
No Recipient	0	0	0	0	0	0	0	0	0	0
One Recipient	0	0	0	5	0	0	0	0	0	5
Two Recipients	0	0	0	271	0	14	62	20	0	367
Three or More	0	0	0	16	0	1	6	2	0	25
80-84										
No Recipient	0	0	0	0	0	0	0	0	0	0
One Recipient	1	0	0	2	0	0	0	1	0	4
Two Recipients	0	0	0	98	0	2	30	8	0	138
Three or More	0	0	0	9	0	0	1	1	0	11
85+										
No Recipient	0	0	0	0	0	0	0	0	0	0
One Recipient	0	0	0	3	0	20	1	0	0	24
Two Recipients	0	0	0	35	0	1 175	9	0	0	1 219
Three or More	0	0	0	2	0	209	1	1	0	213
Total	222	4 554	550	5 658	64	3 056	4 123	2 070	414	20 711
Separated										
50-54										
No Recipient	0	0	0	0	0	0	0	0	0	0
One Recipient	3	0	0	0	0	0	2	3	0	8
Two Recipients	0	133	10	43	2	17	58	22	7	292
Three or More	0	43	10	10	0	5	37	13	3	121
55-59										
No Recipient	0	0	0	0	0	0	0	0	0	0
One Recipient	3	0	0	0	0	0	3	0	0	6
Two Recipients	0	53	5	57	0	15	50	30	5	215
Three or More	0	18	8	13	2	3	13	13	0	70
60-64										
No Recipient	0	0	0	0	0	0	0	0	0	0
One Recipient	0	0	0	0	0	0	2	2	0	4
Two Recipients	0	23	3	127	0	22	57	57	0	289
Three or More	0	0	3	23	0	8	10	8	0	52
65-69										
No Recipient	0	0	0	0	0	0	0	0	0	0
One Recipient	0	0	0	1	0	0	0	1	0	2
Two Recipients	0	0	0	79	0	16	44	36	0	175
Three or More	0	0	0	21	0	2	1	0	0	24
70-74										
No Recipient	0	0	0	0	0	0	0	0	0	0
One Recipient	0	0	0	0	0	0	1	0	0	1
Two Recipients	0	0	0	41	0	4	11	16	0	72
Three or More	0	0	0	4	0	2	2	0	0	8
75-79										
No Recipient	0	0	0	0	0	0	0	0	0	0
One Recipient					0	0	0	0	0	0
Two Recipients	0	0	0	24	0	1	12	2	0	39
Three or More	0	0	0	2	0	0	0	0	0	2
80-84										
No Recipient	0	0	0	0	0	0	0	0	0	0
One Recipient	0	0	0	0	0	0	0	0	0	0
Two Recipients	0	0	0	7	0	1	1	1	0	10
Three or More	0	0	0	2	0	0	0	0	0	2
85+										
No Recipient	0	0	0	0	0	0	0	0	0	0
One Recipient	0	0	0	0	0	0	0	0	0	0
Two Recipients	0	0	0	1	0	0	1	0	0	2
Three or More						0	0	0	0	0
Total	6	270	39	455	4	96	305	204	15	1 394
Total Males	1 602	43 340	8 375	116 456	1 147	24 078	129 699	104 166	2 439	431 302

TABLE 6.2 (*continued*)

		Single source				Multiple sources				
	No income	Labour	Entrep.	Pension	Other	Labour and pension	Other two	Three or more	Unknown sources	Total
Females										
Never married										
50-54										
No Recipient	17	0	0	0	0	0	0	0	0	17
One Recipient	90	92	3	17	2	7	47	17	7	282
Two Recipients	27	1 225	110	622	27	27	180	288	72	2 578
Three or More	0	172	23	132	12	12	20	50	2	423
55-59										
No Recipient	5	0	0	0	0	0	0	0	0	5
One Recipient	73	15	0	20	0	3	17	3	0	131
Two Recipients	25	922	95	818	27	212	860	327	65	3 351
Three or More	0	77	20	110	5	18	110	45	7	392
60-64										
No Recipient	5	0	0	0	0	0	0	0	0	5
One Recipient	73	8	0	32	0	3	5	7	0	128
Two Recipients	7	252	100	1 400	17	267	813	393	20	3 269
Three or More	0	25	20	152	5	27	73	45	2	349
65-69										
No Recipient	0	0	0	0	0	0	0	0	0	0
One Recipient	4	0	1	31	0	2	4	6	0	48
Two Recipients	1	5	4	1 719	0	168	812	359	1	3 069
Three or More	0	0	0	159	0	20	87	44	0	310
70-74										
No Recipient	0	0	0	0	0	0	0	0	0	0
One Recipient	1	0	0	21	0	0	1	0	0	23
Two Recipients	0	0	0	1 421	0	72	675	189	2	2 359
Three or More	0	0	0	149	0	8	68	22	0	247
75-79										
No Recipient	0	0	0	0	0	0	0	0	0	0
One Recipient	0	0	0	14	0	1	1	1	0	17
Two Recipients	0	0	0	1 484	0	26	554	129	1	2 194
Three or More	0	0	0	120	0	4	46	7	0	177
80-84										
No Recipient	0	0	0	0	0	0	0	0	0	0
One Recipient	3	0	0	5	0	1	3	1	0	13
Two Recipients	1	0	0	1 143	0	15	362	71	0	1 592
Three or More	0	0	0	117	0	2	42	15	0	176
85+										
No Recipient	0	0	0	0	0	0	0	0	0	0
One Recipient	4	0	0	7	0	0	2	0	0	13
Two Recipients	1	0	0	756	0	6	186	36	0	985
Three or More	0	0	0	95	0	1	21	2	0	119
Total	**337**	**2 791**	**376**	**10 542**	**93**	**1 063**	**6 084**	**2 058**	**178**	**23 523**
Married										
50-54										
No Recipient	60	0	0	0	0	0	0	0	0	60
One Recipient	1 037	108	15	13	2	17	75	13	13	1 293
Two Recipients	490	16 925	2 000	3 005	727	1 813	16 033	5 505	872	47 370
Three or More	0	9 420	1 693	1 103	393	942	9 480	3 540	470	27 041
55-59										
No Recipient	53	0	0	0	0	0	0	0	0	53
One Recipient	1 430	72	7	17	3	7	23	15	3	1 577
Two Recipients	580	12 685	1 940	8 850	1 078	3 335	16 665	7 490	1 038	53 661
Three or More	0	4 703	1 238	2 477	315	1 228	6 203	2 878	350	19 392
60-64										
No Recipient	43	0	0	0	0	0	0	0	0	43
One Recipient	1 403	17	3	23	0	10	17	3	0	1 476
Two Recipients	400	3 553	1 495	23 833	580	4 692	16 147	8 407	308	59 415
Three or More	0	1 053	697	4 918	115	1 167	3 508	1 853	92	13 403
65-69										
No Recipient	31	0	0	0	0	0	0	0	0	31
One Recipient	53	2	1	18	0	4	11	1	0	90
Two Recipients	11	41	25	28 875	8	2 761	14 022	5 476	29	51 248
Three or More	0	4	13	4 114	1	521	1 981	796	0	7 430
70-74										
No Recipient	9	0	0	0	0	0	0	0	0	9
One Recipient	13	0	0	9	0	1 020	1	1	0	1 044
Two Recipients	0	2	1	20 318	1	155	7 999	2 269	7	30 752
Three or More	0	0	0	2 161	0	1 175	819	207	0	4 362
75-79										
No Recipient	7	0	0	0	0	0	0	0	0	7
One Recipient	1	0	0	7	0	1	0	0	0	9
Two Recipients	0	0	0	12 802	0	379	3 994	781	4	17 960
Three or More	0	0	0	1 094	0	47	345	58	0	1 544

TABLE 6.2 (*continued*)

	No income	Single source				Multiple sources			Unknown sources	Total
		Labour	Entrep.	Pension	Other	Labour and pension	Other two	Three or more		
80-84										
No Recipient	3	0	0	0	0	0	0	0	0	3
One Recipient	4	0	0	2	0	0	0	0	0	6
Two Recipients	1	0	0	5 304	0	85	1 367	249	1	7 007
Three or More	0	0	0	415	0	11	108	11	0	545
85+										
No Recipient	3	0	0	0	0	0	0	0	0	3
One Recipient	0	0	1	0	0	0	0	0	0	1
Two Recipients	0	0	0	1 146	0	10	245	35	0	1 436
Three or More	0	0	0	89	0	2	18	2	0	111
Total	**5 632**	**48 586**	**9 129**	**120 595**	**3 224**	**18 206**	**99 061**	**39 593**	**3 188**	**347 214**
Widowed										
50-54										
No Recipient	0	0	0	0	0	0		0	0	0
One Recipient	7	2	0	13	0	38	5	18	0	83
Two Recipients	3	112	12	603	0	1 260	322	1 308	8	3 628
Three or More	0	17	2	170	0	437	110	453	5	1 194
55-59										
No Recipient	2	0	0	0	0	0		0	0	2
One Recipient	25	3	0	33	0	23	13	30	2	129
Two Recipients	8	125	10	1 332	10	1 427	648	1 360	17	4 937
Three or More	0	25	5	288	2	300	148	332	8	1 108
60-64										
No Recipient	0	0	0	0	0	0		0	0	0
One Recipient	67	2	0	75	0	20	23	18	0	205
Two Recipients	15	87	25	3 317	3	930	1 148	1 063	7	6 595
Three or More	0	8	5	600	0	48	180	178	3	1 122
65-69										
No Recipient	6	0	0	0	0			0	0	6
One Recipient	19	0	0	121	0	14	42	14	0	210
Two Recipients	2	0	0	5 079	1	447	1 606	634	1	7 770
Three or More	0	0	0	845	0	81	295	80	0	1 301
70-74										
No Recipient	0	0	0	0	0	0		0	0	0
One Recipient	13	0	0	140	0	9	41	9	0	212
Two Recipients	0	1	0	5 386	0	221	1428	382	2	7 420
Three or More	0	0	0	866	0	33	219	62	0	1 180
75-79										
No Recipient	0	0	0	0	0	0	0	0	0	0
One Recipient	5	0	1	141	0	2	29	4	1	183
Two Recipients	0	0	0	5 656	0	124	1 346	255	1	7 382
Three or More	0	0	0	966	0	15	206	42	0	1 229
80-84										
No Recipient	0	0	0	0	0	0	0	0	0	0
One Recipient	6	0	0	103	0	2	28	11	0	150
Two Recipients	0	0	0	4 555	0	36	901	154	0	5 646
Three or More	0	0	0	787	0	5	159	15	0	966
85+										
No Recipient	0	0	0	0	0	0		0	0	0
One Recipient	7	0	0	62	0	0	12	1	0	82
Two Recipients	0	0	0	3 321	1	16	536	86	0	3 960
Three or More	0	0	0	523	0	1	87	10	0	621
Total	**184**	**381**	**60**	**34 983**	**17**	**5 580**	**9 534**	**6 522**	**56**	**57 317**
Divorced										
50-54										
No Recipient	18	0	0	0	0	0		0	0	18
One Recipient	90	232	18	45	2	23	123	43	28	604
Two Recipients	10	3 325	167	658	57	495	1 960	603	160	7 435
Three or More	0	672	33	118	13	83	443	130	33	1 525
55-59										
No Recipient	5	0	0	0	0	0		0	0	5
One Recipient	50	47	2	37	0	17	35	18	7	213
Two Recipients	12	1 547	77	1 017	45	395	1 112	485	103	4 793
Three or More	0	242	13	130	2	62	173	70	15	707
60-64										
No Recipient	0	0	0	0	0	0		0	0	0
One Recipient	25	17	3	32	0	10	18	8	0	113
Two Recipients	0	323	30	1 568	3	350	582	310	20	3 186
Three or More	0	58	3	160	2	65	63	30	2	383
65-69										
No Recipient	0	0	0	0	0	0		0	0	0
One Recipient	0	0	0	25	0	4	7	4	0	40
Two Recipients	0	2	0	1 322	1	152	324	158	1	1 960
Three or More	0	1	0	135	0	14	33	12	0	195

TABLE 62. (*concluded*)

	No income	Single source				Multiple sources			Unknown sources	Total
		Labour	Entrep.	Pension	Other	Labour and pension	Other two	Three or more		
70-74										
No Recipient	0	0	0	0	0	0		0	0	0
One Recipient	0	0	0	19	0	1	2	6	1	29
Two Recipients	0	0	0	796	0	47	209	65	2	1 119
Three or More	0	0	0	69	0	5	24	6	1	105
75-79										
No Recipient	0	0	0	0	0	0		0	0	0
One Recipient	0	0	0	12	0	0	1	0	0	13
Two Recipients	0	0	0	565	0	13	113	26	1	718
Three or More	0	0	0	51	0	0	12	4	0	67
80-84										
No Recipient	0	0	0	0	0	0		0	0	0
One Recipient	1	0	0	5	0	0	4	0	0	10
Two Recipients	0	0	0	338	0	4	54	9	0	405
Three or More	0	0	0	35	0	1	6	0	0	42
85+										
No Recipient	0	0	0	0	0	0	0	0	0	0
One Recipient	0	0	0	3	0	0	1	0	0	4
Two Recipients	0	0	0	202	1	1	24	5	0	233
Three or More	0	0	0	11	0	0	1	1	0	13
Total	**211**	**6 465**	**347**	**7 353**	**126**	**1 741**	**5 326**	**1 992**	**375**	**23 936**
Separated										
50-54										
No Recipient	0	0	0	0	0	0	0	0	0	0
One Recipient	2	12	0	0	0	0	7	0	3	24
Two Recipients	2	148	2	27	5	17	65	25	8	299
Three or More	0	50	0	12	3	2	47	12	2	128
55-59										
No Recipient	0	0	0	0	0	0	0	0	0	0
One Recipient	2	5	0	2	0	0	2	0	0	11
Two Recipients	0	83	3	68	2	30	98	30	8	322
Three or More	0	15	0	10	0	5	25	5	0	60
60-64										
No Recipient	0	0	0	0	0	0	0	0	0	0
One Recipient	2	0	0	2	0	0	2	0	0	6
Two Recipients	0	13	2	110	2	18	68	30	0	243
Three or More	0	3	2	17	0	5	8	2	0	37
65-69										
No Recipient	0	0	0	0	0	0	0	0	0	0
One Recipient	0	0	0	0	0	0	1	0	0	1
Two Recipients	0	0	0	101	0	11	24	13	0	149
Three or More	0	0	0	6	0	0	5	1	0	12
70-74										
No Recipient	0	0	0	0	0	0	0	0	0	0
One Recipient	0	0	0	1	0	0	0	0	0	1
Two Recipients	0	0	0	44	0	18	2	2	0	66
Three or More	0	0	0	6	0	1	0	0	0	7
75-79										
No Recipient	0	0	0	0	0	0	0	0	0	0
One Recipient	0	0	0	0	0	0	0	0	0	0
Two Recipients	0	0	0	18	0	6	1	1	0	26
Three or More	0	0	0	4	0	0	0	0	0	4
80-84										
No Recipient	0	0	0	0	0	0	0	0	0	0
One Recipient	0	0	0	0	0	0	0	0	0	0
Two Recipients	0	0	0	7	0	0	0	0	0	7
Three or More	0	0	0	0	0	0	0	0	0	0
85+										
No Recipient	0	0	0	0	0	0	0	0	0	0
One Recipient	0	0	0	0	0	0	0	0	0	0
Two Recipients	0	0	0	2	0	0	0	0	0	2
Three or More	0	0	0	0	0	0	0	0	0	0
Total	**7**	**330**	**8**	**434**	**12**	**91**	**376**	**121**	**22**	**1 400**
Total Females	**6 371**	**58 554**	**9 920**	**173 907**	**3 472**	**26 681**	**120 381**	**50 286**	**3 819**	**453 391**

TABLE 6.3

Number and type of income sources of persons aged 50 and over living in four- or more person households in Finland in 1990 by age, sex, marital status and number of household income recipients

	No income	Single source				Multiple sources				Total
		Labour	Entrep.	Pension	Other	Labour and pension	Other two	Three or more	Unknown sources	
Males										
Never married										
50-54										
No Recipient	0	0	0	0	0	0	0	0	0	0
One Recipient	8	2	0	0	0	0	0	2	0	12
Two Recipients	3	18	7	0	0	0	20	5	3	56
Three or More	22	230	53	185	8	35	157	85	30	805
55-59										
No Recipient	0	0	0	0	0	0	0	0	0	0
One Recipient	0	0	0	2	0	0	2	0	0	4
Two Recipients	12	7	0	3	0	0	5	0	0	27
Three or More	27	118	30	183	0	35	120	62	13	588
60-64										
No Recipient	0	0	0	0	0	0	0	0	0	0
One Recipient	0	0	0	0	0	0	0	0	0	0
Two Recipients	7	3	0	3	0	0	0	0	0	13
Three or More	10	17	13	237	0	18	75	42	2	414
65-69										
No Recipient	0	0	0	0	0	0	0	0	0	0
One Recipient	1	0	0	1	0	0	0	0	0	2
Two Recipients	0	0	0	1	0	0	0	0	0	1
Three or More	1	0	1	162	0	6	34	11	0	215
70-74										
No Recipient	0	0	0	0	0	0	0	0	0	0
One Recipient	0	0	0	0	0	0	0	0	0	0
Two Recipients	0	0	0	0	0	0	0	0	0	0
Three or More	0	0	0	73	0	1	34	7	0	115
75-79										
No Recipient	0	0	0	0	0	0	0	0	0	0
One Recipient	0	0	0	0	0	0	0	0	0	0
Two Recipients	0	0	0	0	0	0	0	0	0	0
Three or More	0	0	0	45	0	0	15	2	0	62
80-84										
No Recipient	0	0	0	0	0	0	0	0	0	0
One Recipient	0	0	0	0	0	0	0	0	0	0
Two Recipients	0	0	0	0	0	0	0	0	0	0
Three or More	0	0	0	29	0	1	4	2	0	36
85+										
No Recipient	0	0	0	0	0	0	0	0	0	0
One Recipient	0	0	0	0	0	0	0	0	0	0
Two Recipients	0	0	0	0	0	0	0	0	0	0
Three or More	0	0	0	17	0	0	6	1	0	24
Total	**91**	**395**	**104**	**941**	**8**	**96**	**472**	**219**	**48**	**2 374**
Married										
50-54										
No Recipient	5	0	0	0	0	0	0	0	0	5
One Recipient	13	40	10	2	3	10	35	8	3	124
Two Recipients	33	667	127	82	23	105	770	443	30	2 280
Three or More	43	5 185	1 125	742	155	903	9 072	8 195	265	25 685
55-59										
No Recipient	0	0	0	0	0	0	0	0	0	0
One Recipient	12	8	3	2	2	2	20	7	2	58
Two Recipients	20	150	55	58	3	28	245	188	8	755
Three or More	33	1 760	672	1 013	62	635	4 433	5 113	90	13 811
60-64										
No Recipient	0	0	0	0	0	0	0	0	0	0
One Recipient	0	2	0	0	0	2	5	2	0	11
Two Recipients	18	23	17	50	0	18	60	83	0	269
Three or More	13	335	265	1 573	12	525	2 337	3 162	12	8 234
65-69										
No Recipient	0	0	0	0	0	0	0	0	0	0
One Recipient	1	0	1	1	0	0	0	5	0	8
Two Recipients	2	1	0	20	1	8	31	35	0	98
Three or More	5	2	6	1 416	1	271	1 259	1 615	4	4 579
70-74										
No Recipient	0	0	0	0	0	0	0	0	0	0
One Recipient	1	0	0	0	0	0	0	1	0	2
Two Recipients	1	0	0	12	0	1	9	12	0	35
Three or More	1	0	0	1 060	0	108	792	692	0	2 653

TABLE 6.3 (*continued*)

	No income	Single source				Multiple sources			Unknown sources	Total
		Labour	Entrep.	Pension	Other	Labour and pension	Other two	Three or more		
75-79										
No Recipient	1	0	0	0	0	0	0	0	0	1
One Recipient	1	0	0	0	0	0	0	0	0	1
Two Recipients	0	0	0	4	0	4	4	7	0	19
Three or More	1	0	0	847	0	56	526	298	0	1 728
80-84										
No Recipient	0	0	0	0	0	0	0	0	0	0
One Recipient	0	0	0	0	0	0	0	0	0	0
Two Recipients	0	0	0	4	0	0	4	1	0	9
Three or More	0	0	0	498	0	13	217	131	0	859
85+										
No Recipient	0	0	0	0	0	0	0	0	0	0
One Recipient	0	0	0	0	0	0	0	0	0	0
Two Recipients	0	0	0	0	0	0	0	0	0	0
Three or More	0	0	0	171	0	1	72	24	0	268
Total	204	8 173	2 281	7 555	262	2 690	19 891	20 022	414	61 492
Widowed										
50-54										
No Recipient	0	0	0	0	0	0	0	0	0	0
One Recipient	0	0	0	0	0	0	0	0	0	0
Two Recipients	2	2	0	0	0	0	2	2	0	8
Three or More	2	23	10	13	0	15	43	45	2	153
55-59										
No Recipient	0	0	0	0	0	0	0	0	0	0
One Recipient	0	0	0	0	0	0	0	0	0	0
Two Recipients	2	2	0	2	0	3	2	2	0	13
Three or More	0	8	7	30	0	20	53	52	5	175
60-64										
No Recipient	0	0	0	0	0	0	0	0	0	0
One Recipient	0	0	0	0	0	0	0	2	0	2
Two Recipients	0	0	0	3	0	2	2	3	0	10
Three or More	0	5	7	88	0	28	67	53	2	250
65-69										
No Recipient	0	0	0	0	0	0	0	0	0	0
One Recipient	0	0	0	0	0	0	0	1	0	1
Two Recipients	0	0	0	4	0	0	2	2	0	8
Three or More	0	0	0	160	0	19	71	53	0	303
70-74										
No Recipient	0	0	0	0	0	0	0	0	0	0
One Recipient	0	0	0	0	0	0	1	0	0	1
Two Recipients	0	0	0	7	0	1	1	1	0	10
Three or More	0	0	0	236	0	18	98	52	0	404
75-79										
No Recipient	0	0	0	0	0	0	0	0	0	0
One Recipient	0	0	0	0	0	0	0	0	0	0
Two Recipients	0	0	0	11	0	0	5	1	0	17
Three or More	0	0	0	349	0	7	119	56	0	531
80-84										
No Recipient	0	0	0	0	0	0	0	0	0	0
One Recipient	0	0	0	0	0	0	1	0	0	1
Two Recipients	0	0	0	6	0	2	2	1	0	11
Three or More	0	0	0	335	0	8	119	29	1	492
85+										
No Recipient	0	0	0	0	0	0	0	0	0	0
One Recipient	0	0	0	0	0	0	0	0	0	0
Two Recipients	0	0	0	1	0	0	2	0	0	3
Three or More	0	0	0	209	0	3	65	19	0	296
Total	6	40	24	1 454	0	126	655	374	10	2 689
Divorced										
50-54										
No Recipient	0	0	0	0	0	0	0	0	0	0
One Recipient	0	2	2	0	0	0	3	3	0	10
Two Recipients	2	57	7	13	2	5	47	17	3	153
Three or More	18	312	45	97	2	48	192	67	37	818
55-59										
No Recipient	0	0	0	0	0	0		0	0	0
One Recipient	3	3	0	0	0	0		0	0	6
Two Recipients	2	10	2	10	0	3	12	12	5	56
Three or More	8	115	28	133	0	33	87	55	13	472
60-64										
No Recipient	0	0	0	0	0	0		0	0	0
One Recipient	2	0	0	0	0	0	2	0	0	4
Two Recipients	0	0	0	8	0	0	3	5	0	16
Three or More	5	22	2	167	0	23	47	22	0	288

TABLE 6.3 (continued)

	No income	Single source				Multiple sources			Unknown sources	Total
		Labour	Entrep.	Pension	Other	Labour and pension	Other two	Three or more		
65-69										
No Recipient	0	0	0	0	0	0	0	0	0	0
One Recipient	0	0	0	0	0	0	0	0	0	0
Two Recipients	0	0	0	2	0	0	0	0	0	2
Three or More	1	0	0	113	0	6	21	11	0	152
70-74										
No Recipient	0	0	0	0	0	0	0	0	0	0
One Recipient	0	0	0	0	0	0	0	0	0	0
Two Recipients	0	0	0	0	0	0	0	0	0	0
Three or More	0	0	0	58	0	2	6	6	0	72
75-79										
No Recipient	0	0	0	0	0	0	0	0	0	0
One Recipient	0	0	0	0	0	0	0	0	0	0
Two Recipients	0	0	0	1	0	0	0	0	0	1
Three or More	0	0	0	29	0	0	8	6	0	43
80-84										
No Recipient	0	0	0	0	0	0	0	0	0	0
One Recipient	0	0	0	0	0	0	0	0	0	0
Two Recipients	0	0	0	0	0	0	0	0	0	0
Three or More	0	0	0	17	0	0	2	1	0	20
85+										
No Recipient	0	0	0	0	0	0	0	0	0	0
One Recipient	0	0	0	0	0	0	0	0	0	0
Two Recipients	0	0	0	0	0	0	0	0	0	0
Three or More	0	0	0	6	0	0	1	1	0	8
Total	**41**	**521**	**86**	**654**	**4**	**120**	**431**	**206**	**58**	**2 121**
Separated										
50-54										
No Recipient	0	0	0	0	0	0	0	0	0	0
One Recipient	0	0	0	0	0	0	0	0	0	0
Two Recipients	0	2	0	0	0	2	5	0	0	9
Three or More	0	27	3	8	2	5	18	12	2	77
55-59										
No Recipient	0	0	0	0	0	0	0	0	0	0
One Recipient	0	0	0	0	0	0	0	0	0	0
Two Recipients	0	2	0	2	0	0	0	2	0	6
Three or More	0	12	2	3	0	3	12	7	2	41
60-64										
No Recipient	0	0	0	0	0	0	0	0	0	0
One Recipient	0	0	0	0	0	0	0	0	0	0
Two Recipients	0	0	0	3	0	0	0	0	0	3
Three or More	0	0	0	17	0	2	10	5	0	34
65-69										
No Recipient	0	0	0	0	0	0	0	0	0	0
One Recipient	0	0	0	0	0	0	0	0	0	0
Two Recipients	0	0	0	0	0	0	0	0	0	0
Three or More	0	0	0	7	0	1	1	0	0	9
70-74										
No Recipient	0	0	0	0	0	0	0	0	0	0
One Recipient	0	0	0	0	0	0	0	0	0	0
Two Recipients	0	0	0	0	0	0	0	0	0	0
Three or More	0	0	0	5	0	0	4	6	0	15
75-79										
No Recipient	0	0	0	0	0	0	0	0	0	0
One Recipient	0	0	0	0	0	0	0	0	0	0
Two Recipients	0	0	0	0	0	0	0	0	0	0
Three or More	0	0	0	2	0	0	1	0	0	3
80-84										
No Recipient	0	0	0	0	0	0	0	0	0	0
One Recipient	0	0	0	0	0	0	0	0	0	0
Two Recipients	0	0	0	0	0	0	0	0	0	0
Three or More	0	0	0	0	0	0	0	0	0	0
85+										
No Recipient	0	0	0	0	0	0	0	0	0	0
One Recipient	0	0	0	0	0	0	0	0	0	0
Two Recipients	0	0	0	0	0	0	0	0	0	0
Three or More	0	0	0	0	0	0	0	0	0	0
Total	**0**	**43**	**5**	**47**	**2**	**13**	**51**	**32**	**4**	**197**
Total Males	**342**	**9 172**	**2 500**	**10 651**	**276**	**3 045**	**21 500**	**20 853**	**534**	**68 873**

TABLE 6.3 (*continued*)

	No income	Single source				Multiple sources			Unknown sources	Total
		Labour	*Entrep.*	*Pension*	*Other*	*Labour and pension*	*Other two*	*Three or more*		
Females										
Never married										
50-54										
No Recipient	0	0	0	0	0	0	0	0	0	0
One Recipient	5	0	0	0	0	0	0	0	0	5
Two Recipients	0	10	0	3	0	0	2	0	0	15
Three or More	13	72	13	122	2	15	62	17	10	326
55-59										
No Recipient	2	0	0	0	0	0	0	0	0	2
One Recipient	3	0	0	0	0	0	0	0	0	3
Two Recipients	0	2	0	2	0	2	0	0	0	6
Three or More	10	35	8	93	0	8	53	15	10	232
60-64										
No Recipient	0	0	0	0	0	0	0	0	0	0
One Recipient	0	0	0	2	0	0	0	0	0	2
Two Recipients	3	0	0	0	0	0	0	0	2	5
Three or More	3	12	7	82	0	10	45	20	2	181
65-69										
No Recipient	0	0	0	0	0	0	0	0	0	0
One Recipient	0	0	0	0	0	0	0	0	0	0
Two Recipients	0	0	0	2	0	1	1	0	0	4
Three or More	0	0	0	108	0	13	31	9	0	161
70-74										
No Recipient	1	0	0	0	0	0	0	0	0	1
One Recipient	0	0	0	0	0	0	0	0	0	0
Two Recipients	0	0	0	0	0	0	0	0	0	0
Three or More	2	0	0	86	0	2	31	4	0	125
75-79										
No Recipient	0	0	0	0	0	0	0	0	0	0
One Recipient	0	0	0	0	0	0	0	0	0	0
Two Recipients	0	0	0	4	0	0	0	0	0	4
Three or More	2	0	0	91	0	0	28	6	0	127
80-84										
No Recipient	0	0	0	0	0	0	0	0	0	0
One Recipient	0	0	0	0	0	0	0	0	0	0
Two Recipients	0	0	0	0	0	0	0	0	0	0
Three or More	0	0	0	71	0	0	21	1	0	93
85+										
No Recipient	0	0	0	0	0	0	0	0	0	0
One Recipient	0	0	0	0	0	0	0	0	0	0
Two Recipients	0	0	0	0	0	0	0	0	0	0
Three or More	0	0	0	75	0	0	15	0	0	90
Total	**44**	**131**	**28**	**741**	**2**	**51**	**289**	**72**	**24**	**1 382**
Married										
50-54										
No Recipient	8	0	0	0	0	0	0	0	0	8
One Recipient	42	5	2	0	0	0	0	0	0	49
Two Recipients	128	267	62	35	2	15	157	55	17	738
Three or More	348	5 852	1 810	665	257	470	6 672	2 858	315	19 247
55-59										
No Recipient	2	0	0	0	0	0	0	0	0	2
One Recipient	5	0	0	2	0	0	0	0	0	7
Two Recipients	53	30	10	5	0	7	22	10	5	142
Three or More	223	1 850	873	1 095	100	585	2 765	1 498	172	9 161
60-64										
No Recipient	0	0	0	0	0	0	0	0	0	0
One Recipient	3	0	0	2	0	0	2	0	0	7
Two Recipients	23	2	2	15	2	3	10	5	0	62
Three or More	135	290	420	1 898	40	532	1 348	697	35	5 395
65-69										
No Recipient	1	0	0	0	0	0	0	0	0	1
One Recipient	0	0	0	0	0	0	0	0	0	0
Two Recipients	1	0	0	16	0	4	12	5	0	38
Three or More	2	2	6	1 915	0	229	896	321	1	3 372
70-74										
No Recipient	0	0	0	0	0	0	0	0	0	0
One Recipient	1	0	0	0	0	0	0	0	0	1
Two Recipients	1	0	0	5	0	0	7	4	0	17
Three or More	1	0	0	1 231	0	53	467	102	0	1 854
75-79										
No Recipient	0	0	0	0	0	0	0	0	0	0
One Recipient	0	0	0	0	0	0	0	0	0	0
Two Recipients	0	0	0	1	0	0	6	0	0	7
Three or More	0	0	0	840	0	26	187	22	0	1 075

TABLE 6.3 (*continued*)

	No income	Single source				Multiple sources			Unknown sources	Total
		Labour	Entrep.	Pension	Other	Labour and pension	Other two	Three or more		
80-84										
No Recipient	0	0	0	0	0	0	0	0	0	0
One Recipient	0	0	0	0	0	0	0	0	0	0
Two Recipients	0	0	0	1	0	0	0	0	0	1
Three or More	0	0	0	286	0	3	68	2	0	359
85+										
No Recipient	0	0	0	0	0	0	0	0	0	0
One Recipient	0	0	0	0	0	0	0	0	0	0
Two Recipients	0	0	0	0	0	0	0	0	0	0
Three or More	0	0	0	51	0	1	14	0	0	66
Total	977	8 298	3 185	8 063	401	1 928	12 633	5 579	545	41 609
Widowed										
50-54										
No Recipient	0	0	0	0	0	0	0	0	0	0
One Recipient	0	0	0	0	0	2	0	0	0	2
Two Recipients	2	0	0	3	0	3	3	5	0	16
Three or More	2	13	3	115	0	180	80	232	0	625
55-59										
No Recipient	0	0	0	0	0	0	0	0	0	0
One Recipient	0	0	0	2	0	0	0	2	0	4
Two Recipients	5	2	0	5	0	10	2	10	0	34
Three or More	2	10	3	225	2	167	135	177	2	723
60-64										
No Recipient	0	0	0	0	0	0	0	0	0	0
One Recipient	0	0	0	2	0	2	3	2	0	9
Two Recipients	0	0	0	12	0	3	7	3	0	25
Three or More	10	7	2	642	2	142	232	185	2	1 224
65-69										
No Recipient	0	0	0	0	0	0	0	0	0	0
One Recipient	0	0	0	1	0	1	1	0	0	3
Two Recipients	0	0	0	32	0	2	8	4	0	46
Three or More	0	0	0	1 324	0	105	376	128	0	1 933
70-74										
No Recipient	0	0	0	0	0	0	0	0	0	0
One Recipient	0	0	0	4	0	0	0	1	0	5
Two Recipients	0	0	0	47	0	1	13	2	0	63
Three or More	0	0	1	1 731	0	51	416	86	0	2 285
75-79										
No Recipient	0	0	0	0	0	0	0	0	0	0
One Recipient	0	0	0	1	0	0	2	1	0	4
Two Recipients	1	0	0	45	0	0	8	1	0	55
Three or More	0	0	0	2 207	0	35	366	79	0	2 687
80-84										
No Recipient	0	0	0	0	0	0	0	0	0	0
One Recipient	0	0	0	3	0	0	0	0	0	3
Two Recipients	0	0	0	17	0	0	4	0	0	21
Three or More	2	0	0	1 610	0	7	226	36	0	1 881
85+										
No Recipient	0	0	0	0	0	0	0	0	0	0
One Recipient	0	0	0	1	0	0	0	0	0	1
Two Recipients	0	0	0	7	0	0	0	0	0	7
Three or More	0	0	1	855	0	2	119	17	0	994
Total	24	32	10	8 891	4	713	2 001	971	4	12 650
Divorced										
50-54										
No Recipient	0	0	0	0	0	0	0	0	0	0
One Recipient	2	2	2	0	0	0	0	2	2	10
Two Recipients	3	22	2	0	0	0	17	0	0	44
Three or More	12	215	13	60	7	45	140	52	20	564
55-59										
No Recipient	0	0	0	0	0	0	0	0	0	0
One Recipient	0	2	0	0	0	0	2	0	0	4
Two Recipients	2	10	0	2	0	3	5	0	0	22
Three or More	7	105	7	80	3	18	80	37	7	344
60-64										
No Recipient	0	0	0	0	0	0	0	0	0	0
One Recipient	0	0	0	0	0	0	0	0	0	0
Two Recipients	0	0	0	8	0	3	5	0	0	16
Three or More	2	17	2	142	0	17	50	27	2	259
65-69										
No Recipient	0	0	0	0	0	0	0	0	0	0
One Recipient	0	0	0	0	0	0	1	0	0	1
Two Recipients	0	0	0	5	0	0	2	0	0	7
Three or More	0	0	0	132	0	15	34	11	0	192

TABLE 6.3 (*concluded*)

	No income	Single source				Multiple sources			Unknown sources	Total
		Labour	Entrep.	Pension	Other	Labour and pension	Other two	Three or more		
70-74										
No Recipient	0	0	0	0	0	0	0	0	0	0
One Recipient	0	0	0	1	0	0	0	0	0	1
Two Recipients	0	0	0	7	0	1	2	0	0	10
Three or More	0	0	0	91	0	4	15	7	0	117
75-79										
No Recipient	0	0	0	0	0	0	0	0	0	0
One Recipient	0	0	0	1	0	0	0	0	0	1
Two Recipients	0	0	0	2	0	0	0	0	1	3
Three or More	0	0	0	60	0	1	13	1	0	75
80-84										
No Recipient	0	0	0	0	0	0	0	0	0	0
One Recipient	0	0	0	0	0	0	0	0	0	0
Two Recipients	0	0	0	1	0	0	0	0	0	1
Three or More	0	0	0	28	0	0	4	1	0	33
85+										
No Recipient	0	0	0	0	0	0	0	0	0	0
One Recipient	0	0	0	0	0	0	0	0	0	0
Two Recipients	0	0	0	0	0	0	0	0	0	0
Three or More	1	0	0	16	0	0	1	0	0	18
Total	29	373	26	636	10	107	371	138	32	1 722
Separated										
50-54										
No Recipient	0	0	0	0	0	0	0	0	0	0
One Recipient	0	0	0	0	0	0	0	0	0	0
Two Recipients	0	0	0	0	0	2	2	0	0	4
Three or More	2	10	3	3	0	2	13	5	0	38
55-59										
No Recipient	0	0	0	0	0	0	0	0	0	0
One Recipient	0	0	0	0	0	0	0	0	0	0
Two Recipients	0	0	0	0	0	0	0	0	0	0
Three or More	0	8	0	2	0	3	3	8	0	24
60-64										
No Recipient	0	0	0	0	0	0	0	0	0	0
One Recipient	0	0	0	0	0	0	0	0	0	0
Two Recipients	0	0	0	0	0	0	0	0	0	0
Three or More	2	0	0	12	0	0	3	7	0	24
65-69										
No Recipient	0	0	0	0	0	0	0	0	0	0
One Recipient	0	0	0	0	0	0	0	0	0	0
Two Recipients	0	0	0	0	0	0	0	0	0	0
Three or More	0	0	0	6	0	1	1	5	0	13
70-74										
No Recipient	0	0	0	0	0	0	0	0	0	0
One Recipient	0	0	0	0	0	0	0	0	0	0
Two Recipients	0	0	0	1	0	0	0	0	0	1
Three or More	0	0	0	1	0	0	0	0	0	1
75-79										
No Recipient	0	0	0	0	0	0	0	0	0	0
One Recipient	0	0	0	0	0	0	0	0	0	0
Two Recipients	0	0	0	0	0	0	0	0	0	0
Three or More	0	0	0	2	0	0	0	0	0	2
80-84										
No Recipient	0	0	0	0	0	0	0	0	0	0
One Recipient	0	0	0	0	0	0	0	0	0	0
Two Recipients	0	0	0	0	0	0	0	0	0	0
Three or More	0	0	0	0	0	0	0	0	0	0
85+										
No Recipient	0	0	0	0	0	0	0	0	0	0
One Recipient	0	0	0	0	0	0	0	0	0	0
Two Recipients	0	0	0	0	0	0	0	0	0	0
Three or More	0	0	0	0	0	0	0	0	0	0
Total	4	18	3	27	0	8	22	25	0	107
Total Females	1 078	8 852	3 252	18 358	417	2 807	15 316	6 785	605	57 470

TABLE 7.1

**Disability status of persons aged 50 and over in Finland in 1990
by age, sex, and number of generations present in the household**

| | | | Receiving a disability pension | | |
| | | | | No | |
		Yes	Live with disabled person	Do not live with disabled person	Total
Males					
Living Alone					
50-54		4 380	0	14 463	18 843
55-59		6 205	0	11 868	18 073
60-64		7 292	0	11 547	18 838
65-69		120	0	15 196	15 316
70-74		0	0	11 145	11 145
75-79		0	0	10 835	10 835
80-84		0	0	8 083	8 083
85+		0	0	4 731	4 731
	Total	**17 997**	**0**	**87 869**	**105 865**
One Generation Households					
50-54		6 692	3 872	35 525	46 088
55-59		14 058	6 243	38 170	58 472
60-64		20 975	7 663	38 547	67 185
65-69		394	7 729	50 107	58 231
70-74		0	2 051	37 779	39 829
75-79		0	608	27 355	27 964
80-84		0	214	13 493	13 707
85+		0	101	4 327	4 428
	Total	**42 119**	**28 482**	**245 303**	**315 904**
Two Generation Households					
50-54		6 877	3 752	56 992	67 620
55-59		8 292	3 865	30 675	42 832
60-64		7 793	3 470	16 482	27 745
65-69		115	3 332	11 420	14 867
70-74		0	1 607	6 094	7 701
75-79		0	1 006	3 706	4 712
80-84		0	615	1 885	2 500
85+		0	307	811	1 118
	Total	**23 077**	**17 953**	**128 064**	**169 095**
Three Generation Households					
50-54		312	168	1 848	2 328
55-59		535	212	1 642	2 388
60-64		728	267	1 512	2 507
65-69		15	331	1 900	2 246
70-74		0	166	1 711	1 876
75-79		0	124	1 548	1 672
80-84		0	98	966	1 064
85+		0	51	398	449
	Total	**1 590**	**1 416**	**11 524**	**14 530**
Four and More Generation Households					
50-54		0	0	8	8
55-59		3	3	13	20
60-64		2	5	7	13
65-69		0	0	0	0
70-74		0	1	1	2
75-79		0	0	2	2
80-84		0	0	0	0
85+		0	0	2	2
	Total	**5**	**10**	**34**	**48**
Unknown					
50-54		213	65	520	798
55-59		247	42	285	573
60-64		140	27	215	382
65-69		0	45	161	206
70-74		0	12	59	71
75-79		0	12	41	53
80-84		0	9	17	26
85+		0	5	10	15
	Total	**600**	**216**	**1 308**	**2 124**
	Total Males	**85 388**	**48 076**	**474 103**	**607 566**

TABLE 7.1 (*continued*)

	Receiving disability pension	Not receiving disability pension		Total
		Live with disabled person	Not living with disabled person	
Females				
Living Alone				
50-54	3 647	0	18 363	22 010
55-59	7 047	0	20 663	27 710
60-64	11 775	0	27 287	39 062
65-69	253	0	49 811	50 064
70-74	0	0	51 891	51 891
75-79	0	0	53 459	53 459
80-84	0	0	39 895	39 895
85+	0	0	22 346	22 346
Total	**22 721**	**0**	**283 714**	**306 436**
One Generation Households				
50-54	6 515	6 443	38 682	51 640
55-59	12 485	9 187	38 572	60 243
60-64	18 013	7 715	41 235	66 963
65-69	285	3 658	53 707	57 649
70-74	0	1 188	36 075	37 264
75-79	0	773	22 902	23 675
80-84	0	554	11 218	11 772
85+	0	440	4 808	5 248
Total	**37 298**	**29 958**	**247 199**	**314 455**
Two Generation Households				
50-54	5 293	6 758	50 563	62 615
55-59	6 382	5 637	26 380	38 398
60-64	6 308	3 868	16 677	26 853
65-69	93	3 378	14 493	17 964
70-74	0	2 347	8 902	11 249
75-79	0	2 056	6 226	8 282
80-84	0	1 390	3 715	5 105
85+	0	723	1 922	2 645
Total	**18 076**	**26 158**	**128 878**	**173 112**
Three Generation Households				
50-54	348	318	1 950	2 617
55-59	585	343	1 918	2 847
60-64	913	305	2 105	3 323
65-69	11	306	3 689	4 006
70-74	0	247	3 461	3 708
75-79	0	325	3 271	3 595
80-84	0	239	1 818	2 057
85+	0	142	694	836
Total	**1 857**	**2 225**	**18 907**	**22 989**
Four and More Generation Households				
50-54	5	3	12	20
55-59	5	7	13	25
60-64	3	0	5	8
65-69	0	1	1	2
70-74	0	0	5	5
75-79	0	2	4	6
80-84	0	5	9	14
85+	0	3	11	14
Total	**13**	**22**	**59**	**94**
Unknown				
50-54	53	3	113	170
55-59	50	7	80	137
60-64	45	5	57	107
65-69	1	11	49	61
70-74	0	9	34	44
75-79	0	7	28	35
80-84	0	6	36	42
85+	0	6	45	51
Total	**150**	**54**	**443**	**646**
Total Females	**80 116**	**58 416**	**679 200**	**817 732**

TABLE 7.2

**Disability status of persons aged 50 and over in Finland in 1990
by age, sex, and primary source of income**

| | | Receiving disability pension | Not receiving disability pension | | Total |
			Live with disabled person	Not living with disabled person	
Males					
	Primary source				
No income					
50-54		33	90	1 045	1 168
55-59		38	82	793	913
60-64		23	40	398	462
65-69		0	12	124	135
70-74		0	1	47	48
75-79		0	0	36	36
80-84		0	0	24	24
85+		0	0	17	17
	Total	**95**	**225**	**2 485**	**2 804**
Labour					
50-54		693	5 978	84 238	90 910
55-59		635	5 907	51 672	58 213
60-64		328	2 350	17 160	19 838
65-69		0	142	1 341	1 484
70-74		0	11	221	232
75-79		0	5	85	89
80-84		0	0	15	15
85+		0	0	5	5
	Total	**1 657**	**14 393**	**154 737**	**170 786**
Entrepreneur					
50-54		537	1 305	18 400	20 242
55-59		995	1 633	15 387	18 015
60-64		1 423	1 443	9 772	12 638
65-69		19	593	3 873	4 485
70-74		0	162	1 498	1 660
75-79		0	36	798	834
80-84		0	32	359	391
85+		0	12	168	180
	Total	**2 974**	**5 217**	**50 254**	**58 445**
Pension					
50-54		17 137	198	2 160	19 495
55-59		27 600	2 420	12 373	42 393
60-64		35 107	7 523	40 320	82 950
65-69		626	10 673	73 278	84 576
70-74		0	3 662	54 907	58 569
75-79		0	1 706	42 504	44 209
80-84		0	904	23 997	24 901
85+		0	452	10 069	10 521
	Total	**80 469**	**27 539**	**259 608**	**367 616**
Property. income					
50-54		32	75	1 420	1 527
55-59		47	117	1 107	1 270
60-64		40	47	418	505
65-69		0	9	136	146
70-74		0	0	89	89
75-79		0	2	53	55
80-84		0	0	46	46
85+		0	0	18	18
	Total	**118**	**250**	**3 288**	**3 656**
Unknown					
50-54		42	210	2 093	2 345
55-59		25	207	1 322	1 553
60-64		8	28	240	277
65-69		0	7	33	40
70-74		0	0	26	26
75-79		0	0	13	13
80-84		0	0	3	3
85+		0	0	2	2
	Total	**75**	**452**	**3 732**	**4 259**
	Total Males	**85 388**	**48 076**	**474 103**	**607 566**

TABLE 7.2. (*concluded*)

| | | Receiving a disability pension | | |
| | | | No | | |
	Yes	Live with disabled person	Do not live with disabled person	Total
Females				
Primary source				
No income				
50-54	25	355	2 187	2 567
55-59	23	423	2 295	2 742
60-64	53	313	2 070	2 437
65-69	0	8	185	193
70-74	0	1	89	91
75-79	0	1	42	44
80-84	0	5	51	56
85+	0	0	71	71
Total	**102**	**1 107**	**6 990**	**8 199**
Labour				
50-54	658	10 582	88 435	99 675
55-59	617	9 387	57 900	67 903
60-64	337	2 585	20 208	23 130
65-69	2	135	1 518	1 655
70-74	0	19	251	269
75-79	0	6	89	95
80-84	0	2	29	31
85+	0	0	8	8
Total	**1 614**	**22 715**	**168 438**	**192 767**
Entrep.				
50-54	308	1 645	12 492	14 445
55-59	390	1 547	8 723	10 660
60-64	408	888	5 867	7 163
65-69	1	138	1 906	2 045
70-74	0	38	678	715
75-79	0	9	380	389
80-84	0	11	222	233
85+	0	12	148	160
Total	**1 108**	**4 288**	**30 415**	**35 811**
Pension				
50-54	14 802	297	2 460	17 558
55-59	25 467	2 980	14 830	43 277
60-64	36 223	7 863	57 383	101 470
65-69	639	7 064	117 821	125 524
70-74	0	3 733	99 155	102 888
75-79	0	3 145	85 240	88 385
80-84	0	2 175	56 306	58 481
85+	0	1 302	29 523	30 825
Total	**77 130**	**28 558**	**462 719**	**568 407**
Property income				
50-54	30	275	2 178	2 483
55-59	37	382	2 250	2 668
60-64	30	153	1 340	1 523
65-69	0	7	265	272
70-74	0	1	160	161
75-79	0	2	118	120
80-84	0	1	73	74
85+	0	0	71	71
Total	**97**	**822**	**6 455**	**7 373**
Unknown				
50-54	38	373	1 932	2 343
55-59	20	462	1 628	2 110
60-64	7	90	497	593
65-69	0	1	56	58
70-74	0	0	35	35
75-79	0	0	20	20
80-84	0	0	10	10
85+	0	0	5	5
Total	**65**	**926**	**4 183**	**5 175**
Total Females	**80 116**	**58 416**	**679 200**	**817 732**